How to Assess
Authentic
Learning

Fifth Edition

To Lois Myers Brown (Mom) and Sue Greaney Brosnan (Aunt Sue) . . .

*Thanks for the unwavering love, heartfelt concern, and daily prayers you provide all
of the members of the Brown, Burke, and Brosnan families. Your unconditional support,
along with the loving memories of Bob Brown, Marylou Brown Nimmo, Lucy Brown, George Brown,
Alice Acheson Myers, Frank Burke Sr., Rita Greaney Burke, and Uncle Red Brosnan,
have sustained and nurtured all of us throughout our lives.*

How to Assess
Authentic
Learning
Fifth Edition

Kay Burke

CORWIN
A SAGE Company

For information:

Corwin
A SAGE Company
2455 Teller Road
Thousand Oaks, California 91320
(800) 233-9936
Fax: (800) 417-2466
www.corwinpress.com

SAGE Ltd.
1 Oliver's Yard
55 City Road
London EC1Y 1SP
United Kingdom

SAGE India Pvt. Ltd.
B 1/I 1 Mohan Cooperative
    Industrial Area
Mathura Road, New Delhi 110 044
India

SAGE Asia-Pacific Pte. Ltd.
33 Pekin Street #02-01
Far East Square
Singapore 048763

Printed in the United States of America.

Library of Congress Cataloging-in-Publication Data

Burke, Kay.
How to assess authentic learning/Kay Burke.—5th ed.
    p. cm.
Includes bibliographical references and index.
ISBN 978-1-4129-6278-0 (cloth)
ISBN 978-1-4129-6279-7 (pbk.)
    1. Educational tests and measurements. 2. Grading and marking (Students). I. Title.

LB3051.B7945 2009
371.26'4—dc22   2009023353

This book is printed on acid-free paper.

    10 11 12 13 10 9 8 7 6 5 4 3

Acquisitions Editor:	Hudson Perigo
Editorial Assistant:	Lesley Blake
Production Editor:	Eric Garner
Copy Editor:	Gretchen Treadwell
Typesetter:	C&M Digitals (P) Ltd.
Proofreader:	Theresa Kay
Indexer:	Judy Hunt
Cover Designer:	Rose Storey

Contents

Acknowledgments

Educators who form a community of learners reach their full potential as professionals when they work together to help their fellow educators and students. I have been privileged to work with so many dedicated district leaders, school administrators, mentors, content specialists, coaches, college instructors, and classroom teachers throughout the years. These educators not only care about their own teachers and students, but are also willing to share their expertise and successes with others. The following people exemplify this community of learners who have graciously organized workshops, facilitated school improvement initiatives, and/or created examples of exemplary work shared in this book:

Carrollton High School, Carrollton City Schools, Carrollton, GA

Thanks to Dr. Kent Edwards (Assistant Superintendent), Jackie Fillingim (Chief Academic Officer), Mark Albertus (Principal), Joy Holley (Assistant Principal), and teachers John Ellison, Keisha Fulton, Stan Gay, Beth Riddle, Kurt Hitzeman, Steve Martin, Terica Oates, Mary Raburn, and Jan Watts.

Carrollton Middle School, Carrollton City Schools, Carrollton, GA

Thanks to Trent North (Principal), Debra B. Williams (Associate Principal for Curriculum), and teachers Cindy Daubenspeck, Denise Little, Tracy Rainwater, and Jill Lyn Rooks.

Charlton County Schools, Folkston, GA

Thanks to teachers Mary Ann Braswell and Beth Roddenberry.

Clarke County School District, Athens, GA

Thanks to Mr. James H. Simms (Interim Superintendent), Dr. Noris Price (Associate Superintendent of Instruction), Dr. Mark Tavernier (Director of Office of Teaching and Learning), Veronica Jackson (Administrative Assistant), Content Specialists Kate Arnold (elementary math), Julie Bower (social studies), Claude Gonzalez (science), Glenda Huff (secondary math), Barbara Michalove (elementary language arts), Instructional Coaches Susan H. Bolen, Molly Efland, Laura W. Forehand, Mia Jordan, Brian D. Madej, Pamela M. Stevens, Claudia W. Taxel, and Donna Ware, Jennifer Starnes (ESOL Teacher), Patty Birchenall (K–12 ESOL Specialist), and Treva Joyce Moeller (Gifted Teacher).

Cobb County School District, Marietta, GA

Thanks to Nancy Larimer (Professional Learning Supervisor), Area Lead Teachers Sheree Altmann, Jeanette Brewer, Rhonda Brewster-McCarthy, Nathifa Carmichael, Kristen Carwile, Elizabeth Cobia, Tracy Guiterrez, April Gwyn, Amy Lacher, Deborah Marker, Mary Jo Martucci, Marcia McComas, Brandi Miller, Marianne Mitchell, Denise Reynolds, Suzanne Schott, Sylvia M. Spruill, Cathy Tyler, Tameka Walker, and teacher Jennifer Hogan.

Thanks to Andrew Smith (Supervisor of Professional Development) and his Advanced Teacher Leaders Allison Grebe, Kim Oden, and Robin Walling, and Area Lead Teacher Nicole Spicer.

Foreign Language Education Program, School of Education, College of William and Mary, Williamsburg, VA

Thanks to course instructor Janet D. Parker (Instructor of Foreign Language Education) and Latin teachers Beth Block, Carl John-Kamp, and Kenneth M. Bumbaco.

A special thanks must go to Frank Burke, my husband of thirty-nine years, for his innate ability to balance my life as I attempt to balance my assessments. Eileen Depka, Chris Jaeggi, Ron Nash, Robin Fogarty, Brian Pete, Ken O'Connor, Patricia Jackson, Nancy Larimer, Andy Smith, Iris Moran, Randee Nagler, Noris Price, Mark Tavernier, Li Massey, Diane Ray, Jackie Fillingim, Donna Ramirez, Aunt Jeanne Brown, and Susan Gray are just a few of the wonderful people who have provided both personal and professional support throughout this journey. I also want to honor the special thirty-year friendship with my former tennis partner, my current golfing buddy, and my lifelong friend Irene Paul, and her equally engaging husband Bill Paul, for always making us laugh and helping us value the true meaning of friendship.

Everyone has a hero to inspire them, and the Brown family wants to thank our uncle, Edward J. Brown, for surviving 110 hours in the shark-infested Pacific Ocean after the USS *Indianapolis* sank in twelve minutes on July 30, 1945. Uncle Ed was one of only 321 survivors out of the 1,196 crew members aboard the ship. It was the worst at-sea loss of life suffered by the Navy, and we are fortunate that our uncle survived and continues to inspire us every day with his political insights and love of life.

It may take a "village" to publish a book, but I needed a whole "state." Hudson Perigo, Executive Editor; Lesley Blake, Editorial Assistant; Eric Garner, Production Editor; Gretchen Treadwell, Copy Editor; and the dedicated editorial staff, permissions department, and production team at Corwin have provided extraordinary support throughout this extensive revision cycle. I truly believe that *assessment drives instruction*, and I appreciate all the talented people who have helped me promote my vision since the publication of the first edition of *How to Assess Authentic Learning* over sixteen years ago in 1993.

Thank you,
Kay Burke
May 2009

About the Author

 **Kay Burke,** PhD, is an author and international consultant who presents practical and interactive professional development workshops to motivate administrators and teachers. She has served as a classroom teacher, department chairperson, dean of students, assistant principal, university instructor, director of a master's degree program, and senior vice-president of a publishing company. Her doctorate from Georgia State University in Atlanta focused on helping students improve their performance on standardized tests. She has received numerous teaching awards including DeKalb County's Teacher of the Year, semifinalist for Georgia Teacher of the Year, STAR Teacher for Georgia, Distinguished Georgia Educator, and a Certificate of Excellence from President Ronald Reagan.

For the past nineteen years, Dr. Burke has facilitated professional development workshops that help educators embed standards into their instruction and improve student achievement by demanding rigor and relevance in their formative and summative assessments. She has presented at conferences sponsored by the Association for Supervision and Curriculum Development (ASCD), National Staff Development Council (NSDC), the National Association of Elementary School Principals (NAESP), the National Association of Secondary School Principals (NASSP), the National Middle School Association (NMSA), the International Reading Association (IRA), and international conferences in Australia and Canada.

Dr. Burke has written or edited fifteen books in the areas of standards-based learning, formative assessment, balanced assessment, classroom management, mentoring, and portfolios. She is a coauthor of *Foundations of Meaningful Educational Assessment* (2009) and the coauthor of *The Portfolio Connection: Student Work Linked to Standards,* 3rd ed. (2008). Some of her other books published by Corwin include *What to Do With the Kid Who . . . : Developing Cooperation, Self-Discipline and Responsibility in the Classroom,* 3rd ed. (2008); *Facilitator's Guide for What to Do With the Kid Who . . . : Developing Cooperation, Self-Discipline, and Responsibility in the Classroom* (2009); and her best-selling book *From Standards to Rubrics in Six Steps: Tools for Assessing Student Learning, K–8,* which was named a 2007 finalist for the Distinguished Achievement Award from the Association of Educational Publishers. She may be contacted through the Kay Burke & Associates' Web site at www.kayburke.com, by e-mail at kay@kay burke.com, or by calling (706) 319–7609.

Introduction

For assessments to become an integral part of the instructional process, teachers need to change their approach in three important ways: They must (1) use assessments as sources of information for both students and teachers, (2) follow assessments with high-quality corrective instruction, and (3) give students second chances to demonstrate success. What makes these changes in approach so difficult, however, is that each change compels teachers to depart significantly from the practices they experienced as students. In other words, teachers must think about and use assessments differently than their teachers did. (Guskey, 2007, pp. 16–17)

For years, the area of assessment was relegated to a secondary role in the educational process. Many educators feel assessment was ignored, misused, and totally misunderstood by administrators, teachers, parents, and students. In the last decade, however, assessment has emerged as one of the major components in the restructured school. One cannot open an educational journal, attend a district workshop, or listen to media reports without hearing about standards-based reform, high-stakes standardized tests, and international testing results.

The emergence of authentic assessment coincides with the ever-increased emphasis on standardized testing. Almost everyone is aware of the controversy surrounding standardized tests. Charges that high-stakes standardized tests do not always measure significant learner achievement, do not focus on thinking skills, and do not accurately reflect students' understanding of important concepts have increased as the variety and number of required tests have increased.

STANDARDIZED TESTS AND CLASSROOM ASSESSMENTS

Standardized Tests

Despite criticisms that standardized tests do not always assess what students are learning, and that their emphasis is on mostly factual knowledge rather than higher-order thinking and application, they are still the yardstick that the public and policymakers use to measure educational progress. Standardized tests are viewed by many people as being valid and reliable and, for the most part, the most effective method to compare students, schools, districts, states, and countries.

Standardized test scores are used to determine many important educational decisions. States use high-stakes standardized tests to promote or retain students, award diplomas, reward administrators and teachers with bonuses if their students perform well, or to fire teachers and school administrators and close schools if students perform poorly. Standardized tests are required for admission at most colleges and graduate schools, and they are used to help determine certification in areas such as law, education, medicine, and accounting.

Recently, however, improvements in terms of tested achievement in the K–12 educational system have reached a plateau. According to Hargreaves and Shirley (2008), "The curriculum is shrinking, classroom creativity is disappearing, and dropout rates are frozen. Top-down prescriptions without support and encouragement at the grass roots and local level are exhausted" (p. 136). Hargreaves and Shirley believe that the data on the existing strategies and the economic need for increased innovation and creativity have necessitated a shift in education reform. They warn that "High-stakes and high-pressure standardization, where short-term gains in measurable results have been demanded at any price, have turned many U.S. schools not into learning-enriched environments, but into enervating 'Enrons' of educational change" (p. 136). With the collapse of the financial sectors of the world, the need for economic innovation and creativity has never been greater and the shift in educational reform will, hopefully, reflect the need for significant educational changes to meet the increasing challenges of the twenty-first century.

Classroom Assessments

Although research-based instructional strategies and classroom management strategies are critical components of teaching, the research on classroom assessment indicates that it is one of the major factors that improve student achievement. Marzano (2006) cites the research by Paul Black and Dylan Wiliam (1998) synthesizing more than 250 studies conclusively showing that formative assessment does improve learning; moreover, the gains are among the largest ever reported for educational interventions. Marzano says, "To the surprise of some educators, major reviews of the research on the effects of classroom assessment indicate that it might be one of the most powerful weapons in a teacher's arsenal" (p. 2).

Teachers usually develop most classroom assessments. These formative assessments consist of a variety of methods including logs, journals, debates, graphic organizers, projects, products, performances, experiments, portfolios, critical or creative writing assignments, skill tests, etc. The purposes of these assessments are to provide feedback for teachers and students, evaluate students' knowledge and understanding of key concepts and standards, and guide the instructional process by differentiating teaching to meet the diverse needs of all learners. Formative assessment provides information to both the teacher and the student about student progress toward learning goals, and the constructive feedback encourages students to self-assess and adjust in order to improve. Effective classroom assessments that are frequent and integrated seamlessly with instruction provide a continuous feedback loop that *informs* instruction.

ASSESSMENT LITERACY

Stiggins (1994) discusses the need to develop "assessment literacy" among all the stakeholders concerned about the quality of schools and the achievement of students. He describes assessment literates as those who understand the basic principles of sound assessment and how this relates to quality instruction. Along with this, teachers must strive to maintain a balanced use of assessment alternatives.

Stiggins says that the educational system will continue to use both standardized testing *and* classroom assessment. Assessments will continue to provide valuable information for important decision making, but they are also valuable teaching tools that should be used to promote meaningful learning for all students.

ACCOUNTABILITY

Elmore (as cited in Crow, 2008) believes that accountability in education today refers to systems that hold students, schools, or districts responsible for academic performance. He believes the current accountability system has further devalued the professional knowledge of the field. Elmore says the consequences of relying so heavily on testing and sanctions reinforces the idea that, "educators already know all that we need to know to solve these problems, and the reasons why schools aren't performing is that educators are just contrary and incompetent people" (p. 46). He recommends that people running the accountability system in the No Child Left Behind (NCLB) legislation review accountability models in Canada, Australia, and Europe in which schools are given feedback on the performance of their students, and they are also given support and challenges to improve. He believes the United States is incredibly overinvested in testing and sanctions, and incredibly underinvested in capacity building.

People know when students and schools are doing poorly, but they need to know the process from taking a school from point A to point B and what organizational structures and resources are necessary. Elmore (as cited in Crow, 2008) states:

> It's not the policy makers who are going to make this period of educational reform successful—it's the people on the ground who are going to do it. They don't have all their best ideas stashed away in some desk drawer somewhere—they're doing what they know how to do. If they're not doing the right thing, we need to figure out how to put them in a situation where they can learn how to do it differently. (p. 47)

The importance of providing high-quality professional development to teachers has never been greater. Beginning teachers, veteran teachers, and second-career teachers all need to experience hands-on training and coaching on the best practices of staff development so they will be able to take schools from point A to point B, regardless of the socioeconomic and academic challenges facing the students.

GRADING

Grades are, unfortunately, an integral part of the American educational system. As early as kindergarten, students receive grades that they might not understand. Ask teachers what they hate most about teaching, and there's a good chance the answer is "giving grades." Many a teacher has agonized over report cards, trying to decide the fate of a student. It is a gut-wrenching task for teachers to translate everything they know about what a student knows, can do, and feels into one single letter or numerical score. That final grade may determine promotion or retention. It may determine placement in a class, school, or participation in an extracurricular activity. It may determine honor roll, class ranking, college admission, college scholarship, or career placement. Currently, in some states such as Georgia and Louisiana, a student's average could prevent him or her from obtaining a scholarship to four years at a state university. Grades are, indeed, high stakes for students and their families. Many important decisions are made on the basis of a grading system that can be inconsistent, arbitrary, and, sometimes, punitive.

Grades affect the self-confidence, self-esteem, motivation, and future of a student. Fortunately, some school systems are moving away from traditional letter and number grades at some levels and adopting performance indicators developed from the standards on report cards. They are also using portfolios, student-led parent-teacher conferences, anecdotal records, checklists, multiple scores, and other more authentic descriptors of a student's progress. But despite attempts to restructure report cards to reflect the emphasis on performance, standards, thinking skills, and other indicators, traditional As, Bs, Cs, Ds, and Fs are still used to pass judgment on students.

With the stroke of a pen or the "bubble" of a Scantron sheet, a teacher can pass judgment on a student. "It [a grade] marks the lives of those who receive it. It may not be imprinted on the forehead, but it certainly leaves an impression" (Majesky, 1993, p. 88). The grade can become the scarlet letter of Puritan days—especially if it is based on trivial tasks or inappropriate behavior, absences, attitude, and punctuality. "As at the last judgment, students are sorted into the wheat and the chaff. Rewards of As and Bs go out to the good, and punishments of Fs are doled out to the bad. 'Gifts' of Ds (Ds are always gifts) are meted out, and Cs (that wonderfully tepid grade) are bestowed on those whose names teachers can rarely remember" (p. 88). Another challenge facing teachers is how their classroom grades correlate to the state's standardized test scores. Parents tend to be displeased if Mary has earned all As in Mrs. Brown's language arts class, but is retained and must attend summer school when she fails the state test. The *disconnect* between "teacher" grades and "standardized test" grades is difficult to explain to the public.

Grading is indeed a complicated issue, and used for accountability, an issue that must be addressed. Airasian (1994) says that grading means "making a judgment about the quality of a pupil's performance, whether it is a performance on a single assessment or performance across many assessments" (p. 281). The judgment, however, should be based upon clear criteria, correlated to course outcomes and state standards, in order to be valid. Arbitrary judgments based on personality, behavior, and effort distort the grade and the inferences that are made from the grade.

O'Connor (2002) believes communicating student achievement is the primary purpose of grades. "Simply stated, if clear communication does not occur, then none of the other purposes of grades can be effectively carried out" (p. 16). Students, parents, and administrators must all be aware of the purposes of the grades and the criteria upon which they are based.

TRADITIONAL COGNITIVE SCIENCE

The methods of assessment used in schools are often determined by beliefs about learning. Early theories of learning indicated that educators needed to use a "building-blocks-of-knowledge" approach whereby students acquired complex higher-order skills by breaking learning down into a series of skills. Every skill had a prerequisite skill, and it was assumed that after the basic skills were learned, they could be assembled into more complex thinking and insight. Therefore, students who scored poorly on standardized tests at an early age would usually be assigned to the remedial or basic skills classes to master those essential basic skills before being exposed to the more challenging and motivating complex thinking skills. In other words, they could not handle the rigor and they went to the "time out" rooms, programs, or grades until they showed they could "merge" back into the regular flow of the general education classes.

Popham (2001) believes that incessant "skill and drill" often turns into "drill and kill." He believes that repetitious instructional activities tend to deaden student's genuine interest in learning. "All the excitement and intellectual vibrancy that students might encounter during a really interesting lesson are driven out by a tedious, test-fostered series of drills" (p. 20). As a result, some students may mentally drop out of schools in the early grades, and physically drop out in high school rather than sit through tedious test-review lessons preparing them to pass high-stakes tests in order to get promoted to the next grade or to graduate from school.

ASSESSMENT AND EVALUATION

Assessment is a global term for gathering information for the purpose of decision making. Chen and McNamee (2007) say, "For classroom teachers, assessment is the process of listening, observing, and gathering evidence to evaluate the learning and development of children in the classroom context" (p. 4). Assessment is the ongoing process of *gathering and analyzing evidence* of what a student can do. *Evaluation* is the process of *interpreting* the evidence and *making judgments* and decisions based on the evidence. If the assessment is not sound, the evaluation will not be sound. Figure 0.1 shows some of the differences between assessment and evaluation, as well as characteristics of performance assessment and portfolios. In most classrooms, teachers assess a student on the basis of observations, oral conversations, and written work. They make instructional decisions based on these assessments. If the assessment is ongoing and frequent, immediate changes can be made to help the student achieve the desired outcome. If the assessment is flawed, the final evaluation will be based upon invalid and unreliable data. The quality of the final evaluation is only as valid as the quality of the ongoing assessment data upon which it is based.

Four Quadrants of Assessment

Assessment	Evaluation
Assessment "for" Learning	Assessment "of" Learning
• Formative • Ongoing feedback in "real time" • Collection of data • Differentiated to meet student needs • "Do Overs" to allow improvements • Helps teachers improve their teaching • Helps students improve their learning	• Summative • Final judgment based on evidence • Analysis and evaluation of data • Standardized to test all students • "Last attempt" to meet standards • Used to evaluate teachers' effectiveness • Used to prove the quality of learning to parents, administrators, and policymakers
Performance Assessment	**Student Portfolio**
• Enriched and integrated curriculum • Meaningful and authentic tasks • Real-life applications of knowledge • Student motivation and engagement • Interactive teaching strategies • Differentiated learning options • Collaborative and cooperative learning • Multiple standards addressed • Metacognition and self-assessment	• Collection of evidence • Development and growth • Progress over time • Process used to produce performance • Final product or performance • Reflections on all work • Self-assessments using rubrics • Framework for learning • Examination of student work

Figure 0.1

Diagnostic evaluations are often administered at the beginning of a course, quarter, semester, or year to assess the skills, abilities, interests, levels of achievement, or difficulties of one student or a class. Diagnostic evaluations should be done informally and are not included in the grade. Teachers use the results to modify programs, determine causes of learning difficulties, and ascertain students' learning levels. By having information about the student's entry-level skills, a teacher assesses how far the student has progressed throughout the course or year. Diagnostic assessments are used as baseline data to find out where the students are before a teacher tries a new intervention to produce desired results. Diagnostic tools include items such as pre-tests, writing samples, problem-solving exercises, skill tests, attitude surveys, or questionnaires.

Tomlinson (1999) discusses the strategy of "compacting" in which teachers assess students before beginning a unit of study or development of a skill.

Teachers analyze the results and create a plan to help the students learn the things they are lacking. Students who do well on the pre-assessment should not have to continue to work on what they already know, and teachers can then create enrichment activities to challenge, extend, and motivate these students so they will not get bored. By analyzing the prior knowledge, ability levels, and personal interests of the students at the beginning of a course or school year, teachers are able to differentiate the content, the products, and the process in order to meet their diverse needs. *One size no longer fits all* in the inclusive class-room and it is important to use diagnostic data to determine the academic and social needs of students and then plan subsequent curriculum opportunities and instructional strategies to meet those various needs.

Formative vs. Summative Assessment

According to Popham (2008), the term *formative* was first introduced in an essay about educational evaluation written by Michael Scriven in 1967. Scriven contrasts formative evaluation with summative evaluation as follows:

> If the quality of an early-version educational program is evaluated while the program is still malleable—capable of being improved because of an evaluation's results—this constitutes *formative* evaluation. In contrast, when a mature, final-version educational program is evaluated in order to make a decision about its continuation or termination, this constitutes *summative* evaluation. (as cited in Popham, 2008, p. 3)

The word "malleable" suggests that an educational program is pliable enough to change, adapt, and improve on an ongoing basis. When the term is applied to students, it sounds like teachers are pulling strategies from their bag of ideas to use with each student who is still "a work in progress."

Formative Assessment

The term *formative assessment* has evolved over the past forty years, but the key idea is that teachers should use evidence of learning to *adjust* instruction. Reviews of research in this area were updated by Black and Wiliam (1998) who concluded that "regular use of classroom formative assessment would raise student achievement by 0.4 to 0.7 standard deviations—enough to raise the United States into the top five countries in the international rankings for math achievement, for example" (Wiliam, 2007, p. 189). Formative assessment usu-ally refers to classroom assessments with teachers providing specific feedback to help students. "Measured in terms of impact on student achievement, the single most important thing to change in teachers' practice is the minute-to-minute and day-by-day use of assessment to adjust instruction" (Wiliam, 2007, p. 188).

Formative assessment has been defined as occurring while the learning is taking place and allows for immediate interventions during the process or activity so teachers can modify the teaching and learning activities. Marzano (2006) says:

> By definition, then, formative classroom assessment can and should begin immediately within a learning episode and span its entire duration.

> Additionally, formative classroom assessment can take a wide variety of formats, both formal (e.g., paper-and-pencil quiz) and informal (e.g., discussion with a student). (p. 9)

Formative assessment calls for those "teachable moments" when effective teachers know how to stop in the middle of a lesson and reteach the skill using another strategy if they see their *malleable* students are still confused.

Summative Assessment

Summative assessment is the term used to grade or make final judgments about what the student has learned at the end of instruction; therefore, it usually occurs at the end of a unit, course, or program. It determines the effectiveness or ineffectiveness of already-completed instructional activities. Once teachers collect the assessment information, Airasian (2000) says they use it to make decisions or judgments about pupils, instruction, or classroom climate. He says:

> Evaluation is the process of making judgments about what is good or desirable as in, for example, judging the quality of pupils' essays or the desirability of a particular instructional activity. Evaluation occurs after assessment information has been collected, synthesized, and thought about because that is when the teacher is in a position to make informed judgments. (p. 10)

Summative assessment, then, is the analysis and evaluation of the data that have been collected throughout the formative assessment process. If the data collected are valid and reliable, teachers interpret them and make appropriate judgments about the students and decisions about the programs.

Once the final evaluation is made, it is too late for teachers to adapt instructional activities to meet the needs of their students. It is over! One experienced educator noted that formative assessment helps teachers help *this year's* students succeed whereas summative assessment only shows a teacher *what went wrong.* While it is too late to help this year's students, it might still help the teacher do better with *next year's* students! Unit tests, final research papers, end-of-course tests, final exams, standardized tests, and report cards are generally classified as summative assessments because they represent the end result with no opportunities for students to have another chance to improve and/or meet standards.

DEFINITIONS OF PERFORMANCE ASSESSMENT

Many terms or phrases are used when discussing the alternatives to conventional objective or multiple-choice testing. Alternative assessment, authentic assessment, standards-based assessment, and performance-based assessment are sometimes used synonymously "to mean variants of performance assessments that require students to generate rather than choose a response" (Herman, Aschbacher, & Winters, 1992, p. 2). Performance assessments are highly engaging for students because they connect their content knowledge with the processes they will use in the real world. Some other characteristics of performance assessments include the following:

- problem scenarios requiring higher-order thinking skills such as analysis, synthesis, and evaluation to solve problems and create original work
- realistic performance tasks correlating to real-life situations faced by students and adults every day
- motivating tasks focusing on producing an authentic product or performance correlated to state standards
- collaboration and group interaction emphasizing both academic and social outcomes
- integration of multiple subject areas highlighting the interdependence of big ideas and essential questions across disciplines

Some other characteristics are included on the performance assessment web in Figure 0.2. Not all of the characteristics need to be present, but they are all important components of effective performance assessment.

Regardless of the different terminologies most of the definitions exhibit two central features: "First, all are viewed as *alternatives* to traditional multiple-choice, standardized achievement tests; second, all refer to *direct* examination of student *performance* on significant tasks that are relevant to life outside of

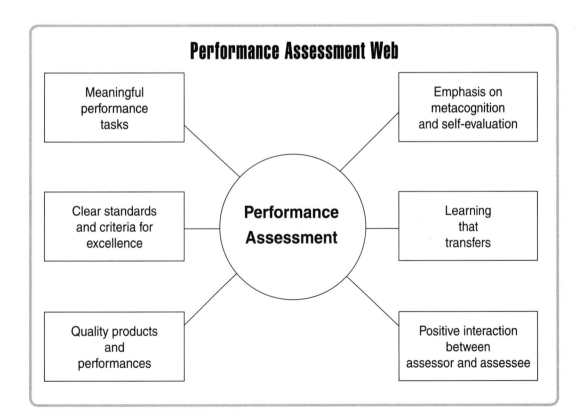

Figure 0.2

school" (Worthen, 1993, p. 445). Almost every state has created "performance standards" for students to demonstrate not only what they know but also how they are able to do things. The final proof is often in the performance.

Archbald and Newmann (1988) describe the term *authentic assessment* as follows: "A valid assessment system [that] provides information about the particular tasks on which students succeed or fail, but more important, it also presents tasks that are worthwhile, significant, and meaningful—in short, *authentic*" (p. 1). Authentic tasks related to real life provide the relevance students need to find meaning in what they are studying. The tasks help students become actively engaged in the learning process, rather than passive receptors of content knowledge.

PORTFOLIOS

A portfolio has been defined as "a *purposeful* integrated collection of student work showing effort, progress, or a degree of proficiency. Portfolios are often defined by the purpose underlying the collection of artifacts and the scope of such purposes is almost unlimited" (Butler & McMunn, 2006, p. 66). Portfolios provide collections of student evidence that show growth and development over time. Portfolios allow students to examine their own work and reflect on their learning. They help students analyze their strengths and weaknesses and set both short- and long-term goals. A portfolio contains both formative and summative evaluations because it is a collection of evidence to show how (or if) students are meeting goals or standards.

Portfolios and e-portfolios include applications of content skills and chronicle students' progress and growth toward meeting curriculum goals and standards. According to Belgrad, Burke, and Fogarty (2008):

> They [portfolios] provide a much richer and more revealing portrait of the student as a learner. Such a picture cannot be captured by a single test score. Within the portfolio process, students become active agents in the acquisition and exposition of their knowledge across the content areas of the grade levels. (p. xv)

One test can be a snapshot of a student on one day, but it does not show the "whole child" or how the student progresses and grows over time. Portfolios also show the process students used to achieve their final products. Many portfolios contain first, second, and third drafts along with the final research paper in order to show the pathway toward improvement.

BALANCED ASSESSMENT

Assessment should not have to generate an "either/or" or a "throw out the baby with the bath water" approach. Most educators agree with Stiggins that we need all the tools at our disposal. Shulman (1988) talks about teacher assessment suggesting that no one piece of evidence is sufficient to provide an evaluation. Teachers need to combine various methods of assessment so that the strengths of one offset the limitations of the other.

Student assessment should follow the same guidelines. No one assessment tool by itself is capable of producing the quality information needed to make an accurate judgment of a student's knowledge, skills, understanding of curriculum, motivation, social skills, processing skills, and lifelong-learning skills. Each single measurement by itself is insufficient to provide a true portrait of the student or learner. If educators combine standardized and teacher-made tests measuring knowledge and content with portfolios measuring process and growth, and performances measuring application, they will provide a more accurate portrait of the individual learner. Fogarty and Stoehr (2007) discuss the balanced assessment model (see Figure 0.3) used to address traditional assessments, portfolio assessments, and performance assessments and subsequently meet the needs of all students.

AND NOW . . . THE TOOLS!

Performance assessments provide teachers with a repertoire—a vast array of tools to measure student growth. The following chapters focus on specific tools teachers need to create a vivid, colorful, and true portrait of students as they develop and grow over the course of a year. In the past, progress was chronicled by a superficial "snapshot" of the student. The snapshot usually consisted of a few pictures of standardized test scores, midterms, final grades, and other one-dimensional scores that lay lifeless in the permanent record file. The grades on the report cards do not adequately describe the skills the students had when they entered a class, as compared to the skills they had when they left the class. Nothing more than a static glimpse of a student can be gleaned from the traditional, cumulative record system that has dominated our school systems for the past two centuries. Teachers who create a repertoire of assessment tools allow students to show what they know and what they can do in multiple formats. Each tool represents a different way to challenge students to succeed and to measure their progress along the way.

Each chapter in this book will introduce an assessment tool to record a student's growth and achievement. The chapters include a description of *what* is the tool, *why* we should use the tool, and *how* we could use the tool. Examples of many of the assessments are provided, and teachers will have a chance to create original tools at the end of each chapter in the "On Your Own" section, as well as self-evaluate their work on the "Reflection Page." The fifth edition of *How to Assess Authentic Learning* presents only a few of the many options available for teachers to add to their repertoire of assessment strategies. As educators review the strategies in this book, they should take some time to reflect on how the tools provide a variety of strategies to help all students meet and exceed the standards.

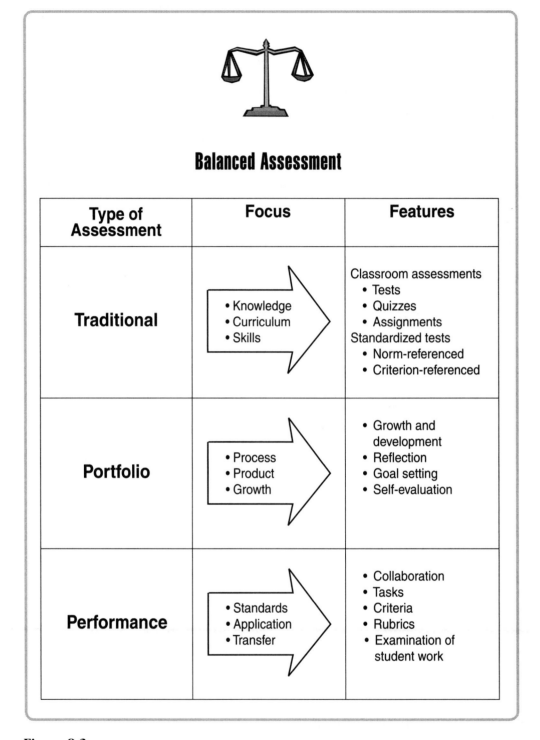

Figure 0.3

Source: Adapted from Fogarty & Stoehr, 2008.

Student Learning Standards 1

WHAT ARE LEARNING STANDARDS AND BENCHMARKS?

Standards are statements of what should be taught. They establish levels of achievement, indicators of a quality performance, and degrees of proficiency expected from students. Some states use the terms *competencies, objectives,* or *goals* in place of standards. Standards are, generally, broad and contain somewhat arbitrary categories of knowledge. Almost every state has established their own standards at all grade levels and in most subject areas. Benchmarks, on the other hand, are used to explicate the standards. Benchmarks explain what students must do in order to meet the standard; they focus on explicit student behaviors or specific products or performances.

Foriska (1998) describes benchmarks as the guideposts that "identify a progression of reasonable expectations detailing what students are capable of learning at different ages with regard to the content standards. This makes the structure of the curriculum appropriate for the cognitive development of the students" (pp. 31–32). Benchmarks provide the framework for teaching and assessing key concepts because they are more specific and concrete than most standards. Marzano and Kendall (1996) suggest that benchmarks can be written as statements of information and skills (declarative and procedural), performance activities, or performance tasks. A standard that requires students to "write a narrative essay" is broad, whereas the benchmarks drill down and tell students to include specific items such as "organizing structure, engaging beginning, plot, context, significance of events, dialogue, figurative language, and sensory language." Benchmarks are the "nitty gritty" of standards-based learning.

Some states use the terms *objectives, competencies, descriptors, indicators,* or *elements* instead of benchmarks. Butler and McMunn (2006) believe "The important thing is not the exact terms that are used but that the definitions of the chosen terms are clear so that everyone in the district speaks the same language and can identify what it is that students are expected to learn" (p. 23). Even though many subject areas have national standards and benchmarks, not all state standards are created equally. Some standards are more descriptive and specific to a content and subject area and, therefore, more helpful for teachers when making decisions about what instructional and assessment strategies would help students. Regardless of the quality of the state standards, teachers must align both their instruction and assessment to the standards and the benchmarks.

WHAT IS THE STANDARDS MOVEMENT?

According to Ardovino, Hollingsworth, and Ybarra (2000), "The standards movement is about assessing 'what was taught and what was learned.' Educators can no longer be independent contractors with multiple game plans. Standards provide cohesiveness that will certify the content our students are learning" (pp. 90–91). Teachers are expected to teach the standards to all students and assess their students' progress toward meeting and exceeding them. In addition, most high-stakes state tests are based upon students' knowledge and understanding of the content and concepts of the standards. Lachat (2004) explains:

> Holding all students to high academic standards is the centerpiece of a national agenda to improve schools and ensure that no child is left behind in the journey towards the American dream. The evolution of standards over the past decade has been driven by the need to define what all students should learn in school in order to participate successfully in the twenty-first century. (p. 1)

Darling-Hammond (1997), in her book *The Right to Learn*, discusses how standards of practice are used to license professionals and guide the work of architects in constructing sound buildings, accountants in managing finances, engineers in assembling space shuttles, and doctors in treating patients. She adds, however, "These standards are not prescriptions; instead they reflect shared norms and knowledge about underlying principles of practice, the effects of various techniques, and decision-making processes" (p. 213). Standards clarify expectations and consensus about what constitutes quality products and practice.

Not all education experts and parents, however, believe that standards contribute to the teaching and learning process. Some would argue that the standards movement has not met the expectations that were predicted when first introduced. Despite the attempts to achieve equity and close the achievement gaps, Moody and Stricker (2009) believe that "contrary to the hopes of legislators and educators involved in the advent of No Child Left Behind, *standards have not proven to be the equalizer they were intended to be*" (p. 4). In fact, some would argue that standards have hurt students by focusing on reviewing and taking tests at the expense of more meaningful educational experiences.

HOW DID THE STANDARDS MOVEMENT BEGIN?

Most educators attribute the publication of *A Nation at Risk* (National Commission on Excellence in Education) in 1983 as the impetus for setting standards at a national level. The concern over education was also the focus of the first education summit, held in Charlottesville, Virginia, in September 1989, where the nation's fifty governors and President George H. W. Bush adopted national educational goals for the year 2000. One of the goals was to establish challenging national achievement standards for five school subjects—English, mathematics, science, history, and geography. As a result of the summit, a number of national organizations representing various subject areas published numerous documents that represented what teachers of mathematics, language arts, and science should be teaching (Marzano & Kendall, 1996).

Diane Ravitch, former Assistant Secretary of Education, is recognized as one of the chief proponents of the standards movement. In 1995, she equated how Americans expect standards for their food, health, and quality of living to how they also expect standards for their schools (as cited in Marzano & Kendall, 1996). Since then, controversy has emerged surrounding the challenges of each state establishing its own standards, implementing how they are used, creating its own high-stakes test, and establishing its own cut-off scores for determining how students perform. Educators and policymakers are concerned with the "nonstandardized" criteria and worry that how students do depends as much on what they know and can do as well as the state where they live. Reeves (2003) says:

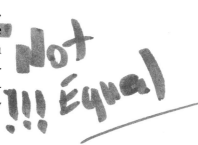

> Unfortunately, the link between the promise of standards and the reality of their implementation is a tenuous one. States that adopt new standards but retain old assessments should not be surprised that the test content will drive educational practice. Unless standards are linked to assessments, the standards become little more than a political slogan full of good, but empty, intentions. (p. 35)

The standards-based movement is much more than having teachers post all the standards in their rooms and administrators asking students what standards they are studying when they do their "walk-throughs" to evaluate staff. The linkage among standards, curriculum, instruction, and assessment has not been made in many cases and that linkage is critical to improved learning for all students.

WHAT ARE PERFORMANCE STANDARDS?

Content standards focus on teaching and testing students' knowledge and skills, and performance standards focus more on how students apply those skills in real life or simulations of real-life situations. The performance standards define levels of learning that are usually labeled as "in progress," "meets standards," or "exceeds standards." Solomon (2002) says that the performance standard is a translation of the content standard and is intended as a clearly discriminated level of the bar or model of acceptance. It answers the question of "how good is good enough?"

A language-arts standard on oral communication states that students in middle or junior high should "speak effectively using language appropriate to the situation and audience." The benchmark describes specific criteria related

to the standard. These criteria can be developed later into a checklist or rubric for assessment purposes.

Checklists

A checklist derived from the vocabulary of the standards provides a step-by-step sequential road map to help students know the steps for completing a project or performance. By using the language of the standards (LOTS), teachers prepare students to complete their oral presentations while at the same time preparing them to recognize and understand the key words from the standards that might appear on their state assessments. Figure 1.1 shows an example of an oral presentation checklist that is correlated to the language of the standards and benchmarks.

Rubrics

A rubric is a scoring tool that uses words and numbers to describe the scaled levels of student achievement necessary to perform a task. Rubrics include indicators or descriptors at different levels that provide written feedback on the students' progress toward meeting and exceeding standards on the performances. Solomon (2002) says that "for the purpose of meaningful assessment of student performance, the standards or performance indicators need to be translated into rubrics" (p. 58). Figure 1.2 on page 18 shows what a rubric would look like if it were developed from the Oral Presentation Checklist shown in Figure 1.1. Note that the language and sequence used on the checklist is repeated on the rubric. The major difference is that the checklist asks the students to merely check off if they have completed an item, but the rubric describes levels of quality using a scale to show levels of graduated performances. The rubric shows "how good is good enough" whereas the checklist just tells students what to do.

WHY DO WE NEED STANDARDS?

Standards provide a blueprint to ensure that all students are learning the necessary knowledge and skills. Once an outcome is established, "effective instructional practices can be designed to teach the standards, and appropriate multiple measures can be developed which are reliable, valid, and fair to ascertain the level at which students are learning the standards" (Ardovino, Hollingsworth, & Ybarra, 2000, p. 90). The expression "begin with the end in mind" signifies the importance of knowing the outcome before planning the instruction. If the end result is mastery of the standards, then standards are the alpha and the omega of education. The teacher begins by knowing the standards students are expected to master and then develops the curriculum and utilizes the instructional strategies that will achieve those goals.

Marzano and Kendall (1996) cite several reasons why standards represent one of the most powerful options for school reform. They believe that the erosion of the Carnegie unit, variations in grading practices, and the lack of concern about educational outcomes have caused states to move toward standards.

Oral Presentation Checklist Correlated to Standard

Oral Communication Standard:
Students will plan oral presentations that use appropriate language and vocabulary, support their main ideas with facts and statistics to clarify main ideas, integrate technology to enhance the presentation, and create effective visual aides appropriate to the audience and the purpose of the speech.

Benchmark:
Deliver planned oral presentations using language and vocabulary appropriate to the purpose, message, and audience; provide details and supporting information that clarify main ideas; and use visual aids and contemporary technology as support.

Criteria/Performance Indicators	Not Yet 0	Some Evidence 1
Did you use language and vocabulary that was . . .		
• Appropriate to the purpose?		
• Appropriate to the message?		
• Appropriate to the audience?		
Did you provide information to support the main idea, such as . . .		
• Details? Give one:		
• Examples? Give one:		
• Statistics? Give one:		
• Quotes? Give one:		
• Anecdotes? Give one:		
Did you select at least two visual aids?		
• Graphic organizer		
• Picture		
• Poster		
• Prop		
• Pamphlet		
• Costume		
Did you select at least two types of technology?		
• Transparencies		
• Slides		
• PowerPoint		
• Audio		
• Digital pictures		

Figure 1.1

| EXAMPLES |

Oral Presentation Rubric Correlated to Standard

Oral Communication Standard:
Students will plan oral presentations that use appropriate language and vocabulary, support their main ideas with facts and statistics to clarify main ideas, integrate technology to enhance the presentation, and create effective visual aides appropriate to the audience and the purpose of the speech.

Benchmark:
Deliver planned oral presentations using language and vocabulary appropriate to the purpose, message, and audience; provide details and supporting information that clarify main ideas; and use visual aids and contemporary technology as support.

Scale: Criteria:	1 Practiced in Front of Mirror (Novice)	2 Enrolled in Toastmaster Course (In Progress)	3 Voted Class President (Meets Standards)	4 Nominated for an Oscar (Exceeds Standards)
Appropriate Language/Vocabulary				
• Purpose • Message • Audience	• Inappropriate language • Limited vocabulary	Language and vocabulary appropriate to purpose	Language and vocabulary appropriate to the purpose and the message	Language and vocabulary appropriate to the purpose, message, and audience
Information Supports Main Idea				
• Details • Examples • Statistics • Quotes • Anecdotes	Limited use of details to support main idea	Use of • details • examples	Use of • details • examples • statistics • quotes	Use of appropriate • details • examples • statistics • quotes • anecdotes
Visual Aids (Minimum of 2)				
• Graphic organizer • Picture • Poster • Prop • Pamphlet • Costume	No visual aids used in presentation	Use of *one* visual aid to support main idea	Use of *two* visual aids to support main idea and keep the attention of the audience	Use of *two or more* visual aids to support main idea, keep the attention of the audience, and motivate the audience
Technology (Minimum of 2)				
• Transparencies • Slides • PowerPoint • Audiotape • Digital pictures	No use of technology	Use of *one* technology tool that supports main idea	Use of *two* technology tools to support main idea and keep the attention of the audience	Use of *two or more* contemporary technology tools to clarify main idea and inspire the audience to action

Student Comment:

Teacher Comment:

Total points _____

Scale 15–16 = A
13–14 = B
9–12 = C
1–8 = Not Yet

Figure 1.2

They also cite the fact that most competing countries have adopted educational standards in their goal to improve student learning. The following section describes the reasons in more depth.

Erosion of the Carnegie Unit and the Common Curriculum

Veteran educators remember the shift away from the standard concept of credit hours (based on the Carnegie unit—a measure of class time) and proliferation of elective courses in the 1960s and 1970s. It was not unusual for students to elect to take "Science Fiction Short Stories" or "Gothic Mystery Writers" in lieu of American literature or composition. Furthermore, studies have shown a disparity among teachers concerning the amount of time spent teaching a particular subject area or skill. How many teachers have spent six weeks covering the Civil War in a history class, and then not have sufficient time for World War I or II? Because teachers sometimes make arbitrary decisions regarding what they teach, there is often a lack of uniformity in a given district or state's curricula and little consistency in the knowledge and skills covered within subject areas.

Variation in Current Grading Practices

Grading has always been an ambiguous process. What does a "B" really mean? How many teachers average effort, behavior, cooperation, and attendance into the academic grade, thus conveying an inaccurate portrayal of a student's achievement? It is difficult to know how a teacher arrives at a grade because grades are often imprecise and sometimes are not indicative of what students know and can do in a subject area. Moreover, some teachers assign zeros for work not attempted, whereas others allow students chances to redo work or drop a number of grades. Other teachers weigh work more at the end of a grading cycle to show improvement. Because of the inconsistency in grading procedures, parents and policymakers often depend on standardized test scores to know whether or not students are improving.

Lack of Attention to Educational Outputs

The outcomes-based education movement attempted to focus attention not so much on the input of instructional delivery, but more on the outcome of the results. Unfortunately, some of the outcomes were difficult to measure objectively, and some parents felt educators should not be measuring outcomes that included values. Glickman (1993, as cited in Schmöker, 1996) feels too much emphasis has been placed on new instructional strategies, the innovation, or the "hot topic" rather than on the results for the learner. For instance, using white boards in classrooms is technologically advanced; integrating the theory of brain-based learning into each lesson is motivating. The bottom line, however, should always be: How does it affect student achievement? Today, schools are paying more attention to results, not intentions. If Nathaniel Hawthorne were writing today, the letter "A" would symbolize accountability.

Competing Countries Do It

The fourth reason for implementing standards for school reform addresses the issue of competition with other countries. Proponents of standards often point to countries such as China, Japan, France, and England to show how setting standards and developing a national curriculum, national exams, and cut-off scores help students attain academic excellence. Many business and community leaders have vigorously supported the establishment of student performance standards to create a world-class workforce. Behind this expectation is the assumption that higher educational standards and student performance are keys to higher workplace productivity (Marzano & Kendall, 1996). Recent research from countries such as Canada, Australia, and Finland show how professional learning communities, an emphasis on teacher training, mentoring, a reduced curriculum load, and formative assessments have improved their students' learning as well as their international performances.

The standards movement has gathered momentum on the basis of these four reasons as well as the public's dissatisfaction with the quality of students the public schools are producing. Headlines about scores on international tests showing the placement of the United States have fueled the groundswell of support for high standards for academic excellence. Moreover, the members of the business community have expressed concern over the skills their employees lack and the inordinate amount of time and money they are spending to teach their employees what they feel they should have learned in public schools. The public seems to support the concept that teachers provide clear and appropriate expectations to students and evaluate their progress accurately.

HOW CAN WE USE STANDARDS?

The introduction of standards into the field of education serves as an essential foundation for the development of curriculum, the emphasis on differentiated instruction, and the creation of performance assessments. Educators are told to "begin with the end in mind" (the standards) and then plan backwards to create curriculum units, implement differentiated instructional strategies to meet the needs of all students, and create valid and reliable formative and summative assessment tools aligned to the standards.

Darling-Hammond (1997) advises that standards can be most useful when used as "guideposts not straitjackets for building curriculum assessments and professional development opportunities, and when they are used to focus and mobilize system resources rather than to punish students and schools" (p. 213). The idea that standards provide guideposts that may differ depending on the student and the situation adds more flexibility and differentiation to the standards-based movement.

Standards as Guideposts

When used by administrators, teachers, and parents effectively, standards target nine important goals:

1. Synthesize Educational Goals

Educators need to focus on attaining important goals that will benefit all students. Establishing a few clear and specific goals focuses a faculty on developing action plans and unifying efforts to achieve the goals. Teachers working in professional learning communities (PLCs) target specific learning goals and work as a team to create meaningful instruction and assessments for all students. (See Figure 1.3.)

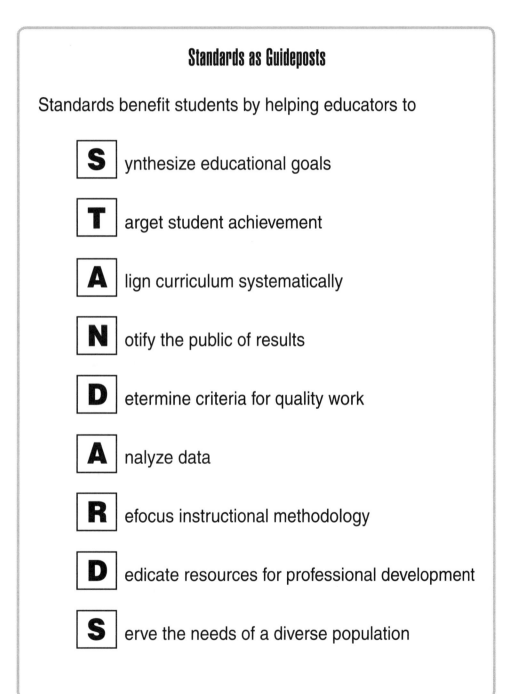

Standards as Guideposts

Standards benefit students by helping educators to

S ynthesize educational goals

T arget student achievement

A lign curriculum systematically

N otify the public of results

D etermine criteria for quality work

A nalyze data

R efocus instructional methodology

D edicate resources for professional development

S erve the needs of a diverse population

Figure 1.3

2. Target Student Achievement

The primary purpose for standards is to focus attention on student work and improved student achievement. The emphasis shifted from the "input" of what teachers teach to the "output" of what students learn. Standards are not really the end; they are a means to achieve the end—improved student achievement. Vocabulary development plays an important role in helping students score well on standardized tests and deepen their understanding of critical concepts. Districts may adopt different textbooks to help their students meet state standards, but teachers need to focus more on the vocabulary, essential questions, and big ideas of the standards. High-stakes state tests target the vocabulary of their state standards rather than the vocabulary included in as many as ten different textbooks that could be adopted by districts or counties in each state.

3. Align Curriculum Systemically

The standards and benchmarks provide guideposts and key concepts that help focus teachers on a relatively small set of core ideas. The curriculum has become so overwhelming that teachers are forced to either cover a great deal of information superficially, or leave out portions of their curriculum. Many districts are also working on curriculum mapping to develop a blueprint of not only *what* essential skills are taught, but also *when* they are taught. A curriculum aligned with meaningful standards and valid assessments provides a pathway to improved student achievement.

4. Notify the Public of Results

One of the reasons the public is demanding standards is because they are concerned about the quality of the schools. Stories about how students in the United States compare with students on international tests, the decline of some standardized test scores, and the rising dropout rate cause alarm among parents and business leaders. Elmore (2002) states that the accountability movement expresses society's expectation that schools will solve the problems that lead to the academic failure of a large number of students and the mediocre performance of many more. "Failure will lead to erosion of public support and a loss of legitimacy" (p. 3). Economic conditions that impact the housing market, the financial sector, the job market, and the credit industry have exacerbated the calls from politicians and policymakers to require educators to prepare students for the new challenges that demand a quality education that emphasizes rigor and relevance. The public expects today's schools to meet these real-world challenges that are not addressed in many textbooks.

5. Determine Criteria for Quality Work

One of the most important by-products of the standards movement is the emphasis on establishing specific criteria for quality work. Teachers often involve students in determining the criteria for assignments and the indicators of quality in order to determine, "How good is it?" Conversations among teachers, parents, and students about what constitutes "A" work and the creation of checklists and scoring rubrics have demystified the grading process. Students know not only the expectations but also the specific steps they need to take to meet the expectations. The emphasis on reflection and metacognition about performance assessments helps students internalize the criteria and become critical self-assessors of their own work.

6. Analyze Data

School personnel have found that if they use standards to drive student achievement, they need to measure a school's progress with hard data. Accurate data such as the analysis of standardized test scores, pass-fail rates in courses, drop-out rates, attendance, and retention and promotion statistics inform teachers, parents, school administrators, and district leaders about what works and what needs more work. Data collection and analysis, therefore, serve as critical components of standards-based education and provide the documentation necessary to adopt or cancel instructional programs and redesign professional development to meet school goals.

7. Refocus Instructional Methodology

The most comprehensive standards in the world will not, by their very existence, improve education. The key to improving student achievement is effective instruction. In order to meet the needs of a diverse student population, teachers need to implement a repertoire of instructional strategies to help all students learn. Though the drill-and-skill lecture method may appeal to some parents and students, fewer and fewer students are responding to that mode of instruction.

Research on brain-compatible learning provides strategies teachers implement to enrich the learning environment, foster reflection and self-evaluation, and stimulate student interest in new areas of study. Darling-Hammond (1997) believes real improvement will come about because "the standards come alive when teachers study student work, collaborate with other teachers to improve their understanding of subjects and students' thinking, and develop new approaches to teaching that are relevant and useful for them and their students" (p. 236). It seems like a contradiction in terms, but a great deal of differentiation by teachers is critical for helping students meet standards and pass standardized tests.

8. Dedicate Resources for Professional Development

Standards-based learning requires dedicated and competent teachers to implement a variety of instructional interventions to help all students learn. The emphasis on qualified teachers goes beyond a deep knowledge of content and skills. Today's teachers must also be trained in how to use diagnostic tests to determine students' prior knowledge. Based on the results of these pre-assessments, teachers differentiate by using a variety of tiered lessons, performance assessments, problem-based learning projects, or experiential learning units. Professional development provides the ongoing training needed to help all teachers succeed with all students. And, just like with students, one size of professional development does not meet the needs of all teachers. Teachers need job-embedded staff development built around their individual needs as well as the individual needs of their students.

9. Serve the Needs of a Diverse Population

One paradox of the standards movement is requiring all students to meet the same standards, regardless of their prior knowledge, ability levels, interests, motivation, socioeconomic status, quality of early education, or effectiveness of previous teachers. Not every student enters school with the same abilities, and Darling-Hammond (1997) says we must allow for "differing starting points and pathways to learning so that students are not left out or left behind" (p. 231). Establishing the standard will not help a student meet the standard. Teachers will have to work with a diverse group of students and experiment with a wide variety of instructional and assessment strategies to see which ones work best. All students may not reach the standard, but teachers and students need to know where they are and what they still need to do. They may all begin "with the end in mind," but they will travel many different roads to arrive at the same destination.

FINAL THOUGHTS

Arthur Costa once addressed an audience at an educational conference and asked, "How many of you are old enough to have been through three back-to-basic movements?" The audience members laughed and nodded their heads. The members of that audience, like so many veteran educators, recognize how many educational movements have come and gone, sometimes sapping the strength and enthusiasm of those involved and making educators somewhat cynical of "innovations" and "systemic reform." New math, transformational grammar, time on task, outcomes-based education, and whole language are just a few of the many educational reforms that have been implemented and, in some cases, abandoned.

The standards movement will probably continue in the twenty-first century, but it is facing many challenges. States have different textbooks with different content, different curriculum frameworks, different criteria for judging the effectiveness of teachers, different high-stakes state tests with a different degree of difficulty, and, in some cases, different cut-off scores for passing. In other words, the standards movement lacks standardization. In addition, the focus of most state standards is performance but the focus of most state tests is knowledge and content skills measured mostly by multiple-choice questions, not performance-based assessments. Teachers know this and are often torn between engaging students in meaningful performances that foster deep understanding or practicing multiple-choice "benchmark testing." Is their job to prepare students to score high on the high-stakes tests or to prepare students for life? Should they do both? The chapters in this book focus on how teachers can and should do both. Each chapter offers strategies to help teachers create assessments to help students meet the standards on tests and also apply the standards in life.

ON YOUR OWN

Checklist Template

Standard: Assignment:	Not Yet 0	Some Evidence 1
•		
•		
•		
•		
•		
•		
•		
•		
•		
•		
•		
•		
•		
•		
•		

Figure 1.4

Source: Adapted from Belgrad, S., Burke, K., & Fogarty, R. © 2008. *The Portfolio Connection: Student Work Linked to Standards, 3rd edition.* Thousand Oaks, CA: Corwin.

ON YOUR OWN

Rubric Template

Standard: _____

Benchmark: _____

Scale:	1	2	3	4
Criteria:				
•				
•				
•				
•				
•				
•				
•				
•				
•				
•				
•				
•				

Figure 1.5

Source: From Burke, K. © 2006. *From Standards to Rubrics in Six Steps: Tools for Assessing Student Learning, K–8.* Thousand Oaks, CA: Corwin.

R E F L E C T I O N

Student Learning Standards

1. Review this chapter and other resources on standards and discuss your ideas with a colleague. Complete the following graphic describing the advantages and disadvantages of the standards-based movement.

STANDARDS-BASED MOVEMENT

	Advantages	Disadvantages
Example:	• It will help teachers focus their curriculum.	• It could become too prescriptive and uniform.
	•	•
	•	•
	•	•
	•	•
	•	•

2. Summarize your feelings by completing the stem question: When I think of the standards-based movement, I wonder . . .

3. Share your reflection on the standards-based movement with a colleague.

Figure 1.6

2 Differentiated Learning

WHAT IS DIFFERENTIATED LEARNING?

Differentiated learning is a term used to describe how students learn differently because of their prior knowledge, ability levels, interests, or learning modalities. Teachers who know how to identify these characteristics are better able to change their teaching and assessment practices by varying the content they teach, the process students use to learn the content, and the products they require students to produce to prove they have met the standards. Fogarty (2001) describes how "differentiated learning" evolved from the phrase "individual instruction" and then changed to "personalized instruction." The phrase "individualized educational plans," or IEPs, is now used to name the required model for developing learning plans tailored for students with special needs, while the preferred phrase in general education today is "differentiated instruction" (p.3).

Gregory and Chapman (2002) discuss the philosophy that "one size doesn't fit all" because students differ from each other in physical abilities, intellectual abilities, and social development. They discuss how teachers used to develop "the lesson" and teach it to all the students, knowing that some were bored because they already knew the material and others were struggling because it was too difficult. They say, "Adjustments should be based on sound knowledge of the learner. This includes what they know already, can do, like, are like, need, or prefer" (p. x). These adjustments involve a repertoire of teaching and learning strategies that go far beyond lecture and seatwork (see Figure 2.1).

Differentiated instruction is the philosophy that encourages teachers to strategically plan to reach the diverse learners in today's inclusive classrooms. Teachers recognize the needs of the students and respond by implementing instructional strategies to help all students meet targeted standards.

Teachers can differentiate the following:

- content that students learn
- assessment tools used to evaluate the work
- performance tasks selected to motivate the students
- instructional strategies used to help students meet the standards

(Adapted from Gregory & Chapman, 2002, p. x)

TOOLS AND STRATEGIES FOR DESIGNING INCLUSIVE CLASSROOMS FOR DIVERSE LEARNERS

Climate	Knowing the Learner	Assessing the Learner	Adjustable Assignments	Instructional Strategies	Curriculum Approaches
• Safe • Nurturing • Encouraging risk tasking • Inclusive • Multisensory • Stimulating • Complex • Challenging • Collaborative • Questioning • Cubing	• **Learning Styles** Dunn & Dunn Gregoric 4Mat Silver/Strong/ Hanson • **Multiple Intelligences** Using observation checklists, inventories, logs, and journals to become more aware of how one learns	• **Before:** **Formal** Written pre-test Journaling Surveys/ Inventories **Informal** Squaring off Boxing Graffiti facts • **During:** **Formal** Journaling/ Portfolios Teacher-made tests Checklists/ Rubrics **Informal** Thumb it Fist of five Face the fact • **After:** **Formal** Post-test Portfolio/ Conferences Reflections **Informal** Talking topics Conversation Circles Donut	• **Compacting** **T.A.P.S.** **Total Group:** Lecturette Presentation Demonstration Jigsaw Video Field trip Guest speaker Text • **Alone:** Interest Personalized Multiple intelligences • **Paired:** Random Interest Task • **Small Groups:** Heterogeneous Homogeneous Task oriented Constructed Random Interest	• **Brain-Research Based** Memory model Elaborative rehearsal • **Focus activities** • **Graphic organizers** Compare & contrast Webbing • **Metaphors** • **Cooperative group learning** • **Jigsaw** • **Role play**	**Centers** **Projects** **Problem-Based** **Inquiry** **Contracts**

Figure 2.1

Source: Gregory, G.H., and Chapman, C. (2007). *Differentiated instructional strategies: One size doesn't fit all, 2nd edition.* Thousand Oaks, CA. Corwin.

The purpose of this book is to help teachers develop performance tasks that will motivate all students to learn as well as to develop a wide range of assessment tools for evaluating the different types of work students create.

WHAT ARE THE MULTIPLE INTELLIGENCES?

In his book *Frames of Mind,* published in 1983, Howard Gardner formulated a theory proposing an alternative to the traditional view of intelligence represented by IQ tests. Based upon his work with brain-damaged veterans at Boston's Veteran Medical Center and with children at Project Zero at Harvard's Graduate School of Education, he hypothesized that in addition to the verbal and mathematical intelligences that are traditionally recognized and fostered in schools, several other intelligences operate. Gardner theorized that human potential encompasses spatial, musical, and kinesthetic, as well as interpersonal and intrapersonal intelligences (adding the naturalist intelligence in 1995). He further suggested that even though the eight intelligences are independent of one another, they do work together.

Gardner postulated the multiple intelligences theory would allow people to assess the talents and skills of the whole individual rather than the narrow definition of IQ measured in traditional tests. Fogarty and Stoehr (2008) believe the theory of multiple intelligences does provide a more holistic natural profile of human potential than an IQ test. One of the key philosophical tenets of performance assessment is that all students can learn, regardless of their IQ or socioeconomic background. Students have many talents and skills and their scores on IQ tests are just one indicator of their intelligence; moreover, teachers need to explore how each student may be "smart" in different ways.

Additionally, Sagor (2003) is concerned that in too many places, the implementation of standards-based education has led teachers to feel that they are supposed to "leave their creativity" at the door. He says often they are handed a canned, sometimes even scripted, curriculum. He also worries that in some locales, teachers are given a pacing chart that tells teachers not only *what* to teach but *when* to teach it. Creating a unit plan incorporating learning experiences and assessments using the multiple intelligences provides a creative way to teach the standards, differentiate instruction, and motivate students to learn in a variety of fun and challenging ways.

WHY SHOULD WE USE DIFFERENTIATION?

When many teachers first began their teaching careers, they taught groups of students who were "tracked" into homogeneously grouped classes based upon intelligence tests or test scores. It was not unusual for a teacher to have one "advanced class," another "regular class," and, of course, the infamous "basic" or "remedial" class. One lesson plan often worked because the teacher could teach to the middle of the class and meet the needs of most of the students. Today, however, teachers face a challenge because their classrooms are in a constant state of flux. Gregory and Chapman (2002) outline a series of factors that influence the constantly changing classroom:

- standard-based classrooms: targeted expectations set by districts, states, and nations
- high expectations for all students: no longer can we leave children behind and just "spray and pray" for success
- multicultural diversity: continuous influx of immigrant children with little or no communication skills or competencies in English
- student diversity: unique learning styles and different levels of multiple intelligences
- new cognitive research on human learning: knowledge of the brain and how it processes memory and makes meaning
- rapid societal and technological change: political and economic revolutions that influence what and how learning takes place (p. xi)

All these factors combine to create a challenging teaching environment. Add to that the explosion of personal technologies that distracts all students. The teacher might be immersed with the ancient Romans and their battles against the Barbarians, but the students are immersed in their text messages and anything else they can hide from the teacher.

HOW SHOULD WE USE THE MULTIPLE INTELLIGENCES?

Teachers are experimenting with a variety of instructional methods and assessment to evaluate students' achievement and progress toward meeting standards. Some educators are also experimenting with integrated instructional units that include learning experiences from all of the multiple intelligences. Using a graphic organizer such as the grid in Figure 2.6 on page 38 helps groups of teachers focus on standards, integrate their curricula, brainstorm learning experiences and assessments, and decide on the key whole-class assessments to capture important concepts in the unit. This approach helps individual or teams of teachers plan a unit that synthesizes cooperative learning, higher-order thinking skills, portfolios, and performance tasks as well as rubrics with the multiple intelligences. Figure 2.2 details learning experiences classified according to Gardner's theory of multiple intelligences.

Learning Experiences Generated by Gardner's Theory of Multiple Intelligences

Visual/Spatial
Images, graphics, drawings, sketches, maps, charts, doodles, pictures, spatial orientation, puzzles, designs, looks, appeal, mind's eye, imagination, visualization, dreams, nightmares, films, and videos

Logical/Mathematical
Reasoning, deductive and inductive logic, facts, data, information, spreadsheets, databases, sequencing, ranking, organizing, analyzing, proofs, conclusions, judging, evaluations, and assessments

Verbal/Linguistic
Words, wordsmith, speaking, writing, reading, papers, essays, poems, plays, narratives, lyrics, spelling, grammar, foreign languages, memos, bulletins, newsletters, newspapers, e-mail, faxes, speeches, talks, dialogues, and debates

Musical/Rhythmic
Music, rhythm, beat, melody, tunes, allegro, pacing, timbre, tenor, soprano, opera, baritone, symphony, choir, chorus, madrigals, rap, rock, rhythm and blues, jazz, classical, folk, ads and jingles

Bodily/Kinesthetic
Art, activity, action, experiential, hands-on experiments, try, do, perform, play, drama, sports, throw, toss, catch, jump, twist, twirl, assemble, disassemble, form, re-form, manipulate, touch, feel, immerse, and participate

Interpersonal/Social
Interact, communicate, converse, share, understand, empathize, sympathize, reach out, care, talk, whisper, laugh, cry, shudder, socialize, meet, greet, lead, follow, gangs, clubs, charisma, crowds, gatherings, and twosomes

Intrapersonal/Introspective
Self, solitude, meditate, think, create, brood, reflect, envision, journal, self-assess, set goals, plot, plan, dream, write, fiction, nonfiction, poetry, affirmations, lyrics, songs, screenplays, commentaries, introspection, and inspection

Naturalist
Nature, natural, environment, listen, watch, observe, classify, categorize, discern patterns, appreciate, hike, climb, fish, hunt, snorkel, dive, photograph, trees, leaves, animals, living things, flora, fauna, ecosystem, sky, grass, mountains, lakes, and rivers

Figure 2.2

Source: Fogarty, R., & Stoehr, J. (2008). *Integrating curricula with multiple intelligences: Teams, themes, & threads.* 2nd edition. Thousand Oaks, CA: Corwin.

Ten Steps to Develop a Differentiated Unit Plan

The following format for developing a unit plan can be adapted to meet the needs of the teacher or a group of teachers:

1. Decide on a unit or theme that will last at least two or three weeks. The unit could be on a specific topic such as oceanography or Greek mythology; a book, Stephen Crane's *The Red Badge of Courage;* or a country, Egypt. Some teachers choose to work on a thematic or integrated unit that connects several content areas. Thematic units might include health and wellness, justice in America, "off to work we go," crime and punishment, a decade (the 1920s), the future, or heroes.

2. Draw a grid on large pieces of newsprint or use a blank grid.

3. Decide on the standards and/or benchmarks that will be the major goals of the unit. What should the students be able to do at the end of the unit?

4. Distribute sticky notes to each participant. Ask participants to brainstorm ideas for learning experiences or assessments for the unit and to write one idea per sticky note. Allow five minutes for individual thinking and writing. Remember to be specific—instead of writing "read a book about oceans," recommend *Chadwick the Crab.*

5. Read each idea and decide where it should go on the grid. Remember that many ideas cross over into other intelligences. For example, holding a mock trial to determine whether President Roosevelt suspected Pearl Harbor was going to be bombed could be classified as interpersonal, bodily/kinesthetic, or verbal/linguistic. Place the idea where it most likely belongs or where more selections are needed.

6. Review the grid to make sure there are five learning experiences or assessments for each intelligence. Remember, many activities are assessments. For example, creating a Venn diagram to compare and contrast Hemingway and Faulkner is a learning experience and it is also an assessment.

7. Decide on four learning experiences from the grid that would benefit the whole class. Consider the following criteria for selecting each experience:
   a. Does the experience help meet the standards?
   b. Does it include several intelligences? (Does it meet the needs of more students?)
   c. Is it worth the time to do it?
   d. Can it be assessed?
   e. Is it doable in my class? (Consider time, resources, money, space, etc.)
   f. Is it fun and motivating?
   g. Will it meet the diverse needs of students?

8. Write the four learning experiences in the boxes on the bottom of the grid. Remember that teachers on the team may select different whole-class experiences based upon their focus for the unit and the individual needs of their students.

9. Decide on how to assess the four learning experiences selected. Remember to combine traditional assessments (quizzes, tests, research reports) with performance assessments (logs, journals, portfolios, projects).

10. Create a culminating event to bring closure to the unit. The event should synthesize all the ideas and provide a showcase for the students to share their learning with a wider audience. Examples of culminating events include mock trials, field trips, portfolio exhibitions, plays, costume days, a medieval banquet, a Renaissance fair, job fairs, and reenactments.

In addition to being a brain-based activity, the multiple-intelligences unit plan enables teachers to make the most of students' individual differences and diversity, since students will gravitate toward their interests and strengths when they choose their projects and some of their portfolio entries. Many teachers feel comfortable developing a multiple-intelligences unit with students because it fosters cooperative learning, integrated curriculum, interdisciplinary teaching, problem-based learning, performance tasks, authentic assessment, portfolios, higher-order thinking, and many other interactive strategies. Such an approach also taps the multiple intelligences of all students and promotes an enjoyable atmosphere of active learning.

Figure 2.3 provides a grid classifying learning experiences and assessments by multiple intelligences. Two examples of unit plans organized by multiple intelligences and five examples of rubrics that can be used for assessment conclude the chapter. Opportunities to devise a unit plan using multiple intelligences and a rubric for a group project are also provided in the "On Your Own" section.

Teachers address the needs of their students by offering multiple learning opportunities and assessments. They vary the type of classroom activities and the projects and performances they assign. Using the multiple-intelligences grid to plan a unit helps teachers organize students' learning experiences and requires teachers to engage in interactive teaching. Effective teachers create meaningful and engaging tasks that challenge students to apply their knowledge and skills to authentic tasks in life. They begin this process by diagnosing where students are in terms of prior knowledge, ability, interest, and learning profile and then scaffold the learning process so each student meets her goal.

FINAL THOUGHTS

Over the years, the terminology to describe how students learn differently has ranged from learning styles, to learning profiles, to multiple intelligences, and to differentiated learning, but regardless of the labels, students *do* learn differently. Teachers who explore multiple strategies for instruction, and provide choices for students to demonstrate their strengths and focus on their weaknesses, differentiate their instruction. Each lesson can be tiered to target different ability levels. The content, process, and product can be changed to target the same standard in different ways.

The inclusive classroom challenges teachers and students to explore techniques and resources that go outside the box to teach and assess students. The students come to school with different academic backgrounds, interests, and social skills. Their diversity challenges educators to meet students' individual needs by implementing appropriate assessment tools.

Learning Experiences

Verbal/Linguistic	Logical/Mathematical	Visual/Spatial	Bodily/Kinesthetic
Speeches Debates Storytelling Reports Crosswords Newspapers Internet	Puzzles Outlines Timelines Analogies Patterns Problem-solving Lab experiments Formulas	Artwork Photographs Math manipulatives Graphic organizers Posters, charts Illustrations Cartoons Props for plays Use of projector	Field trips Role playing Learning centers Labs Sports/games Cooperative learning Body language Experiments

Musical/Rhythmic	Interpersonal	Intrapersonal	Naturalist
Background music Songs about books, people, countries, historic events Raps Jingles Choirs	Group video, film, slides Team computer programs Think-pair-share Cooperative tasks Jigsaws Conferences	Reflective journals Learning logs Goal-setting journals Metacognitive reflections Independent reading Silent reflection Diaries	Outdoor education Environmental studies Field trips (farm, zoo) Bird watching Nature walk Weather forecasting Stargazing Exploring nature Ecology studies Leaf identification

Figure 2.3

EXAMPLES

Greek Mythology

Subject Area: *Integrated Unit—Middle School*   **Timeline:** *4–6 weeks*

Major Goals of Unit: *1. Communicate ideas in writing to describe, inform, persuade, and entertain.*

2. Demonstrate comprehension of a broad range of reading materials related to Greek mythology.

3. Use reading, writing, listening, and speaking skills to research and apply information for specific purposes.

List at least three learning experiences or assessments under each intelligence.

Verbal/Linguistic	Logical/Mathematical	Visual/Spatial	Bodily/Kinesthetic
• *Read* The Iliad. • *Read* The Odyssey. • *Read Edith Hamilton's Mythology.* • *Write an original myth to explain a scientific mystery.* • *Write poems about mythology.* • *Write a eulogy for a fallen Greek or Trojan warrior.*	• *Use a Venn diagram to compare the Greeks and the Trojans.* • *Create original story problems that incorporate the Pythagorean theorem.* • *Draw a family tree of the twelve Olympians and their children.* • *Complete a timeline of Odysseus' trip home from Troy.*	• *Draw the battle plan for the Greeks' attack on Troy.* • *Draw Mt. Olympus.* • *Sketch the Greek gods and goddesses.* • *Create a video of the Olympic games.* • *Draw items that relate to mythology.*	• *Act out a Greek tragedy.* • *Re-create some of the Olympic events.* • *Act out a myth.* • *Create a dance for the forest nymphs.* • *Reenact the battle scene between Hector and Achilles.*

Musical/Rhythmic	Interpersonal	Intrapersonal	Naturalist
• *Write a song for a lyre.* • *Pretend you are Apollo, God of Music, and CEO of Motown.* • *Select music that correlates with each god or goddess.*	• *Interview Helen about her role in the Trojan War.* • *Work in a group to create a computer crossword puzzle about mythology.*	• *Pretend you are a Greek soldier away from home for ten years. Keep a diary of your thoughts.* • *Write a journal about how you would feel if you were Prometheus chained to a rock.* • *Reflect on the effects of war on civilians.*	• *Using scientific data, predict how long it will take before anything grows after the Greeks destroy Troy and sow the fields with salt.* • *Describe the animals and plants on Mt. Olympus.*

1. Whole-class learning experiences:	*Read Hamilton's Mythology*	*Read excerpts from* The Iliad *and* The Odyssey	*Select a group project or performance*	*Portfolio that contains 7–10 items*
	↕	↕	↕	↕
2. Whole-class assessments for learning experiences:	*Teacher-made test*	*Write a paper comparing the Greeks to the Trojans.*	*Rubric to assess each one*	*Rubric created by class*

3. Culminating event for unit:

Hold an exhibition in the school gym where students and teachers dress up as favorite mythological characters. Invited guests view videos, portfolios, artifacts, and an original skit.

Figure 2.4

EXAMPLES

The Red Badge of Courage Novel Unit

Subject Area: *American Literature—High School Social Studies*   **Timeline:** *3 weeks*

Major Goals of Unit: 1. Demonstrate competence in general skills and strategies for reading a variety of literary texts.

2. Demonstrate competence in the general skills and strategies of the writing process.

3. Understand major causes and effects of the Civil War.

List at least three learning experiences or assessments under each intelligence.

Verbal/Linguistic	Logical/Mathematical	Visual/Spatial	Bodily/Kinesthetic
• Read the novel The Red Badge of Courage *by Stephen Crane.* • Write a letter to President Lincoln about your feelings about the Civil War. • Interview a historian about the Battle of Chancellorsville.	• Graph the number of dead and wounded from major Civil War battles. • Compare the number of injured and dead in the Civil War to World War I, World War II, the Korean War, and the Iraq War. • Create a Venn diagram comparing General Grant to General Lee.	• Draw a political cartoon about the Civil War. • Draw a mind map of the Civil War that contains major battles. • Draw a timeline of major events in the war. • Draw a book jacket for The Red Badge of Courage.	• Act out one key scene from The Red Badge of Courage. • Demonstrate marching drills used in the Civil War. • Visit a Civil War battleground, cemetery, or museum.

Musical/Rhythmic	Interpersonal	Intrapersonal	Naturalist
• Sing the songs the troops of the North and South sang while marching. • Learn the dances of the Civil War era. • Make up a ballad about Henry, the protagonist of The Red Badge of Courage.	• Read other books about buddies during war time, such as All Quiet on the Western Front, Catch-22, and For Whom the Bell Tolls. • Write and act out a dialogue between two military buddies in either Iraq, Korea, or World War I or World War II.	• Keep a daily diary of boot camp. • Write a poem about your feelings. • Write a last will and testament in case you die in battle. • Write a eulogy for a soldier who died in battle.	• Find specific passages in The Red Badge of Courage where author Stephen Crane tells about how war destroys nature. • Write how the environment (weather, rivers, terrain) impacts battle decisions. • Research the effects weapons of destruction have on the environment.

1. Whole-class learning experiences:

Read the novel The Red Badge of Courage	*Create a mind map on Civil War battles*	*Select one group project or performance*	*Develop a portfolio that contains 7 items*
↕	↕	↕	↕

2. Whole-class assessments for learning experiences:

Teacher-made test (numerical grade)	*Checklist*	*Rubric to assess key criteria*	*Rubric to assess portfolio*

3. Culminating event for unit:

Hold an exhibition where students display artifacts they selected from the grid to include in their personal portfolios. Invite guests to view videos, slides, and pictures from their projects.

Figure 2.5

ON YOUR OWN

Unit Plan Using Multiple Intelligences Grid

Unit: _____   Grade Level: _____

Subject Area: _____   Timeline: _____

Major Goals of Unit: 1._____

2._____

3._____

List at least three learning experiences or assessments under each intelligence.

Verbal/Linguistic	Logical/Mathematical	Visual/Spatial	Bodily/Kinesthetic

Musical/Rhythmic	Interpersonal	Intrapersonal	Naturalist

1. Whole-class learning experiences:

2. Whole-class assessments for learning experiences:

3. Culminating event for unit:

Figure 2.6

REFLECTION

Reflection on Differentiated Learning

1. List a standard you plan to teach.
   Standard:

2. Develop an assignment, project, or performance to address the standard.

3. Differentiate your assignment, project, or performance using the following guidelines:

   a. Change the *content:*

   b. Change the *process:*

   c. Change the *product:*

4. Why do you think differentiation is so important for students today?

Figure 2.7

3

Portfolios

WHAT IS A PORTFOLIO?

A portfolio is a collection of student work that showcases what students know as well as what students think and feel. "Portfolios and e-portfolios [electronic] can assist teachers in creating these models while also engaging students in both critical and creative thinking. Portfolios provide students with multiple strategies for constructing meaning from information and experiences, and for demonstrating their mastery of standards" (Belgrade, Burke, & Fogarty, 2008, p. xx). A portfolio is more than just a collection of randomly organized materials stuck in a folder. A portfolio has a *purpose* and a *focus*. The organization and the contents of portfolios differ according to the purpose and the type of the portfolio.

A portfolio may contain the following:

1. *Creative cover* to depict the topic.
2. *Letter to the reader* to explain the cover and to welcome the readers.
3. *Table of contents* to display organization.
4. *Six or seven student artifacts* to showcase work selected by teachers and students.
5. *Reflections* to reveal student insight.
6. *Self-evaluation* to analyze strengths and weaknesses.
7. *Goal-setting page* to set new short- and long-term goals.
8. *Conference questions* (optional) to provide the audience with key questions.

Additional items that could be included in a portfolio are

- reflections or comments from peers about the artifacts
- comments from parents or significant others
- descriptions of major concepts learned
- bibliography of sources used

Purpose of the Portfolio

The first step in creating a portfolio is to determine the purpose of the portfolio. The contents need to be aligned to the purpose or rationale for implementing portfolios. Butler and McMunn (2006) would ask if the purpose of the portfolio was to instruct, support learning, or assess. They say that "Answering this question will help determine the types of artifacts the students will collect. For instance, a portfolio assembled solely for summative assessment purpose may contain only best works rather than a continuum of student work" (p. 72). Portfolios can also be an intersection of formative and summative assessment that includes rough drafts and final papers so students can see their growth over time. A portfolio can be used to

1. Document meeting district, state, or national standards.

2. Connect several subject areas to provide an integrated assessment.

3. Chronicle growth and development over extended periods of a semester, year, or clusters of grades (K–2, 3–5, 7–9, 10–12).

4. Document the key concepts taught.

5. Share at a job interview, promotion, or college entrance review.

The purpose of the portfolio will determine the type of portfolio and the process to be used in developing the portfolio. It is not unusual for a portfolio to combine several purposes to meet the needs of the students or school.

Types of Portfolios

Once the primary purpose for creating a portfolio has been determined, educators must select the type of portfolio that would best fulfill the purpose. These types may also be combined to correlate with the purpose for creating the portfolio (see Figure 3.1).

Hansen (1992) advocates using self-created literacy portfolios by asking students to include what they are like outside the classroom. Students can include pictures of relatives, awards, or ribbons won in athletic events, lists of books or magazines about rock stars, sports, hobbies, or anything that interests them. The key to the portfolio is the discussion the items generate. Every adult and student involved in a literacy portfolio project creates one. "Whether or not we know ourselves better than anyone else does, our portfolios give us the opportunity to get to know ourselves better" (Hansen, 1992, p. 66). The potential for reflection and self-assessment in the portfolio process is exciting because the students take more control of their own learning and analyze their own strengths and weaknesses.

Digital Portfolios

As more schools experiment with technology, students are creating digital portfolios or multimedia collections of student work. Since the purpose of the portfolio drives the content, digital portfolios serve many purposes. Those purposes include proving students have met state standards, showcasing their best work, proving they have met all the requirements for promotion or graduation, or communicating with parents (Niguidula, 2005). Digital portfolios could

Types of Portfolios

1. *Writing*—dated writing samples to show process and product.

2. *Process Folios*—first and second drafts of assignments along with the final product to show growth.

3. *Literacy*—combination of reading, writing, speaking, and listening pieces.

4. *Best Work*—student and teacher selections of the student's best work.

5. *Unit*—one unit of study (e.g., Egypt, angles, frogs, elections).

6. *Integrated*—thematic study that brings in different disciplines (e.g., "health and wellness" includes language arts, science, math, health, and physical education).

7. *Yearlong*—key artifacts from an entire year to show growth and development.

8. *Career*—important artifacts (résumés, recommendations, commendations) collected to showcase employability.

9. *Standards*—evidence to document meeting standards.

10. *Goal Setting*—organized focus on setting or meeting academic and personal goals.

Figure 3.1

include videotapes of students' performances, their reading at the beginning of the year and then again at the end of the year to measure growth, or solutions to math problems explaining their processes.

Digital portfolios used as an assessment tool need to address questions about the vision, purpose, audience, technology, logistics, and assessment—just like students producing traditional portfolios. According to Niguidula (2005), technology is, actually, the least important consideration. The focus should be on clear learning goals in a greater assessment. To do this, "schools need to identify the purpose of their portfolios, the kinds of work students should enter into portfolios, and strategies for assessing portfolios" (p. 45). Digital portfolios motivate many students because they have become very adept at all types of technology and enjoy the creative aspect of integrating sound, pictures, and various multimedia programs to express their personalities and showcase their learning.

WHY SHOULD WE USE PORTFOLIOS?

The portfolio helps the classroom environment foster a seamless web of instruction and assessment. "If carefully assembled, portfolios become an intersection of instruction and assessment; they are not just instruction or just assessment, but, rather, both. Together, instruction and assessment give more than either give separately" (Paulson, Paulson, & Meyer, 1991, p. 61). The infinity sign is an appropriate symbol to represent the portfolio. The process provides an ongoing feedback loop of students producing work, reviewing work, sharing work, revising work, conferencing about work, exhibiting work, and then beginning the process again. It is difficult to know where instruction ends and assessment begins because of the overlap in teaching, learning, and assessing.

Portfolios can be used for the following:

- tools for discussion with peers, teachers, and parents
- demonstrations of students' skills and understanding
- opportunities for students to reflect on their work metacognitively
- chances to examine current goals and set new ones
- documentation of students' development and growth in abilities, attitudes, and expressions
- demonstrations of different learning styles, differentiated interests, and cultural diversity
- options for students to make critical choices about what they select for their portfolio
- evidence that traces the development of students' learning
- connections between prior knowledge and new learning

Portfolios provide concrete evidence of student learning. The emphasis on examining student work to see if it meets the standards is critical in the standards-based classroom. The final product is important, but the process is equally important and probably conveys more about how the student learns. The process of metacognition—thinking about one's thinking—helps students become more self-reflective and more empowered as stakeholders in their own learning (see Figure 3.2). Some people use the term *process-folio* to focus on how students learn as much as what they learn.

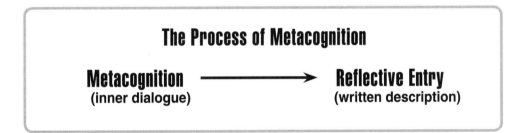

Figure 3.2

HOW CAN WE IMPLEMENT PORTFOLIOS?

Educators have developed a variety of creative and intricate portfolio systems, but for teachers just embarking on the portfolio journey, it might be best to start simply. The portfolio process in its simplest form includes three basic steps of collecting, selecting, and reflecting (see Figure 3.3).

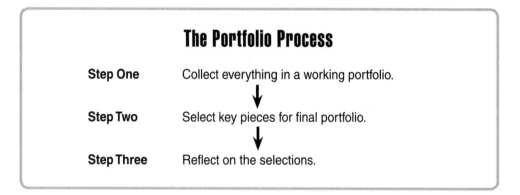

Figure 3.3

Collect

Educators usually recognize the benefits of using portfolios to show the growth and development of their students. Unfortunately, they also recognize the tremendous organizational problems and increased time commitment associated with implementing a portfolio system. The "less is more" philosophy applies to portfolio collection.

Working Portfolios

To simplify the implementation of the system, note the first step in the collection process is to develop a working portfolio. The working portfolio is where students store all the items they have collected before they make their selections for the final, or showcase, portfolio. Various methods for storing items include the following:

- large cardboard boxes
- cereal boxes
- file folders
- accordion files
- computer disks
- compact disks
- file cabinets

Creating a working portfolio is similar to traditional assessment because students usually collect their work in a folder or notebook. Work should still be sent home and brought back. Teachers may choose to make a copy of very important assignments before they are sent home, just in case of loss or damage. Even if students lose some of their work, there should still be enough work left from which to choose for the final portfolio. This first step is not much different than a teacher asking students to keep a folder or a notebook of their work.

Variety of Artifacts

One of the characteristics of working portfolios that sets them apart from more traditional writing folders is that they should contain a *variety* of work that reflects different modalities. Students should have more than just worksheets or homework assignments in their working portfolio; they should collect artifacts including cassette tapes, compact disks (cds), pictures, projects, performances, rough drafts, journals, logs, artwork, musical work, and assignments that feature work from all the multiple intelligences. If the portfolio is to be a true portrait of the student as a learner, it needs to be richly textured and comprehensive. It also must assess more than just one of the multiple intelligences—in this case, usually the verbal/linguistic intelligence. A writing folder is a writing folder. A portfolio is much more.

Select

After most of the quarter or semester is spent collecting items, the selection process usually involves three major questions:

1. Who should select the items that go into the final portfolio?

2. What items should be selected?

3. When should these items be selected?

Who Should Select Items?

In most cases, both teachers and students select the items to be included in the final portfolio. The teacher needs to show evidence that the students met school goals or standards and that they understand the basic concepts of the course. If students were allowed to choose all the items, they would probably select their best or favorite work, but those items wouldn't necessarily provide a balanced analysis to document learning. After the teacher has selected some general items, then students should have the freedom to choose items that they want to showcase their strengths and talents.

In addition, parents and peers sometimes select items for the portfolio and write a comment or reflection about the piece or pieces. The selection process varies, however, depending on the purpose and type of the portfolio (see Figure 3.4). If the purpose of the portfolio were to meet district standards, then the teacher would have to request pieces that provide evidence of meeting those standards. Sometimes the selection could involve both the teacher and the student. For instance, the teacher may require a narrative writing piece to meet standards, but the student can choose which one of the narrative pieces to include. The teacher sets the parameters, but the student has some choice within those parameters.

Regardless of who selects the entries, interested parties need to respond to students' entries. The feedback generates motivation for continued learning.

What Items Should Be Selected?

As stated previously, the motto that educators need to adopt for the selection process, if they are going to maintain their sanity and make this process manageable, is "less is more." It is not necessary to include all of the artifacts in the final portfolio. Even though some students think all of their work is wonderful and they just can't eliminate anything, the very process of reviewing their

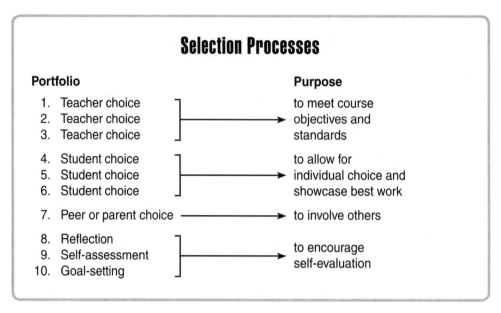

Figure 3.4

work and deciding what is appropriate is metacognitive. Most portfolios contain seven to twelve items. Teachers should not have to bring a wagon to school to haul home portfolios. Keep it simple. Fewer items provide more opportunities for in-depth discussion and more targeted feedback and analysis.

Many teachers like to include selection criteria such as "select a piece that is your most unsatisfying piece and discuss why" or "select the piece you would like to do over and tell why" or "select the piece that you just don't understand and explain why." These criteria provide insightful information about the learners and their learning processes. By viewing the not-so-best work, the audience gets a truer picture of the student's strengths and weaknesses and why particular goals were set for improvement. If students only select their best work for all portfolios, the students may increase their self-esteem, but teachers and parents may develop a distorted or rose-colored opinion of the student's abilities. The "best-work" portfolio sometimes appears "fluffy" and portrays a portfolio more as a "scrapbook of stuff" rather than a collection of evidence that the student met learning standards, district goals, or course objectives. The portfolio must also include rigorous assessments that document a student's ability and help teachers modify instruction or adapt the curriculum to meet each student's needs. The evidence in the final portfolio needs to also correlate to traditional assessments such as teacher-made tests and standardized tests. The portfolio grade will probably be higher than traditional test grades because students have more time to revise and perfect their work.

When Should Items Be Selected?

Teachers usually provide deadlines for selecting items for the portfolio based upon the grading periods. For example, students may select their final items a few weeks before the end of a grading period.

The timing for selecting items for the final portfolio depends, once again, on the purpose and type of portfolio (see Figure 3.5). Many teachers find it more manageable to have the students complete unit portfolios throughout the year. Once the unit is complete, the teacher saves the portfolio contents and returns the notebook or permanent, final-portfolio container to the students for their next unit portfolio. At the end of the year, the teacher distributes the four or five unit portfolios and asks students to select items for their final, yearlong portfolio. The students then choose about ten to twelve items based upon selection criteria such as the following:

1. Select one item from the beginning of the year and a similar item from the end of the year and comment on your growth.

2. Select your favorite artifact and explain why.

3. Select your least favorite artifact and explain why.

4. Select an artifact that will surprise people and explain why.

Timeline Scenarios

Unit Portfolio

1. Collect items for three or four weeks.
2. Select and reflect on items two weeks prior to the end of the unit.
3. Conduct conferences in the last week.
4. Grade portfolio the last week.

Semester Portfolio

1. Collect items the entire semester.
2. Select seven to ten final items for the portfolio four weeks before the end of the semester.
3. Allow one week for students to select, reflect, and organize the portfolios.
4. Allow one week for conferences.
5. Allow one week for grading.

Yearlong Portfolio

1. Collect one to two items each week.
2. Review all items at the end of each quarter and select three or four items. Date all items.
3. Repeat process each quarter. Students write reflections on each item.
4. Four weeks before the end of school, select the final ten to twelve items for the portfolio.
5. Allow two to three weeks for reflection, organization, and conferencing.
6. Allow one to two weeks for grading.

Figure 3.5

Reflect

Portfolios require students to pause and reflect on their learning. The act of reflecting is what makes a portfolio different than a course notebook.

Portfolios enable students to reflect on their progress toward meeting and exceeding learning goals and standards. When students use metacognition to think about their thinking, they achieve a depth of understanding beyond meeting the standards. Martin-Kniep (2000) says:

> Such reflection could be a letter to the reader, an introduction to the portfolio, or reflective statements that accompany the various portfolio entries or artifacts. A portfolio without a student's reflection is not really a portfolio, but rather a collection of work that is hard to decipher without commentary from its author. (p. 67)

Reflection is the heart and soul of the portfolio process and one of the reasons the portfolio is different than traditional and performance assessments. Even though reflection is optional for students for other performances and products, it is required for portfolios.

Labeling

The first and easiest step in the reflection process involves asking students to attach a label to each artifact in the portfolio. The labels could include

- "showcases my interests"
- "best work"
- "most challenging"
- "most creative"
- "a nightmare"
- "first draft—more to come"
- "targets the standard"

Another strategy to introduce students to the reflection process is to have them write their reflections, reactions, or descriptions on sticky notes and then attach the sticky notes to each item. Sometimes they may rewrite these initial reflections when they select the piece for their final portfolio. Other times, they'll just edit them slightly. Occasionally, they'll include their initial reflection from when they completed an item and then add another reflection to provide insight after more time has elapsed.

Stem Questions

Some students become adept at writing descriptions and reflections of their work without any prompts. Many students, however, stare at their portfolio pieces and have no idea what to write. Teachers prime the pump by either assigning a stem question or allowing students to select a stem to complete. Figure 3.6 offers examples of stems that can generate more reflection.

Goal Setting

Goal setting is a part of reflection. Students need to set goals within a predetermined period of time, serving as road maps guiding the student's journey.

Reflective Stems for Portfolio Entries

1. This piece shows I've met standard #__ because . . .

2. This piece shows I really understand the content because . . .

3. This piece showcases my _____ intelligence because . . .

4. If I could show this piece to anyone—living or dead—I would show it to _____ because . . .

5. People who knew me last year would never believe this piece because . . .

6. This piece was my greatest challenge because . . .

7. My (parents, friend, teacher) liked this piece because . . .

8. One thing I have learned about myself is . . .

9. This piece demonstrates I can answer the essential questions of the unit because . . .

10. I understand the big idea of this unit because . . .

Figure 3.6

Pete and Fogarty (2003) say goals "provide the inspiration to begin the journey and the motivation to keep going" (p. 73). Students set both short- and long-term goals in their portfolios. Some goals might be easy to achieve, but others should be "stretch" goals to extend students' thinking and challenge them to exceed expectations. During each portfolio conference, the students reflect on their progress and set new goals. Since the standards movement dictates the outcomes, students should set rigorous goals and try to meet and exceed them.

Mirror Page

Another method to help students gain insight on their work is to ask them to organize their portfolio so that they place the item or piece of evidence on one page and write a description of the piece, followed by a reflection or reaction to it, on the facing page (see Figure 3.7). The proximity of the reflection to the piece of evidence helps the portfolio creator as well as the reader focus on examining the piece more carefully alongside references to the elements being described.

The description requires the students to explain the piece of work and share their understanding of its importance. Also, the description provides the teacher with a more in-depth analysis of student learning. The description could be elaborated upon during the conference, but the written description helps to clarify whether or not the student understands the basic concept of the

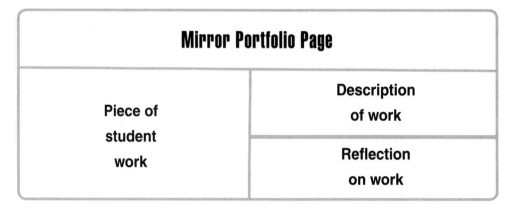

Figure 3.7

assignment. The reflection, on the other hand, helps students understand how they feel about each piece by asking themselves questions such as the following:

1. What does this piece show about me?

2. What did I do well in this piece?

3. How can I adjust my learning to improve?

4. What help do I need?

5. Why is this piece important?

6. How does this piece demonstrate my understanding of the essential questions and big ideas?

Student Reflection

A seventh-grade student was asked to include his most difficult math assignment in his portfolio and write why it was his most difficult piece. He included an assignment on word problems and wrote the following piece, entitled "My Most Difficult Work."

If I had to choose one, I would choose the word problems that we did. I found them the most difficult out of the things that we did. I found them the most difficult because I had to think about them for a while before I could get an answer, especially since I work at a slow pace. We didn't have enough time for me to be able to take my time and think them over. I was able to find the answer most of the time, but other kids work at a faster rate than I do so they were able to get more of the answers. I was glad we got to work in groups because it showed me that I was not the only kid who was having trouble with them. I think that it also helped me because some people could understand parts of the problem better than others and we could also learn how they found out the answers that will help us out in the future. I am going to try to correct it by getting a book on word problems and tips on how to solve them. I am also going to be an engineer so I will need to get good at them and take classes that deal with them when I get older.

Seventh-Grade Student, Maryland

The teacher was amazed when she read the reflection because she had always thought mathematics came very easily to the student. She said she gained new insight on the student as a learner and a person by reading his reflection. Her comment was, "I ask you, does this child understand the content, the process, and himself?" (Personal correspondence, 1996). Clearly, the power of the portfolio is derived from the descriptions, reactions, processing pieces, and metacognitive reflections that help students achieve their goals.

Examining Student Work

Blythe, Allen, and Powell (2008) advocate examining student work either individually or collaboratively by reviewing portfolios together, having students sit in on one another's portfolio exhibitions, or scoring their own work and the work of others with a common rubric. Teachers will learn more about an individual student's response to an assignment and, in the process, learn more about their own teaching and assessment practices. Conducting teacher-student conferences and peer conferences to discuss the portfolios helps synthesize the learning and celebrate the successes.

The formative feedback provided to the students from both the written and the oral comments helps improve students learning. What, then, are the characteristics of good formative feedback? Gareis and Grant (2008) believe effective formative feedback should be (1) honest, (2) accurate, (3) specific, (4) constructive, and (5) timely. Along with stressing the importance of using all five characteristics, they explain, "To maximize the instructive effect of feedback, it must also be honest, constructive, and timely. Teachers, therefore, are wise to consider practical ways to provide formative feedback to students in their own classrooms" (p. 167). One of the greatest challenges, of course, involves the time constraints for providing written feedback to each student when teachers have thirty-five students in the class. It also takes a special type of classroom management to provide oral feedback to individual students while simultaneously scanning the other thirty-four students. Teachers soon learn how to talk one-on-one with a student without losing control of the entire class. Sometimes the best time to provide individual feedback is when the class is working in small groups and engaged in a project or cooperative activity. By moving around the room, teachers can engage in quick conversations with many individual students during one class period. Brief feedback can be effective if it is specific, clear, and focused. Once again, the "less is more" philosophy prevails.

Assessing the Portfolio

Students need to know the criteria for grading the portfolio in advance. Teachers should provide a criteria checklist and a rubric to show students the expectations for quality work. Butler and McMunn (2006) explain how a scoring guide can lessen frustration for students when choosing content, and also ease the challenge for teachers. "Through careful planning, the teacher does not have to dread the moment he must confront a huge mound of papers, wondering what he will find in the contents of the portfolio his students have constructed" (Butler & McMunn, 2006, p. 73). Using a checklist and rubric will also help students self-assess their own work and assess the work of their peers.

Students should then have opportunities to improve their work before submitting it for the summative evaluation.

This chapter has just addressed the tip of the iceberg about portfolios, but the three basic steps remain the key: collect, select, reflect. For educators and students just beginning the portfolio process, start small. Once teachers introduce the first portfolio, prepare to alter, extend, and elaborate on the process to meet the needs of the teachers and the students.

FINAL THOUGHTS

Portfolios have been one type of classroom assessment used by some teachers for many years. Portfolios, however, continue to have a rollercoaster existence. They ride a cycle where they are very popular for a while and then they almost disappear. The "best work" portfolios of the 1980s were criticized because parents only saw students' best work. They were understandably upset if a student's grades were not as high because the final grade on the report card included *all* the student's work and the average was lower. Digital portfolios became popular when schools incorporated more advanced, and accessible, technology. In the last few years, standards-based portfolios have emerged to document each student's ability to meet the standards. Additionally, special education students and English language learners often provide work samples in portfolios to document evidence they can meet the standards, even though their scores on standardized tests may be lower.

Portfolios will probably play a bigger role as the emphasis on examining student work intensifies. They show students' formative, or "in progress," drafts as well as their summative "final attempts." The connection between assessment "for" learning and assessment "of" learning is showcased in one document for all to see. The growth, progress, and process of each student is transparent. Hopefully, teachers will devote the time and resources necessary once they see how their students' personalities, creativity, and academic growth are showcased in the portfolios.

EXAMPLES

Portfolio Examples by Level and Discipline

ELEMENTARY

SPIDERS PORTFOLIO

Integrated Unit on Spiders

Table of Contents

1. Letter to parents about what students have learned
2. Book review of *Charlotte's Web*
3. Web graphic organizer
4. Watercolor artwork
5. Audio tape of student reading story about spiders
6. Original narrative (first and final drafts) about a spider
7. Science research report on arachnids
8. Spider rap song created in cooperative group
9. Pictures of group project on spiders
10. Checklists or rubrics for book review, narrative, and science report

MIDDLE SCHOOL

GEOMETRY PORTFOLIO

Table of Contents

1. My *Math Phobia* Journal
2. Three original geometry problems
3. Glossary of geometry terms
4. Drawings of geometric shapes with labels
5. Three problem-solving logs with explanations
6. String geometric design poster
7. CD of group project on angles
8. Essay on video, *Why Math?*
9. Research on math-related careers and academic requirements
10. Checklists for poster, CD, essay, and research
11. Checklist and rubric for portfolio
12. Three goals for next quarter

HIGH SCHOOL

BIOLOGY PORTFOLIO

Table of Contents

1. Research reports on careers related to the field of biology
2. One lab report (checklist provided)
3. One problem-solving log (checklist)
4. Pamphlet on diabetes as a group project (rubric)
5. Multimedia presentation on the circulatory system
6. Informative essay on germ warfare
7. Research paper on genetic engineering
8. Interview with college biology professor about new fields of study
9. Self-evaluation of portfolio using checklist and rubric
10. Goal-setting web
11. Reflection page on how this course will influence the student's life

COLLEGE

CIVIL WAR PORTFOLIO

Table of Contents

1. Annotated bibliographies of five books written about the Civil War (checklist)
2. Reference list for 20 sources related to the Civil War
3. One abstract of a research article (checklist)
4. Audiotape of interview with local historian
5. Journal entries of trip to Gettysburg Battlefield
6. Map of the Battle of Gettysburg
7. Oral presentation on Pickett's charge
8. Research paper on military tactics used at the Battle of Gettysburg
9. Venn diagram comparing Battle of Gettysburg and Battle of Chancellorsville
10. Critique of TV miniseries *The Civil War*
11. Peer evaluation of portfolio using checklist and rubric

Figure 3.8

EXAMPLES

Self-Assessment Portfolio Checklist

Standard: Use reading, writing, listening, and speaking skills to research and apply information for specific purposes.

CRITERIA:	SCALE:	1	2	3	4
Form: Did you check for correct…					
• spelling?					
• grammar?					
• sentence structure?					
Visual Appeal: Did you include creative…					
• cover?					
• artwork?					
• graphics?					
Organization:					
• Is your portfolio complete?					
• Did you turn the portfolio in on time?					
• Did you include an accurate Table of Contents?					
Knowledge of Key Concepts: Did you demonstrate your…					
• knowledge of the facts?					
• understanding of important concepts?					
• ability to apply your knowledge to new situations?					
Reflections: Did you…					
• write a reflection for each piece?					
• reveal the depth of your thoughts?					
• demonstrate your ability to self-assess your work?					

Figure 3.9

EXAMPLES

Weighted Rubric for Portfolio

(Developed from Checklist)

Student: _____ Subject: _____ Date: _____

Standard: Use reading, writing, listening, and speaking skills to research and apply information for specific purposes.

Criteria	Indicators	Does Not Meet Standards 1	Approaching the Standards 2	Meets State Standards 3	Exceeds State Standards 4	Score
Form	• Spelling • Grammar • Sentence structure	2–3 errors	1 error	0 errors	0 errors and a high level of writing	__ x 3 __ (12)
Visual Appeal	• Cover • Artwork • Graphics	Includes 1 element	Includes 2 elements	Includes all 3 elements	All 3 elements are creatively and visually appealing	__ x 4 __ (16)
Organization	• Completeness • Timeliness • Table of contents	Includes 1 element	Includes 2 elements	Includes all 3 elements	All 3 elements demonstrate high level of organization	__ x 5 __ (20)
Knowledge of Key Concepts	• Key concepts • Evidence of understanding • Application	Evidence of key concepts included in portfolio	Evidence of basic level of understanding of key concepts	Evidence of high level of understanding of key concepts	Evidence of ability to apply knowledge to new situations	__ x 6 __ (24)
Reflections	• One per piece • Depth of reflection • Ability to self-assess	Includes reflections for some pieces	Includes reflections for most pieces	Includes insightful reflections for all pieces	Reflections show insightfulness and ability to self-assess	__ x 7 __ (28)

Student Comment:

Teacher Comment:

Scale
A = _____
B = _____
C = _____
D = _____

Final Score: _____ (100)

Final Grade: _____

Figure 3.10

ON YOUR OWN

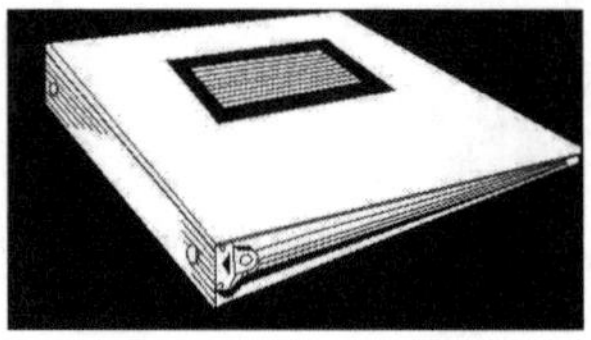

Portfolio Planner

Purpose of portfolio: _____

_____

Type: _____   Standards addressed: _____

Timeline: _____   _____

Working Portfolio Process	**Final Portfolio Process**

Items to collect:

_____

_____

_____

Three stem questions for reflections:

1. _____

2. _____

3. _____

Figure 3.11

REFLECTION

Reflection on Portfolios

Review this graphic organizer and write your own ideas about using portfolios.

Portfolios
Why should I assign a portfolio?
What problems can I anticipate?
How will my students benefit?

Figure 3.12

4 | Performance Tasks

WHAT ARE PERFORMANCE TASKS?

Performance tasks require students to apply their knowledge and skills in order to solve problems, create original products, or demonstrate particular skills. The subjectivity of the task and the creativity of the possible responses require a criteria-based assessment rather than an objective-style test. Performance tasks may appear in many different types and formats, but Gronlund (1998) explains that the majority involve solving realistic problems, engaging in oral or psychomotor skills without producing a product, and writing or demonstrating a psychomotor skill that produces a product.

Solving realistic problems usually entails a problem scenario based upon a relevant challenge requiring students to engage in collaboration and problem solving. It usually requires more than just content knowledge because students have to research information and formulate an action plan. Topics could include developing an environmentally friendly playground or revamping school lunches to meet federal health guidelines. Oral or psychomotor activities usually include presenting a speech to an audience, using equipment such as saws and hammers or food processors, repairing things, or demonstrating athletic skills. Students who engage in a debate or a mock trial, or run for student council, demonstrate their speaking abilities in an oral context and do not necessarily produce a finished product to support their skills. The last category, however, involves psychomotor skills such as writing or typing, but a product must be produced. This type of performance could be a research report, a lab report, or a birdhouse created in a wood craft course. All of these examples are considered performance tasks because they require students to apply their knowledge and skills to demonstrate their abilities beyond answering test questions.

Gronlund (1998) uses the term *restricted performance* to refer to performance tasks that tend to be highly structured to fit a specific instructional objective (e.g., read aloud a selection of poetry or construct a graph from a given set of data). Students have to perform a task, but it can be done in one or two class periods. Some educators refer to this as a *single-focused* performance because it usually targets one or two standards. Another example of a restricted task would be for students to write a letter to a pen pal describing how their state government works. The letter may contain multiple criteria, such as content (social studies), organization, letter format, usage, conventions (language arts), and computer skills (technology), but the task could be completed in one or two class periods. Figure 4.1 is an example of a restricted task that includes a motivating scenario that could be completed by an individual or a group over a short period of time.

Organizing and Graphing

Restricted Performance Task

Standard: Organizing and Graphing   **Grade: 4**

Key Standard, M4D1: Students will gather, organize, and display data according to the situation and compare related features.

> **Know and Do:** Collect data and create a bar graph.

> **Task:** The PE teacher wants to know what is the favorite Field Day activity for fourth graders. Collect data from the students in your homeroom to find the answer. The choices are "sack race," "water-balloon relay," "tug-of-war," "student vs. teacher soccer game," or "baseball."
>
> She would like you to
>
> - Plan and create a table to record all the data that you collect.
> - Collect data in an organized format (table, frequency table).
> - Create a bar graph to represent your data.
>
> Don't forget to include all the important parts of the graph.

> **Differentiation:**
>
> - Sort the data by boys and girls.
> - Collect data from all fourth-grade homerooms and display the data in a triple-bar graph.
> - Limit the choices of activities to two or three.
> - Survey just the boys or just the girls in your homeroom.

Figure 4.1

Source: © Created in 2008 workshops sponsored by Dr. Mark Tavernier, Director of Curriculum and the Clarke County Curriculum Department and facilitated by Kay Burke. Used with the permission of Brian Madej, Molly Efland, Laura Forehand, Joyce Moeller, Jenna Stames, and the Clarke County School District, Athens, GA.

The term *extended performance* refers to tasks that are so comprehensive that numerous instructional objectives and standards are involved. Extended performance tasks, also known as *multi-focused* tasks, tend to be less structured, broader in scope, and more time-consuming (Gronlund, 1998).

An extended task for a Latin class titled "Operation: Restore Pompeii" could last for several weeks. This unit was first developed for students in a Latin One course that covers grades 7–10 for a curriculum unit on Roman life. The teachers justify the time involved based on its application of five Virginia Standards of Learning (SOLs). The unit also addresses essential questions such as (1)What are the structures of a typical Roman town? (2) How do these structures contribute to the well-being of the community? (3) How do societies make decisions about their needs and the allocations of their resources? It also focuses on the big idea of the unit, "The students will understand how the various structures and buildings of a typical Roman town all contribute to the welfare of the community as a whole." The format of extended performance tasks can vary, but they could include a problem scenario, whole-class instruction, group work, individual work, and methods of assessment used throughout the unit. Figure 4.2 is an example of this extended performance task.

Extended performance tasks, or performance-task units, allow for traditional, whole-group instruction while they also allow for differentiation in the types of group work assigned, as well as the types of presentation methods groups may select. Often, students select a group based upon their prior knowledge or interests or because they prefer the type of product or performance as a match for their learning styles.

An example of an extended math performance task for high school students involves group work as well as individual work correlated to the state standards. The unit "'For a Good Time Call . . .': 1–900-Math-Model Performance Task" addresses the math standard, "Students will explore and interpret the characteristics of functions using graphs, tables, simple algebraic techniques" as well as three other math standards (see Figure 4.3 on page 62). It also addresses language-arts standards because the students will write an explanation of their math findings. Most importantly, the problem scenario will motivate high school math students because it shows how they can apply the mathematics skills they learn to a real-life practical problem related to their own lives as well as the business community, and it helps answer the question, "Why do we have to learn this?" When students write their report for the Federal Communications Commission (FCC), teachers can provide a checklist for additional assistance. Figure 4.4 on page 63 shows an example of questions students should ask themselves as they prepare to write the explanation.

Another example of an extended performance task involves the entire school in a fifth-grade music project that also addresses character education. The task targets music standards related to performance critiques, melody, notation, and creation as well as social skills related to character education (see Figure 4.5 on pages 64–65). All of the work is completed in groups and the students are engaged in a competition motivating them to use their best efforts to help their group and their school. This type of task works well for teachers who teach a large number of students each week in areas such as chorus, band, art, or physical education.

It is important for teachers to identify potential areas of integration when planning a performance task unit. "When appropriate, merging concepts from two or more disciplines can make for a powerful and lasting learning experience" (Jacobs, 1997, p. 20). Jacobs explains how curriculum maps can be useful guides for identifying an appropriate merge. "Whether the focus is a topic, theme, issue, or problem-based study, elementary and secondary teachers can use [curriculum] maps to find natural connections that will expand and

(Continued on Page 66)

Operation: Restore Pompeii

A Latin One Cultural Unit

Problem Scenario: Pompeii has been damaged by an earthquake. The town planners are looking to rebuild quickly, but they only have limited funds and labor to work with. As members representing a particular segment of the community, it is your task to convince officials that your interests should be given top priority.

Whole-Class Instruction: List the content or skills that will be introduced as instruction to prepare students for the group and individual work:

- organizations and structures of a Roman town or city with Latin vocabulary as needed
- the historical background of Pompeii in particular related to the earthquake in 62 AD
- daily practices in a provincial town of the early Roman Empire

Pre-Assessment: Give students the problem scenario; ask them to brainstorm what elements are important parts of the Roman town and should be rebuilt first. As a class, share possible responses.

Group Work: Students may select their group topic or presentation method. Topics:

1. Entertainment: amphitheater, theater, circus, bath complex
2. Commerce: market/shopping district, granaries/warehouses, guild halls
3. Public Works: gates/walls, roads, aqueducts, harbor
4. Residences: insulae, villae, prison
5. The Forum Government Administration: temples, courthouse/basilica, municipal offices (treasury, record office, meeting building)

Oral Component: Each group must lobby for their cause by making an oral presentation. They can choose their own format, provided that each member participates and that their presentation is persuasive. Some possibilities would be a skit, a formal persuasive argument, or an editorial on a news program.

Visual Component: Each group must also have a visual for their presentation. The visual should represent all of their individual structures and their cause as a whole. The visual is the group's choice. Some possibilities include poster, brochure, PowerPoint presentation, model, an architectural blueprint, or a map.

Individual Work: Each student will complete the following:

The Narrative: The students will become experts on a particular structure within the group's category. They will write a narrative about its structure, history, and importance within the community.

The Ballot: After hearing all of the presentations, students will have to rank the five most important structures they feel are necessary in the new community. They will explain in writing their rationale for the two most important choices.

Methods of Assessment: List all the methods of assessment used in this unit:

- oral component (group)
- visual component (group)
- narrative (individual)
- ballot (individual)

Figure 4.2

Source: © This performance assessment created by Kenneth M. Bumbaco, Beth Block, and Carl John-Kamp is the result of a collaborative project assigned to preservice teachers in the foreign language education program in the School of Education at the College of William & Mary. The course instructor is Janet D. Parker. Used with permission.

"For a Good Time, Call . . ."
1-900-Math-Model Performance Task

Key Standards, MM1A1: Students will explore and interpret the characteristics of functions, using graphs, tables, simple algebraic techniques.

MM1A1a: Represent functions using function notation.

MM1A1d: Investigate and explain the characteristics of a function: domain, range, zeroes, intercepts, intervals of increase, intervals of decrease, maximum and minimum values, and end behavior.

MM1A1e: Relate to a given context the characteristics of a function and use graphs and tables to investigate its behavior.

Problem Scenario: The FCC needs your help! Our class has been recruited to analyze cell phone usage and trends. Your mission (if you choose to accept it) is to

1. Gather current data on cell phone usage and do a statistical analysis on the data?

2. Research the history of cell phones and their use and create a timeline illustrating it.

3. Create a brochure describing different cell phone plans and the consumers these plans best fit.

4. Plan a debate of the pros and cons of cell phone usage.

5. Produce a video of careers involving cell phones.

The FCC mandates completion by _____.

Whole-Class Instruction:

- data collection and organization
- scatter plot
- correlation coefficient
- calculator use
- regressions

Group Work:

<u>Group 1</u> Debate the pros and cons of cell phones.	<u>Group 2</u> Create a brochure for plan analysis.	<u>Group 3</u> Develop a timeline showing changes in appearance and features, and consumer profile (cost, etc.).	<u>Group 4</u> Film a video of career opportunities associated with cell phones.

Individual Work:

Students will write a report for the FCC containing personal experiences regarding cell phones. The report will include a regression, an interpretation of the intercepts, an analysis of the rates of change, and a prediction of the future of cell phones.

Methods of Assessment:

- teacher-made tests (whole-group materials)
- checklist/rubric for each group and individual tasks

Figure 4.3

Source: © Used with the permissions of John Ellison, Keisha Fulton, Stan Gay, Beth Riddle, Steve Martin, Sandra Ofili, Mary Raburn, and Jan Watts, teachers at Carrollton City High School; and the permission of the Carrollton City Schools, Carrollton, GA.

("For a Good Time, Call...")
FCC Report: Individual Assessment

Assignment: Students will write a report for the FCC containing personal experiences regarding cell phones. The report will include a regression, an interpretation of the intercepts, an analysis of the rates of change, and a prediction of the future of cell phones.	Not Yet 0	Some Evidence 1
Usage and Mechanics		
• Did you check your grammar?		
• Did you use complete sentences?		
• Did you check your spelling?		
Personal Experience Component		
• Did you develop reader interest?		
• Did you report a real-life experience of your own or someone you know? _____		
Regression Component		
• Did you use technology to display your data on a scatter plot?		
• Did you include a linear regression equation? _____		
• Did you interpret the intercepts of your graph for the reader?		
• Did you analyze the rate of change for the graph? _____		
• Did you use your data to make a prediction about future cell phone use? Prediction:_____		

Grading Scale: Total Points:

10–9 = A

  8 = B

  7 = C

6 or below = Unacceptable

Figure 4.4

Source: © Used with the permissions of John Ellison, Keisha Fulton, Stan Gay, Beth Riddle, Steve Martin, Sandra Ofili, Mary Raburn, and Jan Watts, teachers at Carrollton City High School; and the permission of the Carrollton City Schools, Carrollton, GA.

Recording Artists
Fifth-Grade Music Performance Task

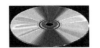

Music Standards: Performance critique, melody, notatation, creation.

Problem Scenario: We could win $20,000 for our school! A competition is on for our school to create a Character Education CD featuring original songs by our fifth-grade class. You may choose to create one track of the CD from the following words:

- "Rappin" to Respect
- "March" of Integrity
- "Rock 'n' Roll" Responsibility
- "50s or 60s" Citizenship
- "Classy" Compassion
- "12-Bar Blues" Tolerance
- "Country" Commitment
- "New Age" Accomplishment

Group Work:

Each group will complete the following:

1. Write an "AABB" rhyme-scheme poem about your character-education word that includes a definition and examples.
2. Compose a melody that supports your poem.
3. Notate melody and rhythm for your composition in 4/4 meter.
4. Orchestrate your piece using classroom instruments.
5. Perform your composition for the class.

Let's get to work, recording artists! It's showtime for the recording studio!

Student Checklist for Performance Critique Fifth grade – Music Standard PS4 **5th Grade** *Idol Unplugged* Paula and Randy are sick with the flu. You have been called by the fifth-grade *Idol* producers to help evaluate tonight's musical performances. Please use the following checklist to critique your classmate's musical works.	**Not Yet (0)**	**Some Evidence (1)**
Organization – Does your evaluation have:		
♪ your name on the page?		
♪ your teacher's name?		

♪ your grade level?		
♪ the title of the musical work?		
Musical mechanics included in the critique:		
♪ Did the performer observe 4/4 time?		
♪ Did the performer keep a steady beat?		
♪ Did the performer use at least one group of 16th notes?		
♪ Was the song singer-friendly?		
♪ Did the performance "rock" or "roll"?		
Written critique:		
♪ Did you use at least four music terms in your critique? List them: 1._____ 2._____ 3._____ 4._____		
♪ Did you include a "Positive-Paula" comment?		
♪ Did you make musical suggestions on how to improve the performance? What? _____ _____		
♪ Did the performance convey a musical style? What? _____ _____		
♪ What timbres did the performance include? _____ _____		
♪ What was the form of the musical performance? _____ _____		

Student's Signature: _____

Teacher's Signature: _____

Parent's Signature: _____

Comments: _____

_____

_____.

Scale
13 – 15 = O
10 – 12 = S
7 – 9 = N
Not Yet

Figure 4.5

Source: © Created in the 2007 Advanced Teacher Leader Institutes facilitated by Andrew Smith, Supervisor of Professional Development, and Kay Burke. Used with the permission of Allison S. Grebe and Kim Oden and the Cobb County School District in Georgia.

underscore students' learning" (p. 20). Integrated units also save time by targeting multiple content objectives and learning standards.

The following task, "Anchorman Performance Task," outlined in Figure 4.6, demonstrates how teachers can integrate social studies and language arts. The task combines group and individual work to cover topics such as nationalism, world leaders, technology, trade and industry, war/genocide, terrorism, and minority advancement during the 1980s, 1990s, and 2000s. The Anchorman Student Checklist provided in Figure 4.7 on page 68 helps guide the students as they prepare their individual oral newscast to the class. Rather than a traditional lecture covering these topics over three decades, the students assume ownership for their learning by engaging in research, analysis, visual communication, and oral communication.

Gronlund (1998) describes how performance tasks and the assessments built into them usually have several characteristics. The tasks are more complex because they relate to real-life situations and problems. They are also less structured and require students to use higher-order thinking skills to arrive at multiple solutions that are both original and creative. Because of the complexity of the tasks, students need more time to perform the required operations and present their findings. In addition, Gronlund explains how teachers need more time for assessment and a "greater use of judgment in scoring (due to the complexity of tasks, originality of the responses, and, in some cases, the variety of possible solutions)" (p. 136). The time factor can be critical because even though many teachers may feel these performance tasks are motivating and worthwhile, they cannot assign more than one or two a year because they are responsible for covering a broad curriculum and multiple standards.

One of the key elements in performance tasks is authenticity. Authentic learning embeds real-world problems into the classroom and encourages students to think critically and creatively to solve problems. Groeber (2007) says, "The authentic-learning classroom is a learner-centered environment in which students are encouraged to become active learners. The tasks in an authentic-learning classroom are relevant to students' real-life experiences" (p. 1). The authenticity of the tasks motivates the students to engage more fully in their own learning. Performance tasks will motivate students if they relate to grade-specific topics that interest the students. Petitioning the cafeteria manager to change the school lunches may appeal to elementary students; petitioning the school board to allow cell phones may appeal to middle school students; and launching a campaign to allow students to participate in service learning projects may appeal to high school students.

WHY SHOULD WE USE PERFORMANCE TASKS?

Darling-Hammond et al. (2008), through synthesis of recent research on effective teaching, found that looking across domains, studies consistently find that highly effective teachers support the process of meaningful learning by creating ambitious and meaningful tasks that reflect how knowledge is used in the field.

Anchorman Performance Task

Key Standards, Social Studies-World History (Grades 9–12): The student will examine change in the world since the 1960s. The student will analyze globalization in the contemporary world.

Problem Scenario: VH1 has a new contest reality show (*Keep It Classy, VH1*)! The station is trying to find new hosts for its *I Love the 80s, 90s, and 00s* shows. They are looking for three people who can really capture what it was like to live in these decades. Each student will be assigned to a group of three. Each group must select one of the decades mentioned above and design three mini-newscasts that include historical facts from each of these time periods. At the end of presenting these newscasts, the class will peer assess and vote for a winner.

Whole-Class Instruction: Whole-class instruction and background will be achieved through

- assigned readings
- brief lectures and discussions
- viewing of select videos from United Streaming

Group Work: Group work will include research, development of group themes, gathering of resources, and construction of television "sets."

Individual Work: Each student will be responsible for completing the following:

- five-minute "newscast" or presentation*
- background prop or screen to supplement news topics
- selection of theme music for each decade's newscast
- selection of a decade-themed costume

*Each five-minute newscast must include three of the following topics from the selected decade: nationalism, world leaders, technology, trade and industry, war/genocide, terrorism, minority advancement.

Methods of Assessment: The following methods of assessment will be used:

- Accuracy of Information – 20%
- Completeness – 20%
- Creativity/Presentation – 20%
- Peer Assessment – 25%
- Participation and Use of Class Time – 15%

Figure 4.6

Source: © Used with the permissions of Kurt Hitzeman and Terica Oates, teachers at Carrollton High School; and the permission of the Carrollton City School System, Carrollton, GA.

Anchorman Student Checklist

Key Standards, Social Studies-World History (Grades 9–12): The student will examine change in the world since the 1960s. The student will analyze globalization in the contemporary world.

Assignment: Give an oral "newscast" from one of the following decades: 1980s, 1990s, or 2000s (five minutes). You must dress in period clothing and enter to period music. A background board or screen must be created to supplement the information in your report. Include at least three categories in your report from the following: nationalism, world leaders, technology, trade and industry, war/genocide, terrorism, or minority advancement.

Scale: Criteria:	1	2	3	4
Accuracy of Information				
• Did you give sources within your newscast?				
• Was your dress and music from the correct decade?				
Completeness				
• Did you include three categories of information?				
• Did you provide facts (not opinions)?				
• Did your backdrop support your oral presentation?				
Creativity/Presentation				
• Did you dress for your time period? Music?				
• Did you remain in character as a news anchor throughout?				
• Did you successfully link together your different categories to provide smooth transitions?				
Peer Assessment				
• Did you speak to your audience (eye contact, volume, etc.)?				
• Did you keep your audience interested and entertained?				
• Did you use proper vocabulary?				
Participation and Use of Class Time				
• Did you participate in discussions and fully use your time in class to help your group?				

Figure 4.7

Source: © Used with the permissions of Kurt Hitzeman and Terica Oates, teachers at Carrollton High School; and the permission of the Carrollton City School System, Carrollton, GA.

These tasks engage the students in active learning that draws connections to students' prior knowledge and experiences. Teachers are able to diagnose what students know and don't know and scaffold the learning process to help them meet the standards while at the same time providing constructive feedback to guide their way. In addition, Darling-Hammond et al. (2008) say that ambitious and meaningful tasks "Encourage strategic and metacognitive thinking, so that students can learn to evaluate and guide their own learning" (p. 5). The ultimate purpose of evaluation is to have students become their own best critics. When they analyze their work, review the criteria for quality performances, and adjust or revise their work to improve it, they are using metacognitive thinking to "think about their thinking" and strategically plan for the future.

Performance tasks and the checklists and rubrics used for assessment address all of these characteristics of effective teaching. Another important reason to use performance tasks is student motivation. If students don't want to participate in their own learning, if they don't want to come to school, or if they decide to drop out of school because they see no relevance to their lives, how much learning is taking place? Price (2008) believes that the issue of student motivation deserves more attention. He says:

> Although the issue of student motivation receives scant attention from proponents of testing and tough love, the truth (at least according to many researchers) is that student motivation really does matter. So do its conceptual siblings: conscientiousness, self-confidence, self-discipline, and responsibility. Children begin life ready and willing to learn. But as they progress through the primary grades, a great many lose their natural curiosity and enthusiasm for learning. Rekindling this enthusiasm is one of the keys to improving student achievement, and the community has an essential role to play in this effort. (p. 24)

What causes so many students to lose their natural curiosity and love for learning as they progress through the years? The research shows that what and how much is learned is influenced by each learner's motivation to learn. Students' motivation to learn is influenced by their emotional state, their interests, and their goals. McCombs and Miller (2007) believe that creativity, ability to use higher-order thinking skills, and natural curiosity contribute to motivation to learn. Intrinsic motivation is stimulated by novel tasks, appropriate level of difficulty (not too easy but not too hard), personal interests, some personal choice, and some control over their learning. McCombs and Miller are concerned because, in most schools, students' natural interests and curiosity are not consistently aroused. "It then becomes the teacher's job to figure out how to make what students have to learn more meaningful, interesting, and relevant to their interests and experiences" (p. 53). Appealing to students' interests is also a key component of differentiating learning, and effective teachers are always searching for that "hook" to capture the students so that they want to learn and look forward to coming to class.

Wiggins and McTighe (2008) discuss the specific challenges confronting high school teachers. They believe that high school students often become bored, passive, or apathetic because the external pressures from tests demand superficial coverage of content. The fast pace of the "coverage" does not allow sufficient time for them to learn how to apply their knowledge to real problems. Wiggins and McTighe believe, "The mission of high school is not to cover content, but rather to help learners become thoughtful about, and productive with, content" (p. 36). This preparation and later application is more significant than being "good at school" while they are there, since the problems students will face when they leave school will pose challenges beyond those covered in the textbooks. Teachers who search for ways to make the content fresh and interesting, as well as relevant, are better able to improve student achievement. It goes without saying that students who come to school more often and pay attention more carefully score higher on standardized tests. Attendance is half the battle in helping students achieve academic success. Moreover, if students enjoy working with classmates in group projects, they also tend to be better adjusted socially and involved in their school experiences. And, they want to come to school.

Another important aspect of performance tasks is collaboration. Students are required to work in cooperative groups to complete part of the performance. Vygotsky (1978) believes that a learning community is important because learning takes place in a social context and relies on communication and interaction with others. With cooperation as a highly important goal of education, teachers should structure learning experiences to foster teamwork. "Teachers skillfully design and manage group work so that it is purposeful, used to support accomplishment of productive tasks, and generative of both stronger relationships and more insightful problem solving" (Darling-Hammond et al., 2008, p. 197). Collaboration is a skill that is critical for success in personal relationships, education, business, as well as local, state, national, and international relations. Fostering appropriate social skills and positive interactions are important life skills educators must teach and reinforce at each grade level. Teachers should never assume those skills are taught in the homes or in the lower grades.

HOW SHOULD WE CREATE PERFORMANCE TASKS?

Some assignments in a performance task will be standardized because all students are expected to demonstrate their mastery of a specific state standard. For example, if a state standard requires "all students to produce informational writing," then that is the target goal. Teachers can use a variety of differentiated instructional tools to help each student use different approaches, but the bottom line is that each student, regardless of prior knowledge, ability level, learning preference, or interests, *must* produce an informational writing piece that meets the criteria of the standard.

The group work included in an extended performance task, however, allows more flexibility for differentiation. Tomlinson (1999) says that

> differentiation of instruction is a teacher's response to learners' needs guided by general principles of differentiation such as respectful tasks,

flexible grouping, and ongoing assessment and adjustment. Performance tasks help teachers differentiate the content, process, and product according to students' readiness, interests, and learning profiles. (p. 15)

Teachers differentiate the group work by *tiering.* Tomlinson and Edison (2003) define tiering as a process of adjusting the degree of difficulty of a question, task, or product to match a student's current readiness level. One way to tier is to develop multiple versions of the task at different levels of difficulty, ensuring that all versions focus on the essential knowledge, understanding, and skills. The different options for group work in an extended performance task allow teachers to tier the groups, addressing different levels of difficulty while ensuring that all students master the content and concepts of the standards.

Figure 4.8 provides some guidelines to help develop an extended performance task that includes the standards, task, whole-group instruction, cooperative group work, individual work, and methods of assessment.

An example of a task using the format in Figure 4.8 is the Language Arts Performance Task in Figure 4.9 (page 73), focusing on health.

HOW SHOULD WE ASSESS PERFORMANCE TASKS?

One of the challenges of assessing performance tasks is subjectivity. The essence of performance-based learning calls for originality and creativity to address a problem and offer logical and pragmatic solutions. Content knowledge and some skills can be assessed with traditional tests comprised of true-false, multiple-choice, fill-in-the-blank, matching, and essay questions. Performance tasks, on the other hand, should be assessed on the basis of criteria that require students to prove to what degree they have met or exceeded the standards.

Criteria checklists for group and individual work provide students with clear expectations for quality work. The language of the standards (LOTS) should be included in the criteria to show students the pathway to mastering the concepts and skills embedded in state standards and required for high-stakes state tests.

Chapter 5 describes how to create criteria checklists that show students how to organize and *complete* their work according to guidelines and rubrics, as well as show them how to *improve* their work, answer the essential questions, grasp the big ideas, and exceed the standards. Other parts of the performance tasks can be assessed with quizzes, teacher-made tests, logs, journals, observations, interviews, conferences, or portfolios. There are multiple assessment opportunities in a performance task to evaluate content, process, and product. The Resources at the end of this book contain sample performance tasks and the checklists and rubrics that are used to assess the work.

Equitable assessment methods are necessary because students need to know the expectations for quality work *before* they begin a performance or project. If teachers do not establish clear learning goals and a roadmap toward completing the task, students sometimes perceive the task as unfair and become either apathetic or disruptive based on their frustration over the confusion on

Anatomy of a Performance Task Unit

Title/Topic: _____ Grade Level/Subject: _____

Standards/Benchmarks: Target power standards that address processes such as writing, reading, problem solving, and technology as well as content standards from social studies, science, mathematics, and language arts.

Task Description:
- Hook/Motivator
- Outside Audience (You have been asked by:)
- Problem Scenario
- Group Work (4 or 5 different performances)
- Due Date

Whole-Group Instruction:
- Direct Instruction
- Readings/Internet
- Guest Speakers
- Videos
- Class Discussions

Small Groups: Selected by Students (Variety of multiple intelligences)

Group One	Group Two	Group Three	Group Four	Group Five
Research	Artwork (Poster)	Brochure	PowerPoint	Skit

Individual Work: Each student will complete the following:

These must match the standards and should be accompanied by checklists and rubrics.

Methods of Assessment:
- Quizzes, teacher-made tests
- Checklists, rubrics, logs/journals
- Portfolios, interviews, conferences
- Observations

Figure 4.8

Source: Burke, Kay. (2006). *From Standards to Rubrics in Six Steps: Tools for Assessing Student Learning, K–8.* Thousand Oaks, CA: Corwin.

Language Arts Performance Task

1. ***Language Arts Standards (Middle/Junior High School):***
   Benchmark 3a: Compose persuasive writings for a specified audience.

2. *Benchmark 4a: Deliver planned oral presentations using language and vocabulary appropriate to the purpose, message, and audience.*

Subject Area: *Language Arts/Health*   **Grade:** *8th Grade*

Task Description: As part of the school's Health Fair Week, the Cancer Prevention Association has asked your class to develop a plan for eliminating all smoking areas from local businesses. The project will include (1) a statistical analysis of research data; (2) a brochure; (3) an antismoking poster; and (4) a five-minute PowerPoint presentation selling your ideas to business owners. Be prepared to present your antismoking campaign to members of the Cancer Prevention Association on February 3 at their monthly meeting.

Direct Instruction for Whole Class: The whole class will be involved in the following learning experiences:
- Guest lecture from the school nurse on the effects of secondhand smoke
- Lectures and discussions on the health risks related to smoking
- Readings from articles and textbooks
- Oral presentation techniques
- Statistical analysis of research data

Group Work: Students select one group project.

Group One	Group Two	Group Three	Group 4
Prepare a **statistical analysis** using charts and graphs showing the effects of smoking.	Prepare a **brochure** that depicts health risks related to smoking.	Prepare an **antismoking poster** to display in local stores.	Prepare a five-minute **PowerPoint presentation** to local business owners.

Individual Work: In addition to the group project, each student will complete two individual assignments:
1. Write a letter to the editor of the local newspaper trying to convince business owners to ban smoking in their establishments.
2. Deliver a five-minute presentation to local business owners at the Chamber of Commerce meeting.

Methods of Assessment:
- Teacher-made test on the health risks related to smoking
- Criteria checklists to assess each of the four group projects
- Checklists and rubrics to assess the letter to the editor and the persuasive speech

Figure 4.9

what they are supposed to do, or on the difficulty of the assignment. Providing guidelines for cooperative group work and clear expectations for the task will alleviate potential classroom management problems.

FINAL THOUGHTS

Sternberg (2007/2008) is concerned about today's emphasis on taking a multiple-choice or fill-in-the-blank test when, in the real world, people have to demonstrate why they are qualified for a job. He says:

> When I look at the skills and concepts I have needed to succeed in my own field, I find a number that are crucial: creativity, common sense, wisdom, hard work, knowing how to win and how to lose, a sense of fair play, and lifelong learning. But memorizing books is certainly not one of them. (p. 20)

Sternberg concludes that teachers need to assess what students need in order to become active and engaged citizens of the world in which they live. He says, "Oddly enough, a lot of models can prepare students for the roles they will play in their world. Traditional schooling just does not happen to be one of them" (Sternberg, 2007/2008, p. 21). Performance-task units will prepare students for the roles they will play in their world. Teachers who are willing to take the extra time and effort to work as a team to create the tasks will help all of their students become active and engaged citizens of the world.

EXAMPLES

"All by Myself" Math Performance Task

Key Standard, Math (Grade 7): Students will understand the meaning of positive and negative rational numbers and use them in computation. **Language Arts:** Writing skills.

Note to Teachers: Introduce this activity by playing the song "All by Myself" by Eric Carmen or Celine Dion. Give the students approximately ten minutes per class period to work on this activity and calculate their income and/or expenses.

Directions: Students can use ledger sheets or plain notebook paper to keep up with their accounts. Each day, you (the teacher) will have students draw a "Life Card," and students will use this information to adjust their accounts. Students must keep up with their own accounts until the end of the four-week period. It will be helpful if they have to keep up with all of their cards so their work can be double checked. At the end of the project, students can exchange projects and evaluate each other's work. Ask students to write a 3–5 paragraph reflection on the project describing how well they did (or didn't do) "all by themselves."

Performance Task:

Welcome to the real world! For the next four weeks, you will be working, paying bills, and going to school like many adults! You have just been hired, through our work-study program, by _____ Industries at (minimum wage or another $) per hour. You will be required to work a minimum of 20 hours per week, but you will have the option of working up to 45 hours per week. Any work-time over 40 hours per week will earn you overtime pay of time and a half; however, you can only work a maximum of 5 hours overtime every other week. Your net pay will show a tax deduction of 10 percent of your gross income. Since this is a work-study program, the following guidelines have been preapproved and established with your employer:

While working 20–45 hours per week, you are expected to complete all math assignments in the allotted time (including homework), pass every graded math assignment (including daily activities), and pass all math quizzes/tests. If at any time during the four-week period you fail to complete an assignment on time, or fail a math assignment, test, or quiz, then you will be required to stay after school for 1 hour to complete makeup work. This means that you will lose 1 hour of pay each time you need to stay after school for makeup work. (Optional: You will be charged $5.00 for incomplete or missed assignments.)

Furthermore, your parents have decided that you will now be responsible for your own monthly expenses. Those expenses include the following and are due at the end of this project (in four weeks):

Monthly Expenses

- Rent: $100 plus any damages
- Utilities: $50
- Cell Phone: $45 plus any overages
- Internet Access: $10
- Cable TV: $20 plus any show/movie rentals at $2 each
- Food: $150 for the basics, plus any extras such as eating out, gratuity, & snacks
- Medical Expenses: $50 (Those braces aren't free, you know!)
- Pet Fee: $15 for food and vet visits per pet, plus $1 fee for any "accident" clean ups.
- Entertainment expenses will be your decision, and your parents said that you tend to spend at least $50 per week on movies, games, activities, etc. that you enjoy regularly.
- Clothing expenses will be your decision, and your parents said that you tend to cost them at least $100 per month on shoes and clothing, unless you hit a growth spurt and then you're talking about a whole new wardrobe.

Your parents also request that you put at least $50 per month into a savings account.

(Continued)

(Continued)

Sample Life Cards

You were just dumped by your sweetie. After a quick trip to the corner market, you find you spent $5 on ½ gallon of ice cream and a box of tissues.	You're language arts essay was excellent! You won the contest! Your prize is $20.
You got a new sweetie. You must make an impression so you buy a new shirt for $10.	You neighbors went out of town and asked you to walk their dog while they're gone. You just made an easy $15.
You made $15 babysitting your neighbors' kids for 3 hours.	Grandma came to visit and slipped you $20 because (shh) you're her "favorite"!
Ouch! You got stung by a bee . . . and you're allergic. Doctor's visit & medication cost you $35.	You went over your cell phone minutes and must pay an extra $15 for overage fees.
What a cute doggie! You find a stray and your heart is way too big to let it go hungry. You must now add your pet expense.	Your boss asked you to work an extra 4 hours today. (That is overtime!)
You made $10 by giving skateboarding lessons to your boss's teenager.	You went out with your friends for a movie and burger. You spent $20.

Figure 4.10

Source: © Used with the permissions of Beth Roddenberry and Mary Ann Braswell, 7th/8th grade teachers of mathematics at Charlton County High School, Charlton County Schools, Folkston, GA.

ON YOUR OWN

Performance Task Template

Subject Area: _____ **Grade Level:** _____

Learning Standards: _____

Task Description:
Direct Instruction for Whole Class: The whole class will be involved in the following learning experiences:
Group Work: Students may select their group and their task.   Group One   Group Two   Group Three   Group Four
Individual Work: In addition to the group project, each student will complete the following individual assignments:
Methods of Assessment:

Figure 4.11

REFLECTION

Why Performance Tasks?

Performance tasks can address the following educational practices:

- Standards-Based Teaching
- Response to Intervention (RTI)
- Differentiated Learning
- Cooperative Learning
- Interdisciplinary Learning
- Formative Assessment
- Student Motivation
- Independent Learning
- Mastery Learning
- Experiential Learning
- Teaching for Understanding
- *Other best practices?*

Decide on three reasons you feel students would benefit by engaging in performance tasks.

1. _____

2. _____

3. _____

Write one sentence to summarize your feelings about using performance tasks.

_____

_____

Figure 4.12

Checklists and Rubrics **5**

WHAT ARE CHECKLISTS?

The checklist is an effective formative assessment strategy to monitor specific skills, behaviors, or dispositions of individual or all students in the class. Checklists provide clear criteria that focus on the intended benchmarks in a standard. Checklists also show students how to organize their tasks into sequenced steps that will lead to the successful completion of a complex task. They provide clear expectations for quality work and they "chunk" the learning into smaller segments so students can master each step before tackling the next chunk. Teachers can use criteria checklists for formative assessments by focusing on specific behaviors, thinking skills, social skills, writing skills, speaking skills, or athletic skills. Peers can use checklists to assess the progress of another student. In group work, cooperative members can monitor the entire group's progress. These checklists can then be shared and discussed among group members to determine who needs additional help in different areas and how the whole group is performing overall.

Popham (2008) advocates using a *learning progression,* and he describes it as

[a] sequenced set of subskills and bodies of enabling knowledge that, it is believed, students must master en route to mastering a more remote curricular aim. In other words, it is composed of the step-by-step building blocks students are presumed to need in order to successfully attain a more distant, designated, instructional outcome. (p. 24)

Popham also talks about "subskills" that students need to meet in order to master the more advanced cognitive skill. An example would be students' need to master the complex cognitive skill of writing a narrative essay. But, in order to master that complex multistep process, they need to master smaller subskills such as

- creating an interesting opening paragraph to hook the reader
- organizing the essay into paragraphs
- developing topic sentences, support sentences, and concluding sentences
- using descriptive language and sensory details to describe the story
- checking for mechanics (capitalization, punctuation, and spelling)

Some educators use the term *chunking* to classify a big task into smaller chunks that serve as building blocks toward mastering the abstract learning goal. For instance, with writing, some students need to focus on the concrete process of mastering one step at a time rather than tackling the more abstract five-paragraph narrative essay process.

Criteria for Checklists

Once the performance task is designed, the next very important step involves developing the criteria to determine the adequacy of the student's performance. Bear in mind that a common dictionary definition for a criterion is a standard on which a judgment or decision may be based. Popham (1999) explains when teachers set criteria, they are trying to make a judgment regarding the adequacy of student responses, and the specific criteria used will influence the way a response is scored. If a student is giving a speech, the criteria could include eye contact, gestures, organization, visual aid(s), opening, closing, etc.

It is important to review the standards to see if specific criteria or indicators are listed. Teachers should incorporate the vocabulary and criteria from the benchmark into the checklists and rubrics to ensure validity. Once teachers design the performance task, they need to develop a checklist to help students complete the task. Notice how the task in Figure 5.1 motivates students to work first in a group and then as an individual.

WHY SHOULD WE USE CHECKLISTS?

The checklist provides a quick and easy way to observe and record many of the skills, criteria, and behaviors prior to the final test or summative evaluation. Too often, teachers do not realize a student needs help until it is too late. Checklists show teachers and students the areas of concern early enough to be able to help students before failing a test or unit. They also provide teachers the opportunity to "change gears" in a classroom if a large percentage of the students are not doing well.

Checklists also provide formative assessments of students' learning and help teachers monitor whether or not students are on track to meet the standards. According to Chappuis and Chappuis (2007/2008), "[Feedback] functions as a global positioning system, offering descriptive information about the work, product, or performance relative to the intended learning goals. It avoids marks or comments that judge the level of achievement or imply that the learning journey is over" (p. 17). Checklists also occur in the "do over" time period when, if teachers check "not yet," students still have time to complete the task successfully with constructive feedback from their peers, parents, and teachers. Notice how the checklist in Figure 5.2 on pages 82–83 helps students do the individual assignment in their "Can We Save Georgia?" performance task. The results helps students decide which techniques were most efficient based upon each group's findings.

Can We Save Georgia?
Science Performance Task

Key Standard: Soil Conservation   **Grade Level:** Sixth   **Subject:** Earth Science

Standard: 1. Students will investigate the scientific view of how the earth's surface is formed. 2. Explain the effects of human activity on the erosion of the earth's surface. 3. Describe methods for conserving natural resources such as water, soil, and air.

Problem Scenario: The drought in Georgia is still raging! The Hurricane Emergency Center, however, has just announced that a level-2 hurricane is headed our way. The grass is dead and the topsoil is exposed and fragile! Due to your extensive knowledge about soil conservation, the governor has asked our class to devise a way to conserve our soil at all costs! The hurricane is predicted to hit land on September 13. We need to divide our class into groups to analyze the problem and report back to the governor before it's too late. Here are our assignments. Group 1: Brainstorm which soil conservation techniques will be the most effective against a hurricane; Group 2: By majority vote, choose two of the soil conservation techniques to utilize in your model; Group 3: Create your model to be tested by wind and water; and Group 4: After the test analyze the results of your model's effectiveness using the guiding questions provided. Let's get busy. The governor needs our recommendations NOW!

Group Work: Groups will construct an erosion-free environment for the sample of soil. The soil sample will be given to each group by the teacher to ensure the consistency of each sample. The teacher will make the following items available for each group to construct their erosion-free model: Popsicle sticks, pipe cleaners, and modeling clay.

Individual Work: 1. Using the chart provided on the individual checklist, illustrate each of the group's findings. Use the chart to collect data that will clearly demonstrate which techniques were most efficient. 2. Write a response that describes your findings. Your response should include the answers to the following guiding questions:

Why were the materials that you used effective or not effective?

How did the design prevent erosion for wind, water, or both? Explain your answer.

What could you have done differently to make a more efficient model?

Then write a letter to the governor with your recommendations based upon your findings and analysis. The *Can We Save Georgia?* Checklist for the Individual Work that follows in Figure 5.2 will help students collect their data, analyze their results, and write their letter with their recommendations to the governor before another disaster hits Georgia!

Figure 5.1

Source: © Created in the 2007 Advanced Teacher Leader Institutes facilitated by Andrew Smith, Supervisor of Professional Development, and Kay Burke. Used with the permission of Robin Walling, science teacher, and Nicole Spicer, Area Lead Teacher, and the Cobb County School District in Georgia.

Can We Save Georgia? Individual Work

Topic/Focus: Soil Conservation
Grade Level/Subject: 6th Grade Earth Science
Standard: Students will investigate the scientific view of how the earth's surface is formed. Explain the effects of human activity on the erosion of the earth's surface. Describe methods for conserving natural resources such as water, soil, and air.

Assignment: Use the "Analyzing Your Results" chart to demonstrate which techniques were most efficient based upon your group's findings.

Analyzing Your Results Chart	Amount of Wind Erosion	Amount of Water Erosion	Total Amount Eroded
Contour Plowing			
Terracing			
Conservation Plowing			
Windbreaks			

SCALE: CRITERIA:	No (0)	Yes (1)
Analysis of Data • Did you use the guiding questions?		
• Why were the materials that you used effective or not effective?		
• How did the design prevent erosion for wind, water, or both? Explain your answer.		
• What could you have done differently to make a more efficient model?		
Structure of Analysis • Did you establish the context of your response?		
• Does your response demonstrate understanding of soil conservation techniques?		

	No (0)	Yes (1)
• Is your analysis interpretive, analytical, evaluative, and reflective?		
• Is your response an interpretation based on several clear ideas, premises, or images?		
Letter Format		
• Date		
• Inside Address		
• Salutation		
• Body		
• Closing		
• Signature		
Mechanics		
• Capitalization		
• Punctuation		
• Spelling		
Usage		
• Grammar		
• Sentence Structure		
• Transitions		

Figure 5.2

Source: © Created in the 2007 Advanced Teacher Leader Institutes facilitated by Andrew Smith, Supervisor of Professional Development, and Kay Burke. Used with the permission of Robin Walling, science teacher, and Nicole Spicer, Area Lead Teacher, and the Cobb County School District in Georgia.

Helping Students With Special Needs

Lougy, DeRuvo, and Rosenthal (2007) discuss how students with attention-deficit/hyperactivity disorder (ADHD) often lack age-appropriate organizational skills to help them sequence the steps needed to complete a task, leaving them unable to even begin a project without outside support. A checklist that asks the students specific questions about a project and guides them through the process will help them stay focused. When students are introduced to high-interest and engaging tasks that motivate them to learn, children with ADHD can be as attentive as students without ADHD. "[W]hen involved in high-interest activities, they can be hyper-focused—so focused on what they are doing that they are oblivious to what is happening around them" (Lougy, DeRuvo, & Rosenthal, 2007, p. 15). Checklists can help focus all students as they complete the meaningful assignments that are relevant to their lives.

Observing Intelligent Behaviors

Costa (2008) recommends that characteristics of intelligent behavior such as persistence, listening, flexibility in thinking, metacognition, and checking for accuracy as well as precision can be taught and observed by students, parents, and teachers. Observation checklists are tools for checking whether or not a student can demonstrate the skill or attribute being measured. Observation checklists also focus on observable performances or criteria that are often more meaningful or authentic than paper-and-pencil tests. By focusing on two or three concrete skills or criteria, teachers and students can monitor growth or pinpoint a need for improvement more easily.

Creating Observation Checklists

Checklists also serve as a record-keeping device for teachers to keep track of who has mastered the targeted skills and who still needs help. Effective observation checklists include the student's name, space for four to five targeted areas, a code or rating to determine to what degree the student has or has not demonstrated the skill (+ = frequently; * = sometimes; o = not yet), and a space for comments or anecdotal notes. Some teachers find it useful to date the occurrences so they can see developmental growth or use the checklists for student and parent conferences.

Observation is one of the most effective tools to find out what children can do and determine their learning needs. By observing children interacting with their peers, reading, speaking, using technology, and solving problems, teachers can learn a great deal about how a student performs and thinks. By charting students' progress on note cards, observation checklists, sticky notes, or portfolios, teachers learn about students' learning styles, learning needs, attitudes, initiative, likes and dislikes, and need for assistance.

HOW SHOULD WE USE CHECKLISTS?

Teachers can determine which specific areas to include in the observation checklist and then make sure the students are aware of the areas that will be observed. If students are going to observe their peers or perform a self-assessment, they should be trained in what each skill looks like and sounds like. It is imperative that the skills and processes being observed are modeled and taught to the students prior to the observations.

Observing Process and Progress

Teachers are accustomed to grading students' final products and performances. It is more difficult, however, to assess the process used to arrive at their final products and the progress they make throughout the grading period. Checklists help make abstract traits and attitudes more concrete. Guskey and Bailey (2001) believe teachers need to classify grading criteria into three broad categories: product, process, and progress.

- *Product* criteria describe what students know and are able to do at a particular point in time. Teachers use product criteria to grade final products such as reports, projects, portfolios, and performances.
- *Process* criteria describe how students achieve the final product. Teachers consider student effort, class behavior, work habits, daily work, regular quizzes, homework, class participation, punctuality of assignments, or attendance.
- *Progress* criteria describe how much the students actually gain from their learning experiences. This might include learning gain, improvement grading, value-added grading, and educational growth. Progress criteria look at how far the students have come rather than where students are, allowing for a very individualized judgment of students' "learning potential" (adapted from pp. 40–41).

One of the first steps in creating an observation checklist is to develop specific indicators that describe the skills, actions, or behaviors that are expected in terms of a criterion. Students need concrete examples. Asking a student to be more attentive or more persistent is abstract. Listing specific behaviors or skills is concrete. It is sometimes developmentally appropriate to start with specifics on a checklist and then move to the abstract after students know the expectations. A checklist could be as simple as criteria with a 0 for not observed and a 1 for observed. A kindergarten-skills checklist could consist of the following (Figure 5.3):

Kindergarten Skills Checklist

Indicators:	Not Yet 0	Yes 1
1. Can write name		
2. Knows phone number		
3. Can write address		
4. Recognizes different colors		
5. Can count to 25		
6. Knows alphabet		
7. Speaks in complete sentences		
8. Knows directions to school		

Figure 5.3

Checklists can also help students walk through the process and help them think through what they are doing.

Criteria for Checklists

State standards and benchmarks provide the criteria that should be used in checklists in order to ensure validity. Sometimes, however, teachers need to add additional criteria to help students get organized. Figure 5.4 provides possible criteria for checklists.

WHAT ARE RUBRICS?

As used today in education, a *rubric* refers to a scoring guide or scoring dimension used to evaluate the quality of students' constructed responses, usually related to a performance. Because the performance task is usually more subjective and creative, it is necessary to provide some evaluative criteria to distinguish acceptable responses from unacceptable responses for the students who are completing the work and the educators who are assessing the work (Popham, 2006). A rubric can also be defined as a set of rules specifying the criteria. The set of rules should specifically match the task as well as the standards and benchmarks being assessed. Students preparing an oral presentation, for example, would know in advance that their presentations will be judged on evaluative criteria such as focus on the topic, support information, quality of facts and statistics, logical arguments, appropriate eye contact, facial expressions, gestures, rate of speed, effective visual aide, and adherence to time limits and guidelines. The rubric would address each of these criteria.

Martin-Kniep (2000) defines a rubric as a rating scale that defines and differentiates levels of performance. Checklists indicate the presence or absence of an attribute, but a rubric defines the completeness and quality or development in a process, product, or performance—therefore supporting learning. It also identifies the different levels of quality that can range from "in progress" to "exceeding standards" on a continuum.

Solomon (1998) states, "[R]ubrics are a set of guidelines for distinguishing between performances or products of different quality. They should be based on the results of stated performance standards and be composed of scaled descriptive levels of progress towards the result" (p. 120). Rubrics describe levels of quality so that students know exactly what they have to do to achieve the higher levels. Rubrics take a great deal of the subjectivity out of the grading process.

WHY SHOULD WE USE RUBRICS?

Rubrics provide clear and specific guidelines for creating quality performance tasks. They help students internalize the criteria from the standards and provide

ON YOUR OWN

Criteria for Checklists

Writing

Grammar and Usage

Sentence structure
Subject-verb agreement
Comma splices
Plurals of nouns
Pronouns/agreement
Verb tenses
Use of adjectives
Use of adverbs
Fragments
Run-on sentences

Mechanics

Capitalization
Commas
Semicolons
Colons
Question marks
Apostrophes
Spelling

Organization

Outline
Introduction
Topic sentences
Support sentences
Transitions
Conclusion

Research Skills

Selection of topic
Review of literature
Working bibliography
Thesis statement
Outline
Paraphrasing
Documentation
Final bibliography
Proofreading

Speaking and Reading

Speaking Skills

Eye contact
Facial expression
Voice inflection
Enthusiasm
Organization
Use of facts
Visual aids
Movement
Persuasiveness
Body language
Gestures

Oral Reading

Pronunciation
Enunciation
Expression
Fluency

Study Skills

Prereading
Webs
Venn diagrams
KWL
Surveys
Q3K
Idea wrapping
Think-pair-share

Reading Readiness

Chooses to read during
   free time
Visits school library
Begins reading quickly
Talks about books

Social Skills

Formation of Groups

Forms groups quietly
Sits face to face
Makes eye contact
Uses first names
Shares materials
Follows role assignments

Support

Checks for understanding
Offers help
Asks the group for help
Encourages others
Energizes the group
Disagrees with the
   idea—not the person

Communication

Uses a low voice
Takes turns
Makes sure everyone speaks
Waits until speaker is finished
   before speaking

Conflict Resolution

Disagrees with the idea—not
   the person
Respects the opinion of
   others
Thinks for self
Explores different points of
   view
Negotiates and/or compro-
   mises
Reaches consensus

Problem Solving

Critical Thinking

Analyzing bias
Attributing cause and
   effect
Classifying
Comparing
Contrasting
Decision making
Drawing conclusions
Evaluating
Inferring
Prioritizing
Sequencing
Solving analogies

Creative Thinking

Brainstorming
Generalizing
Hypothesizing
Inventing
Making analogies
Recognizing
   paradoxes
Personifying
Predicting
Problem solving

Intelligent Behaviors

Persistence
Listening
Flexibility in thinking

Metacognition
Checking for accuracy
Precision

Figure 5.4

guideposts for achieving escalating indicators of excellence. Rubrics can be a critical tool in the evaluation process because they do the following:

- provide scaffolding for improving work through a continuum of quality
- showcase students' progress toward meeting and exceeding the standards
- help teachers grade subjective work consistently, fairly, and objectively
- help students self-assess their own work, and adapt and improve their skills
- help parents understand how work is graded and the expectations for quality work
- help students know in advance the criteria for work

Rubrics also help ensure both teacher and student accountability. Flynn and Flynn (2004) believe that teachers sometimes take on too much of their students' responsibilities. With rubrics, they believe that "students are held accountable for their work. They know exactly what is expected, when parts are due, and how they will be graded. It then becomes the *student's* responsibility to ensure that all requirements of the assignment are met" (p. 5). Students who understand rubrics are also better able to self-assess their own work and work more independently because they know the expectations for quality work.

Creating Scales for Rubrics

Typically, a numerical scale is used for each criterion. Sometimes the scale points are accompanied by verbal descriptors and even visuals, while scales can also contain only verbal descriptors with no numbers. Numerical scales assign points to a continuum of performance levels. According to Herman, Aschbacher, and Winters (1992), the length of the continuum or the number of scale points can vary from three to seven or more. However, a shorter scale will result in a higher percentage agreement and a larger scale will take longer to reach consensus if more than one person is evaluating the performance. Most educators find that even-numbered scales (e.g., 0–1–2–3 or 1–2–3–4 or 1–2–3–4–5–6) work best because odd-numbered scales (e.g., 1–2–3 or 1–2–3–4–5) tend to cause the evaluator to select the middle number. The even-numbered scales force the evaluator to select a side—either low or high—with no middle ground for compromise. Figure 5.5 highlights various types of scales, with a descriptive scale illustrated in Figure 5.6.

Creating Quality Indicators for Rubrics

Performance assessments usually focus on the application of knowledge to a real-life experience. For example, identifying the parts of a letter requires factual knowledge, but writing a letter with a purpose and audience requires a real performance—the act of writing the letter. The judging criteria, or rubric, for students' responses identify the factors to be considered when determining the adequacy of a student's performance. Teachers provide feedback on the goals in both formative measures throughout the process and summative

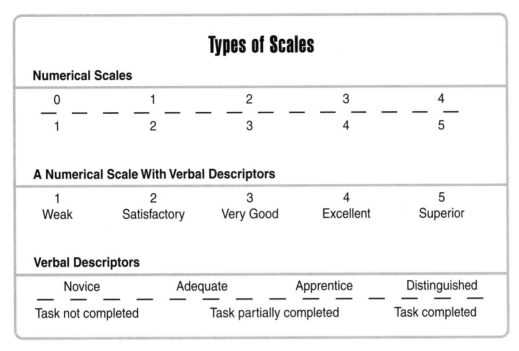

Figure 5.5

Descriptive Scale

Criterion: Eye Contact During Speech

No Evidence	Minimal Evidence	Partial Evidence	Complete Evidence
Does not look at audience	Looks some of the time at some of the audience	Looks most of the time at most of the audience	Looks all of the time at all of the audience

Figure 5.6

measures for the final product or performance. The criteria are usually discussed with the students before they prepare their product or presentation. Criteria by themselves provide a guideline for students to follow when preparing their performance, but the indicators or descriptors of what constitutes a quality performance to attain the standard or earn an A or B are usually described in the rubric. Figure 5.7 shows how the criteria for the letter are listed on the left and each column progressing across the scale provides indicators necessary to achieve each rating necessary to score a 1-2-3-4 for writing a letter to the editor.

Letter to the Editor Weighted Rubric

Standard: Students will be able to write a persuasive letter by using appropriate organization, arguments, information as well as correct usage, conventions, and letter format.

Criteria The student:	1 Do Over!	2 One More Edit!	3 Editor Considers!	4 Editor Publishes!	Score
Purpose of the Letter • Persuade • Call to action • Generate support	Evidence of 1 element	Evidence of 2 elements	Evidence of 3 elements	The letter persuades the reader to agree with author's opinion.	__ x 6 =
Organization • Thesis Statement • Support Sentences • Concluding Sentences	Evidence of 1 element	Evidence of 2 elements	Evidence of 3 elements	The organization is logical, coherent, and fluent.	__ x 5 = __
Arguments • Logical • Factual • Use of Statistics • Use of Quotations	Evidence of 1 element	Evidence of 2 elements	Evidence of 3–4 elements	Arguments use appropriate logic, facts, statistics, and expert quotations to convince readers.	__ x 6 = __
Letter Format • Date • Inside Address • Salutation • Body • Closing • Signature	Includes 1–2 elements	Includes 3–4 elements	Includes 5–6 elements	The writer follows standards of formal letter writing and capitalizes and punctuates all elements correctly.	__ x 4 = __
Usage • Complete Sentences • Correct Grammar • Correct Subject/ Verb Agreement	Evidence of 1 element	Evidence of 2 elements	Evidence of 3 elements	Writer demonstrates correct usage and uses appropriate transitions for coherence.	__ x 2 = __
Conventions • Capitalization • Punctuation • Spelling	4 or more errors that damage writer's credibility	2–3 errors that distract from the message	1 error—a result of careless proof-reading	Polished and professional mechanics that editors admire and publish.	__ x 2 = __

Figure 5.7

HOW CAN RUBRICS BE USED?

Generalized Rubrics

There are different types of rubrics that are used when applied to different targets. A *generalized* rubric focuses on large and complex questions such as: What is an expert scientist? What is the description of a good teacher? What makes a skilled mathematician? A generalized rubric can also focus on large tasks such as, "What is the description for an excellent oral presentation?" or "What makes an outstanding science experiment?"

Musial, Nieminen, Thomas, and Burke (2009) explain that while a generalized rubric is useful for targeting "the critical attributes of a task or professional as a single entity" (p. 251), they can be imprecise due to the more abstract language necessary to include various contexts. In many cases, generalized rubrics are used by states to evaluate writing samples from every student in the state. Generic criteria such as content, focus, organization, voice, and mechanics are used to evaluate thousands of essays, regardless of the topic. The feedback generated from generalized rubrics is not very specific and it is used more for summative assessments where students will not be allowed to improve their work. It is usually used for the final judgment.

Analytical Rubrics

Analytical rubrics require teachers to identify specific knowledge and skills that are critical to completing specific tasks. They yield more precise results than generalized rubrics, but they cannot be generalized across different contexts. The analytical rubric lists indicators such as understanding of concept, applications of concept, thinking strategies, process skills, and other valued learning targets. It then assigns a rating such as "complete" or "in progress," or "meets expectations" or "exceeds standards," to describe how the students mastered each indicator. The analytical rubric provides a separate score for each of the multiple dimensions implicit in each student's work.

Analytical scoring allows for more specific observation and detailed feedback than generalized rubrics. Clear evaluation criteria help teachers define excellence, communicate goals, score performances consistently and fairly, and document the judgments they make about student work. Musial, Nieminen, Thomas, and Burke (2009) explain:

> Carefully crafted analytical rubrics not only point to the key learning dimensions that should be assessed, but, like all good assessments, they also illuminate instruction. Since analytical rubrics specify the key indicators of learning within a task, teachers can quickly note if one of those task indicators is consistently not evident in students' work. Immediately, the teacher has a specific target for further instruction. (p. 255)

Analytical rubrics are sometimes called "teaching rubrics" because they inform teachers on how to adjust their instruction. In the proceeding section, "The Checklist-Rubric Connection" (Figure 5.9 on page 95) provides an example of an analytical rubric to assess a debate, with Figure 5.11 (page 100) showing an example of an analytical rubric to assess informational writing.

Weighted Rubrics

Both generalized and analytical rubrics can be *weighted* to reflect the importance of each criterion in a specific assignment. Targeted criteria may sometimes carry more weight than other criteria based upon the key components of the standard, the focus of the teaching, and the timing of the assessment. For example, if the focus of the instruction for one week was how to write motivating hooks or leads to capture the readers' attention, the teacher might weight the criterion of "hook or motivator" more heavily when administering the practice rubric at the end of the week. If the focus of the lesson the next week centered on "mechanics," then that criterion for mechanics would be weighted more on that practice rubric. Formative assessments reflect the major purpose of a lesson in order to provide the immediate feedback in "real time" that teachers need to provide students who have not yet mastered that "chunk" of information before moving on to another topic.

The checklist usually contains one point for every criteria met. For example, students completing a narrative essay would receive one point for the following: organization, hook or motivator, coherence, paragraph structure, storyline, descriptive language, usage, and mechanics. The checklist simply shows there is some evidence of completion. The rubric describes the degrees of quality of each criterion.

A weighted rubric could show that the topic sentence was weighted x1, but the organization was weighted x4, and the paragraph structure was weighted x3. The teacher adjusts the weight based upon the main purpose of that specific assessment. Groeber (2007) states, "Because the teacher distributes the rubrics at the start of the research unit, students are aware of this expectation before they begin their research" (p. 3). Figure 3.10 in Chapter 3 is an example of a weighted rubric for a portfolio, as is the rubric for the letter to the editor shown earlier in Figure 5.7.

WHAT IS THE CHECKLIST-RUBRIC CONNECTION?

While many educators use checklists and rubrics to assess student work, sometimes neither the checklists nor the rubrics use the language of the standards to improve validity. Rarely do educators see the connection between creating a checklist first to help students organize and complete their work in a sequential order before describing indicators of quality. Payne (2008), when discussing nine powerful practices that help raise the achievement of students living in poverty, shows how checklists and rubrics can also achieve two of these strategies. One strategy is to "monitor progress and plan interventions" and another is "translate the concrete into the abstract" (pp. 50–51). Checklists and rubrics do both since they help teachers identify learning gaps, choose appropriate interventions, and monitor progress toward helping all students meet academic goals.

Checklists and rubrics provide graphic organizers and mental models for students to help them translate the concrete into the abstract. While it is usually more difficult to construct the checklist because it must include all the criteria from the state standard, the checklists and rubrics are really quite similar. The checklist is written in a sequential order that makes sense to the student and the process. Once the checklist is finished, it can be easily converted to the rubric by adding descriptors of quality at each level. Since all assessments begin with the end in mind, it is important to use the wording of the standard.

Sometimes teachers feel the checklist is a sufficient form of assessment and it is not necessary to create a rubric for the students. Other times, the standard is important enough to offer a rubric that details levels of quality. Figure 5.8 shows a debate checklist that will be helpful for students, but since this is a high school assignment, the teachers felt the students needed to push themselves toward exceeding the standards in preparation for college. Figure 5.9 on page 95 shows how the checklist can be extended to include more specifics about the students' ability to not only conduct a debate, but win it!

By using the language of the standard and the critical ideas and concepts to develop the checklist first, the creation of the rubric is much easier. Converting the checklist into the rubric provides a guidepost for evaluating the dimensions of quality for work.

HOW DO WE CREATE COMMON ASSESSMENTS?

Common assessments are those used by one or more teachers in a grade level, subject area, or across grade levels. They correlate to the state standards and are essential if teams of teachers in a school or district want to work together to shift their focus from *teaching* to *learning* by asking the question: "Are students really learning what they are supposed to be learning?" Graham and Ferriter (2008) say that teams often struggle with this question while first developing common assessments. They believe, however, that "Shared assessments force teachers to define exactly what students should learn and what evidence is necessary for documenting success" (p. 40). Common assessments require common checklists and rubrics based on clearly defined criteria that communicate the important dimensions in a product or performance to all the stakeholders. Wiggins and McTighe (2007) recommend using common rubrics throughout a department, grade-level team, school, or district to achieve a more consistent evaluation of all students and to support standards-based grading and reporting. Vertical teams that include teachers from several grade levels or from grades K–12 in schools and districts examine the common concepts, big ideas, or language of the standards that thread throughout subject areas and grade levels.

Teachers who use common rubrics often work in teams to grade student work. They internalize the qualities of what makes a solid performance to help them focus on those qualities in their own teaching, benefitting the students as well (Wiggins & McTighe, 2007). Creating common rubrics also helps teachers define the criteria, share instructional strategies they use to teach the criteria, and clarify in their minds any confusion about what the standards require.

Protocol for a Debate Checklist
Grade 8

Standard/Benchmark: 8th Grade—The student participates in student-to-student verbal interactions. The student displays appropriate turn-taking behaviors. The student offers own opinion forcefully without domineering. The student responds appropriately to comments and questions. The student gives reasons in support of opinions expressed. The student clarifies, illustrates, or expands on a response when asked to do so….	Not Yet 0	Some Evidence 1
Organization and Clarity: Students will…		
• Know the rules of debate		
• Agree on debate order in advance		
• Challenge respectfully		
Use of Arguments: Students will…		
• Refute in rebuttals		
• Defend position		
• Check speech time		
Use of Rebuttal: Students will…		
• State contentions clearly		
• Use formal language		
• Speak with intensity		
Use of Examples: Students will…		
• Use experts as references for resources		
• Use anecdotes and quotes		
• Bring closure to subject		
Presentation Style: Students will…		
• Stand to speak		
• Not patronize or condescend opponents		
• Know other teams' positions		

Figure 5.8

Source: © Created in a 2007 workshop for Area Lead Teachers facilitated by Nancy Larimer, Professional Learning Supervisor, and Kay Burke and used with the permission of Rhonda Brewster-McCarthy, Cathy Tyler, and Jeanette Brewer and the Cobb County School District in Georgia.

Protocol for a Debate Rubric

Standard/Benchmark: 8th Grade—The student participates in student-to-student verbal interactions. The student displays appropriate turn-taking behaviors. The student offers own opinion forcefully without domineering. The student responds appropriately to comments and questions. The student gives reasons in support of opinions expressed. The student clarifies, illustrates, or expands on a response when asked to do so.

SCALE: CRITERIA:	1 Novice	2 Rookie	3 Runner-up	4 Winner	Score
Organization and Clarity: Viewpoints and responses are organized and clear	Poorly organized	Organized and clear in some parts	Organized and clear in most parts	Organized and clear throughout	
Use of Arguments: Reasons are given to support viewpoint	Few or no relevant reasons given	Some relevant reasons given	Most reasons are relevant	All reasons given are relevant and support arguments	
Use of Examples and Facts: Examples and facts are given to support reasons	Few or no relevant supporting examples/facts	Some relevant examples/facts given	Many examples/facts given; most are relevant	Many relevant supporting examples and facts are given	
Use of Rebuttal: Arguments made by the other teams are responded to and dealt with effectively	No effective counter-arguments made	Few effective counter-arguments made	Some effective counter-arguments made	Many effective counter-arguments made	
Presentation Style: Tone of voice, use of gestures, and level of enthusiasm are convincing to audience	Few style features were used but not convincingly	Few style features were used convincingly	All style features were used effectively; most used convincingly	All style features were used effectively and convincingly	

Total Points: ____

Comments:

Scale:
18–20 = A
16–17 = B
14–15 = C
Not Yet!

Figure 5.9

Source: © Created in a 2007 workshop for Area Lead Teachers facilitated by Nancy Larimer, Professional Learning Supervisor, and Kay Burke and used with the permission of Rhonda Brewster-McCarthy, Cathy Tyler, and Jeanette Brewer and the Cobb County School District in Georgia.

Teachers go from working independently to working in professional learning communities striving for common assessments and common goals.

Many teachers work in vertical teams to create common assessments that cross over into other grades. It is important to examine the standards and see the similarities from grade to grade. Rather than create separate assessments, teachers together find common criteria. There is more synergy when teachers from grades 3, 4, and 5 examine all their standards and target the ones that are similar. Sometimes school teams use curriculum mapping to see the standards-based connections among all grade levels and subject areas. Review the wording of the following writing standard for informational writing in fourth grade, and notice how similar it is in the writing standard for informational writing in fifth grade. There are only two areas that differ.

English Language Arts Informational Writing Standard: Grade 4

Standard ELA4W2: The student demonstrates competence in a variety of genres.

The student produces informational writing (e.g., report, procedures, correspondence) that:

a. Engages the reader by establishing a context, creating a speaker's voice, and otherwise developing reader interest.

b. ***Frames a central question about an issue or situation.***

c. Creates an organizing structure appropriate to a specific purpose, audience, and context.

d. Includes appropriate facts and details.

e. Excludes extraneous details and inappropriate information.

f. Uses a range of appropriate strategies, such as providing facts and details, describing or analyzing the subject, and narrating a relevant anecdote.

g. Draws from more than one source of information, such as speakers, books, newspapers, and online materials.

h. Provides a sense of closure to the writing.

Source: Reprinted with permission from the Georgia Department of Education's Georgia Performance Standards. © 2009 Georgia Department of Education. All rights reserved.

English Language Arts Informational Writing Standard: Grade 5

Standard ELA5W2: The student demonstrates competence in a variety of genres.

The student produces informational writing (e.g., report, procedures, correspondence) that:

a. Engages the reader by establishing a context, creating a speaker's voice, and otherwise developing reader interest.

b. ***Develops a controlling idea that conveys a perspective on a subject.***

c. Creates an organizing structure appropriate to a specific purpose, audience, and context.

d. Includes appropriate facts and details.

e. Excludes extraneous details and inappropriate information.

f. Uses a range of appropriate strategies, such as providing facts and details, describing or analyzing the subject, and narrating a relevant anecdote.

g. Draws from more than one source of information, such as speakers, books, newspapers, and online materials.

h. Provides a sense of closure to the writing.

i. **Lifts the level of language using appropriate strategies including word choice.**

Source: Reprinted with permission from the Georgia Department of Education's Georgia Performance Standards. © 2009 Georgia Department of Education. All rights reserved.

Fourth- and fifth-grade teachers at Carrollton City Middle School in Carrollton City, Georgia, reviewed the writing standards and worked as one team to create a checklist and a rubric for informational writing to use with their students in both grades. The students in the fourth grade work all year trying to meet the standard and then they continue their mastery of the standard the next year. This continuity provided by teams working together to create common assessments helps teachers plan their teaching, provide valid and reliable assessments, and prepare students for summative high-stakes standardized tests because they are embedding the language of the standards in all their formative classroom assessments. The connection between formative and summative assessments is essential for students to meet challenging academic standards and achieve deep understanding of the major concepts. Figure 5.10 shows the "Informational Writing Checklist" used by teachers to introduce and reinforce the process and Figure 5.11 on page 100 shows the "Informational Writing Rubric" created by the teachers to use with their students as the summative assessment to determine whether or not the students mastered the standard of informational writing along with all the subskills embedded in the writing process.

FINAL THOUGHTS

The standards-based movement has contributed a great deal to the construction of valid rubrics. Before each state had specific standards that contained criteria and indicators, teachers felt free to develop their own scoring guides, use examples from books and workbooks, and download examples from various Internet sites. But, on the high-stakes standardized tests, questions come from the vocabulary and concepts on the standards. It is critical, then, that teachers use the vocabulary of their state standards when they create the checklists and rubrics to guide their students in the completion of an authentic performance task. Often, teachers have to add additional criteria to clarify the task, but all the key words and ideas from the standards should be embedded in all scoring guides. Checklists and rubrics provide effective responses to intervention for all students—not just those who are struggling. The mantra of assessment is to "begin with the end in mind" and the rubric is the final outcome of the targeted standard.

Informational Writing Checklist

Standard: ELA4W2, ELA5W2 The student demonstrates competence in a variety of genres.

Checklist: Informational Writing

Assignment: Self-assess your own informational writing piece to see how well you have met the standards.	**Not Yet (0)**	**Some Evidence (1)**
Did you create an organizing structure? (check which one)		
• Chronological order (order in which things happen)		
• Cause and effect (reasons for things happening and the things that happen)		
• Similarity and difference (how things are alike and different)		
Did you engage the reader?		
• Did you establish a context? Who is your audience? Who will read this? _____ What is your purpose? Why are you writing this? _____		
• How did you create a speaker's voice? 1st person (I, we) ___ 2nd person (you) ___ 3rd person (he, she, it) ___		
• Did you develop your readers' interest? Explain how.		
Did you develop a controlling idea?		
• What are you teaching your reader? _____		
• What is the main idea? _____		
• What are you trying to say? _____		
• What perspective did you convey on your subject? Did you include different points of view? ___ Give 2 examples _____ _____ What is your personal point of view? _____		
Did you draw from more than one source of information? Check sources used.		
Speakers _____ Books _____ Newspapers ____ Online materials ____ Other _____		

• Did you tell a relevant anecdote (important personal story)? What?		
Did you use a range of appropriate strategies?		
• Did you describe or analyze the subject? How did you break it down?_____		
• Did you provide facts (true statements)? List 3 facts 1)_____ 2)_____ 3)_____		
• Did you give details (statements that back up the facts)?		
Did you exclude extraneous information?		
• Did you leave out extraneous details (things that are true, but do not apply to the topic)?		
• Did you leave out inappropriate information?		
• Did you stay focused and on topic?		
Did you provide closure (an ending)?		
• Did you summarize the main points?		
• Did you restate the controlling idea in a new way? How?		

Total Points: ____

Reflection:

How did you do?

What can you revise to make the paper better?

What help do you need?

Student Signature: _____ Date: _____

Figure 5.10

Source: © Used with the permissions of Cindy Daubenspeck, Tracy Rainwater, Denise Little, and Jill Lyn Rooks, teachers at Carrollton City Middle School, Grades 4–5, and the permission of the Carrollton City School System, Carrollton, GA.

Informational Writing Rubric

Student Name _____

Standard: ELA4W2, ELA5W2 The student demonstrates competence in a variety of genres.

Criteria The Student:	1 **Below the Standard**	2 **Approaching the Standard**	3 **Meets the Standard**	4 **Exceeds the Standard**	Score
Creates an Organizing Structure	Organizational structure is not evident	Structure is evident but not maintained throughout the paper	Structure is evident and maintained throughout the paper	Well-designed structure that flows from opening through closing	
Engages the Reader	Does not engage the reader	Attempts to engage the reader but lacks interest	Interesting introduction and point of view that engages the reader	Engaging hook that grabs and retains the reader's interest	
Develops a Controlling Idea	Controlling idea is not developed	Controlling idea is partially developed	Controlling idea is developed with the main idea clearly stated	Controlling idea is clearly developed using rich vocabulary	
Draws From Multiple Sources of Information	Draws from one source and that source is weak	Draws information from one or two reliable sources	Clearly draws from multiple sources of information	Multiple sources are clearly used and creatively developed	
Uses a Range of Appropriate Strategies	Range of strategies is not used	A range of strategies is used but they are not used correctly	A variety of appropriate strategies are used effectively	Appropriate strategies are embellished with vivid details	
Excludes Extraneous Information	Many extraneous details included throughout paper	Only a few extraneous details included	Extraneous information is not included	Topic is consistently and effectively developed and excludes all extraneous information	
Provides Closure	Closure is not evident	Closure is attempted but is confusing	Closure is included and clearly stated	Creative use of language to restate main idea in unique closing	

Total Points: _____

(out of 28)

Grade Equivalents:
A = 25–28 points (90%)
B = 22–24 points (80%)
C = 20–21 points (70%)
19 or below—Not Yet

Figure 5.11

Source: © Used with the permissions of Cindy Daubenspeck, Tracy Rainwater, Denise Little, and Jill Lyn Rooks, teachers at Carrollton City Middle School, Grades 4–5, and the permission of the Carrollton City School System, Carrollton, GA.

EXAMPLES
Four Examples of Checklists

PRIMARY

SOCIAL SKILLS CHECKLIST

ASSESSMENT OF SOCIAL SKILLS

Date: 10/21
Class: 3rd Grade
Teacher: Forbes

Ratings:
+ = Frequently
✔ = Sometimes
○ = Not Yet

Skills (diagonal headers): Listening, Using first names, Taking turns, Encouraging, Sharing

Who	Skill 1	Skill 2	Skill 3	Skill 4	Skill 5	Comments
1. Lois	✔	✔	○	✔	✔	
2. Connie	+	+	○	✔	+	Dropped in 2 areas
3. James	✔	✔	✔	✔	✔	
4. Juan	+	+	✔	+	+	
5. Beth	○	○	+	✔	✔	Improved in 2 areas
6. Michele	✔	✔	○	✔	✔	
7. John	✔	✔	○	✔	✔	
8. Charles	+	+	○	✔	+	
9. Mike	✔	✔	✔	✔	✔	Went from 5 0s to this in 2 months
10. Lana	+	+	✔	+	+	

Notes: Work with Lois on a regular basis. Change her seat and group.

MIDDLE SCHOOL

OBSERVATION CHECKLIST

Student: Denise   Class: Science   Date: 12/5
Type of Assignment: Work habits

☑ Teacher   Date _____   Signed _____
☑ Peer   Date _____   Signed _____
☑ Self   Date 12/5   Signed Denise Smith

	Not Yet	Sometimes	Frequently
WORK HABITS			
• Gets work done on time			X
• Asks for help when needed		X	
• Takes initiative		X	
STUDY HABITS			
• Organizes work			X
• Takes good notes			X
• Uses time well			X
PERSISTENCE			
• Shows patience		X	
• Checks own work	X		
• Revises work		X	
• Does quality work			X
SOCIAL SKILLS			
• Works well with others		X	
• Listens to others		X	
• Helps others		X	

COMMENTS: I always get my work done on time, and I am really organized. I just need to check my own work and help my group work.

Future goal: I need to be more patient with my group and try to work with them more. I worry about my own grades, but I don't do enough to help group members achieve their goals.

HIGH SCHOOL

BASKETBALL SKILLS

Teacher: Ms. Moses   Class: 5th Period P.E.   Date: 11/22
Target Skill: Students will develop basketball skills and teamwork.

STUDENTS DEMONSTRATE THE FOLLOWING

Ratings:
+ = Frequently
✔ = Sometimes
○ = Not Yet

Skills (diagonal headers): Dribbling skills, Passing skills, Free throw skills, Team spirit, Sportsmanship

Names of Students						Comments
1. Toni	✔	+	○	○	✔	
2. Casey	+	+	○	✔	+	
3. James	✔	✔	○	✔	✔	
4. Juan	+	+	✔	+	+	Real potential
5. Beth	✔	✔	✔	✔	✔	
6. Michele	✔	✔	○	✔	✔	Practice free throws
7. Judy	+	○	✔	+	+	
8. Charles	○	○	+	✔	✔	Does not like team sports
9. Dave	✔	+	○	✔	+	
10. Lisa	+	+	✔	+	+	Excellent player

COLLEGE

WRITING CHECKLIST

Key:
+ = Good
✔ = OK
○ = Not Yet

☑ Teacher
☑ Peer
◼ Self

Student: Robin   Class: English 102
Paper: Teaching for transfer

	Date: 9/1	Date: 11/5	Date: 1/2
Usage			
1. Topic sentence	+	+	+
2. Complete sentences	+	+	+
3. Complex sentences	○	○	○
4. Wide vocabulary	○	✔	+
Mechanics			
5. Capitalization	+	+	+
6. Punctuation	✔	✔	✔
7. Spelling	○	✔	+
8. Grammar	✔	✔	+

Strengths: My topic sentences, sentence structure, and capitalization are good.
Not Yet: I need to write more complex sentences. Most of my sentences are simple.

Figure 5.12

ON YOUR OWN

Observation Checklist

Directions: Select the skills you want to observe and write them on the five slanted lines at the top of the numbered list.

Teacher: _____ Class: _____ Date: _____

Target Skills: _____

Ratings:
  + = Frequently
  ✔ = Sometimes
  ○ = Not Yet

Names of Students						Comments
1.						
2.						
3.						
4.						
5.						
6.						
7.						
8.						
9.						
10.						
11.						
12.						
13.						
14.						
15.						
16.						
17.						
18.						
19.						

Figure 5.13

ON YOUR OWN

Individual Observation Checklist

Directions: Select criteria you want to observe and list specific indicators that describe those criteria.

Student: _____ Class: _____ Date: _____

Type of Assignment: _____

☐ Teacher Date _____ Signed _____

☐ Peer Date _____ Signed _____

☐ Self Date _____ Signed _____

	Not yet 0	Sometimes 1	Frequently 2
• _____	_____	_____	_____
• _____	_____	_____	_____
• _____	_____	_____	_____
• _____	_____	_____	_____
• _____	_____	_____	_____
• _____	_____	_____	_____
• _____	_____	_____	_____
• _____	_____	_____	_____
• _____	_____	_____	_____
• _____	_____	_____	_____
• _____	_____	_____	_____
• _____	_____	_____	_____

Comments:

Figure 5.14

Checklist/Rubric Template

Standard: _____

SCALE:	1	2	3	4
CRITERIA:				
•				
•				
•				
•				
•				
•				
•				
•				
•				
•				
•				

Figure 5.15

Source: From Burke, K. © 2006. *From Standards to Rubrics in Six Steps.* Thousand Oaks, CA: Corwin.

Rubric Template

Standard: _____

Assignment: Create a rubric and reflect on how it helps students excel.

Criteria The student:	1 Below the Standard	2 Approaching the Standard	3 Meets the Standard	4 Exceeds the Standard	Score

Figure 5.16

Source: From Burke, K. © 2006. *From Standards to Rubrics in Six Steps.* Thousand Oaks, CA: Corwin.

REFLECTION

Reflection on Checklists and Rubrics

1. Why do you think checklists help struggling students get organized?

2. What are some differences between checklists and rubrics?

3. How do you feel about working with a team to create common assessments?

4. Self-assess your feelings about rubrics by rating how you feel below:

A rubric is a rubric is a rubric!

Show me the Scantron!	Rubrics are our friends!	Rubrics rock!	Rubrics rule!

Explanation:

Figure 5.17

Metacognitive Strategies 6

WHAT IS METACOGNITIVE REFLECTION?

The term *reflect* is defined in *Webster's New World Dictionary of the American Language* as "to think seriously; contemplate; ponder" (1974, p. 1193). Jonson (2002) takes this a step further: "Without such reflection, past events and occurrences disappear into history. Whether they have been dealt with well or not, they are done. With reflection upon past events, though, they become stepping-stones to improvement, opportunities for growth" (p. 114). Within today's fast-paced educational agenda, it becomes very challenging to pause and reflect on what has gone before in order to adjust thinking to address current and future issues. Moreover, when people think about education, the term *cognition* comes to mind; it is important to teach students knowledge and thinking skills. However, the thinking often is overshadowed by the information. Mansilla and Gardner (2008) discuss how most students in most schools memorize animal taxonomies, atomic weights, the organs in the respiratory system, and the effects of the Industrial Revolution. "From a subject-matter perspective, students come to see the subjects of history and science as the collection of dates, actors, facts, and formulas catalogued in textbooks and encountered in rooms 458 and 503, in second and third period" (p. 15). Teachers can rapidly present large quantities of information to students and easily test this information.

In recent decades, however, cognitive psychologists have documented a phenomenon of vital importance for anyone interested in education. "Although students have little trouble spewing forth information that they have committed to memory, they display great difficulty in applying knowledge and skills to new situations" (Mansilla & Gardner, 2008, pp. 15–16). Cognition is important, but *metacognition* may help the students integrate their facts and apply them to solve problems in the real world. "Metacognition" can be defined as *above* or *beyond* one's cognitive thinking. Metacognition is basically "thinking about your thinking" and becoming more aware of one's own thought processes. Students who can label their own thinking, such as *"analyzing* the experiment to see what went wrong," show they are learning from the past in order to prevent the same problems from occurring in the future. Doing "more of the same when the same does not work" is not metacognitive.

Teaching students to think is a clear goal of education because it leads to intellectual development. Noddings (2008) says that writers often distinguish among such thinking categories as critical thinking, reflective thinking, creative thinking, and higher-order thinking. Noddings qualifies thinking as a "mental activity" using "facts to plan, order, and work toward an end; seeks meaning or an explanation; is self-reflective; and uses reason to question claims and make judgments. This seems to be what most teachers have in mind when they talk about thinking" (p. 9). Teachers today, while knowing how to encourage their students to think, are often constrained by the amount of time required. It takes time to engage students in inquiry and allow them sufficient opportunities to construct knowledge and gain deeper understanding on their own. With the emphasis on standards and preparing for high-stakes tests, they admit that sometimes there is little time available for thoughtful questioning and reflection.

Bellanca and Fogarty (2003) believe that teachers face a great challenge when they try to promote student reflection or metacognition. They believe that the challenge is most difficult when students seem very comfortable in their passive roles of "information acquirers" who "sit and get" the information because there are such low expectations for active thinking and student-to-student interaction. However, once a goal for "active mental engagement" (p. 201) is under way, teachers see the benefit of undertaking this challenge. "They [teachers] focus not on *what* students think but on *how to use* students' developing thinking skills to increase learning and encourage higher achievement" (p. 201). Teachers, therefore, need to introduce and model strategies that promote metacognition. Moreover, students need to learn ways to self-reflect regularly so they can become adept at monitoring, assessing, and improving their own performances and their own thinking.

One of the key components of meeting the challenges of the twenty-first century involves using self-assessments and peer-assessments to navigate the complexities of a global community. While covering course content, meeting state standards, and preparing students for high-stakes tests, teachers sometimes neglect the critical piece that allows everyone to step back, reflect on what went well, what could be done differently the next time, and whether or not help is needed. Individual students, cooperative groups, and teachers need to take more time to process what they have done and reflect on their own learning. If students make connections between past learning and new learning, they are more likely to make sense of the meaning and retain the learning.

WHY SHOULD WE USE METACOGNITIVE REFLECTION?

Learning to think begins with recognizing how we are thinking. Costa (2008) believes that metacognition calls on "our emotions, bodily sensations, ideas, beliefs, values, character qualities, and the inferences we generate from interactions with others. When confronted with perplexing, ambiguous situations, skillful thinkers engage in an internal mental dialogue that helps them decide on intelligent actions" (p. 23). Teachers foster metacognition by posing a series of self-reflective questions to help students think about their own thinking, such as "What do I already know about this?" or "How can I break this problem down into more manageable chunks?" or "Do I need help from others to solve this problem?" By encouraging students to verbalize their plans and strategies, teachers actively monitor their progress, evaluate their results, and offer constructive feedback to help them improve their thinking processes.

Transfer

A critical relationship exists between metacognition and transfer. In order to transfer knowledge or skills from one situation to another, students must be aware of the skills they used in order to apply those skills again when a similar situation occurs. Students' ability to *transfer* the skills they learn in class to new situations in school or life is the ultimate goal of all learning. Some educators use the phrase "making thinking visible" so that students know the name of what specific thinking skill they used. Telling a student "I like the way you predicted what was going to happen in the story" helps the student affix a label to what he did. By knowing the meaning of the verb "predict" as well as knowing how to predict what is going to happen next, the student is more likely to use the skill again while reading a story. Hopefully, the student will also be able to use the skill in other content areas, such as predicting the results of a science experiment, estimating a mathematical solution to a problem, or predicting which team should win a game based on players' statistics.

Some educators believe that students automatically apply or transfer the skills learned in their classes to other classes or situations outside of school. Yet, students often do not connect what they learn in English class to social studies class, or what they learn in math class to a mathematical problem they encounter at work or in life. Transfer of knowledge plays a key role in metacognition. (An example of a transfer journal appears in Figure 6.9 on page 124.) Understanding what a word or concept means in one context helps students realize how it could be used in a similar context. Transfer does not happen automatically—teachers have to teach for transfer. Journals, thoughtful questioning, goal setting, problem-based learning, and self-assessments help students become more aware of their thought processes and, therefore, more able to transfer those strategies to other situations.

Transfer is an integral component of the learning process. Every day teachers refer to past learning to make new learning more understandable and meaningful. Students are expected to transfer the knowledge and skills they learn in school to the context of everyday life. Sousa (2001) states, "It is almost axiomatic that the more information students can transfer from their schooling to the context of everyday life, the greater the probability that they will be good communicators, informed citizens, critical thinkers, and successful problem solvers" (p. 139). The more connections students are able to make between past learning and new learning, school learning and life learning, the more likely they are to be successful in both school and life.

Bellanca and Fogarty (2003) believe that in most ordinary learning situations, students just do more of the same thing in the same situation. Real transfer happens when people carry over something they learned in one context to a significantly different context. They created the graphic organizer in Figure 6.1 to illustrate the situational dispositions for transfer, using six birds to represent the different models of transfer and symbolize how people act or react in different situations. Sometimes people "soar like Samantha the eagle" when they create original ideas or products. Other times, that same person resembles "Dan the duplicator" when it comes to a different situation. Dan either does not

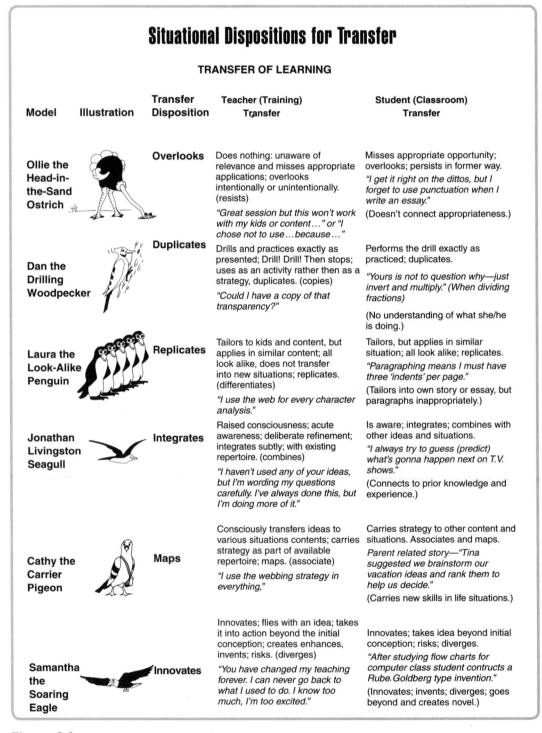

Figure 6.1

Source: Bellanca, J., & Fogarty, R. (2003). *Blueprints for Achievement in the Cooperative Classroom.* Thousand Oaks, CA: Corwin.

understand what is expected or does not care. He is content to copy what some-one else has done rather than spend the time and effort to delve deeper to achieve greater insight and understanding.

Successful transfer can be enhanced with thematic units and an integrated curriculum. Sousa (2001) believes that an integrated approach to learning helps students see the commonalities among diverse topics and reinforces understanding and meaning for future applications. When students make con-nections among topics, themes, or concepts, they begin to see the bigger pic-ture, and begin to answer the essential questions and grasp the big ideas.

English Language Learners

One of the biggest challenges for teachers is building in enough time in their lessons to allow students to think about their thinking and self-assess their own work. Many English language learners may need more time to reflect on the processes and products of their learning in their native language first, before transferring their thoughts to English. Gottlieb (2006) believes self-assessment is important because it does the following:

- provides a venue for students to convey their depth of understanding
- invites students to take responsibility for their own learning
- honors student input in the assessment process
- recognizes the student perspective as a valid data source
- fosters the creation of a shared set of expectations between teachers and students
- encourages students to do their best work
- helps students set realistic goals based on their accomplishments
- offers personalized feedback to teachers
- promotes students becoming lifetime learners (pp. 141–142)

In today's differentiated classrooms, students may need more time or they may need different types of techniques to learn how to reflect on their own learn-ing and self-assess their work. Gottlieb (2006) warns that the concept of self-assessment may be new to some English language learners, especially students who have been schooled out of the United States where student voice and feel-ings are not encouraged or acknowledged. She recommends, "Teachers should gradually introduce this idea, perhaps initially as a whole-group language expe-rience. Later, individual students can express their thoughts on learning through interactive journal writing where teachers provide feedback, prior to engaging in self-assessment independently" (p. 142). This technique can greatly ease discom-fort in students unfamiliar with a more interactive model of education.

HOW SHOULD WE USE METACOGNITIVE REFLECTION?

Metacognitive reflection can be threaded throughout teaching experiences in all content areas, at all grade levels, and by all teachers. Since reflection is critical to learning and transfer, it needs to be embedded in all curriculum development, instructional strategies, and assessments. As Knight (2007) says, "*Reflection* is believing that learning can be enhanced when we have numerous opportunities to consider how what we're learning might impact what we have done in the past, what we are doing now, and what we will be doing in the future" (p. 54). The following strategies provide opportunities for students to evaluate things done in the past in the light of new information they have learned. Hopefully, they can analyze what they are currently doing and make decisions about how to change or improve what they do in the future.

WHAT ARE LEARNING LOGS AND JOURNALS?

Learning logs and reflective journals have been used by teachers as formative assessment tools for years, but mostly by middle and high school English teachers. Logs and journals, however, play an even broader role in today's reflective classrooms with teachers in all content areas and grade levels.

Logs consist of short, objective entries that contain mathematical problem-solving entries, observations of science experiments, questions about the lecture or readings, lists of outside readings, homework assignments, or anything that lends itself to keeping records. The responses in these logs are usually brief, factual, and impersonal.

Journals, on the other hand, are usually written in narrative form and are more subjective since they deal more with feelings, opinions, or personal experiences. Journal entries usually contain longer descriptions and are more open-ended and free flowing than logs. Journals are often used to respond to pieces of literature, describe events, comment on reactions to events, reflect on personal experiences and feelings, and connect what is being studied in one class with another class, or with life outside the classroom. Journal writing provokes more reflection and encourages students to take charge of their learning and their feelings. Journals help students make connections between what is really important to them, the curriculum, and the world. The Venn diagram in Figure 6.2 shows similarities and differences between learning logs and journals.

Reflective-Lesson Logs

A reflective-lesson log is an effective method to help students select key ideas from a lecture, discussion, or video and write down important facts, insights, or questions that will lead to better understanding. Jensen (1998) believes, "Teachers need to keep attentional demands to short bursts of no longer than the age of their learners in minutes. For a first grader, that's about six consecutive minutes; for a high school student, that's up to fifteen minutes" (p. 43). This practice of "chunking" lessons allows students time to hear the new information via direct instruction, reflect on its meaning, and ask questions for clarification.

Since it is important for students to interact with the teacher, the textbook, and each other, teachers often use logs and journals to help students process information during lectures. Teachers give direct instruction in short chunks

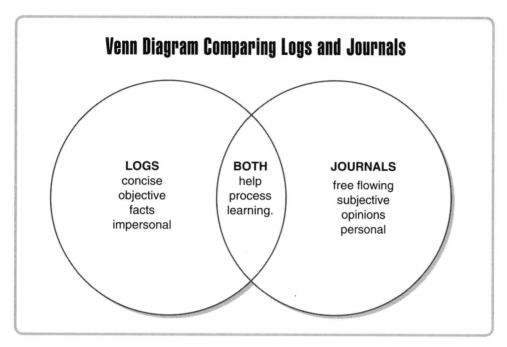

Figure 6.2

appropriate to chronological age and then ask students to write down key ideas, questions, connections, or reflections. The students use this time to think about the material, clarify areas of confusion, discuss key ideas with group members, and process the information before the teacher moves on to the next segment or chunk of direct instruction. The following is an example of such a reflective lesson log technique.

Using a Reflective-Lesson Log

1. The teacher presents information to the class (five–fifteen minute chunks, depending on students' ages).

2. Students spend time writing in their reflective-lesson log using the format in Figure 6.3 (two–five minutes).

3. Students then share their logs with a partner or group members. They discuss the key facts they recorded with other students and see if they captured them correctly and clarify any misunderstandings (three–five minutes).

4. The teacher conducts a brief discussion with the whole class to hear some of the big ideas generated by the groups, as well as any connections students made with the information to other subject areas or life experiences (three–five minutes).

5. The teacher asks students to share any other essential questions about the topic and the class discusses how and where students can research additional information to share at their next meeting (three–five minutes).

Reflective-Lesson Log

Name: _____   Topic: _____   Date: _____

Key facts from this discussion:

_____

_____

Big idea from this discussion:

_____

_____

Connections I can make with other ideas, different content areas, current events, or personal life experiences:

_____

_____

Essential questions I still have about this topic:

_____

_____

Follow-up research I could do to answer these questions:

_____

_____

Summary statement:

_____

_____

Figure 6.3

6. The teacher asks for someone to summarize what the class has just discussed so everyone feels comfortable with that chunk of information and can anticipate additional information that will be provided the next day (one–two minutes).

7. The teacher continues with the next chunk of direct instruction. The cycle repeats if there is time, or students complete logs for homework.

8. The next day, students in pairs or small groups discuss their logs as a review, and clarify any confusion about yesterday's lesson or the homework. The whole class finds out the answers to their questions from the students who volunteered to research additional information that was of interest to the class (three–five minutes).

This process obviously takes too long for every lesson, but teachers learn methods to modify it and use only one or two steps as needed.

The advantages of structuring lessons to include the use of a reflective-lesson log include the following:

1. Students retain key ideas.

2. Students improve their writing skills.

3. Students with special needs have more time to process information.

4. Students increase interaction and collaboration among peers.

5. Students study logs for quizzes and tests.

6. Students discuss the essential questions and big ideas as well as facts.

7. Teachers assign grades for selected logs or "log books" (daily grades or weekly grades).

8. Students who are absent can get logs from friends to keep up with work and the important ideas they missed.

9. Teachers sense during the lesson if there is confusion or misunderstandings about information and adjust their instruction accordingly.

10. Students connect ideas they learn to real life and use inquiry to explore points of further interest to meet their needs.

It is important for teachers to build in class time for students to reflect. If teachers don't provide adequate time for students to process information, they may have to spend additional time reteaching the information later. Many teachers feel pressured to keep up with the district's pacing calendar or prepare for periodic benchmark tests. Students with learning disabilities and English language learning challenges may need more time to master the concepts. Teachers, however, are often forced to focus on preparing all students to take standardized tests, at the expense of differentiating instruction for their students with diverse needs.

WHY SHOULD WE USE LEARNING LOGS AND JOURNALS?

Research by Brownlie, Close, and Wingren (1988) and Jeroski, Brownlie, and Kaser (1990a) recommend using logs and journals on a regular basis in the following ways:

1. *Record* key ideas from a lecture, movie, presentation, field trip, or reading assignment.

2. *Predict* what will happen next in a story, movie, or experiment; with the weather; or in school, national, or world events.

3. *List* essential questions surrounding big ideas of the lesson.

4. *Summarize* the main idea of a book, movie, lecture, or reading.

5. *Reflect* on the information presented and pose additional questions to extend learning.

6. *Connect* the ideas presented to other subject areas, current events, or to personal lives.

7. *Monitor* change in an experiment or event over time.

8. *Respond* to questions posed by the teacher or peers.

9. *Brainstorm* ideas about potential projects, papers, or presentations.

10. *Identify* problems.

11. *Record* problem-solving techniques.

12. *Track* the number of problems solved, books read, or homework assignments completed.

By using a variety of logs and journals, teachers vary their instruction enough to meet the needs of students' learning styles and prevent students from becoming bored by doing one type of journal writing the entire year. The key is to introduce a repertoire of appropriate log and journal options that correlate to the purpose of the lesson. Brownlie, Close, and Wingren (1990) identify certain prompts or lead-ins that promote higher-level thinking. They suggest using prompts at the beginning, middle, and end of a lesson, and to comment on the group process.

Some examples of prompts or lead-ins include the following:

At the beginning of lesson:

- What questions do you have from yesterday?
- Write two important points from yesterday's lesson.

In the middle of lesson:

- What do you want to know more about?
- How is this like something else?
- Is this easy or hard for you? Explain why.
- Could someone in the class explain it in another way?

At the end of lesson:

- What did you learn that surprised you?
- What would you like to learn more about?
- How will you use this outside of class?

About the group process:

- How did you move the group's thinking forward?
- How did your group members help clarify your thinking?
- Can you give an example of how your group collaborated today?

Stems or lead-ins for log entries should encourage responses that reflect analysis, synthesis, and evaluation.

Examples of log stems include the following:

- One thing I'm excited about is _____ because . . .
- I hate it when _____ because . . .
- This is like another movie I saw, _____, because . . .
- When I compare _____ and _____, I find these similarities . . .

Along with reflecting on learning in logs and journals, it is equally important to encourage students to ask good questions showing how they integrate the information and achieve deeper understanding of the key concepts. Garner (2007) believes teachers can assess understanding by encouraging students to formulate their own questions rather than answering questions in the back of chapters in the textbook. She says, "The true level of understanding is evident in the kinds of questions students ask. Teachers who model asking open-ended questions stimulate student reflection and the need to know more" (p. 26). Students who ask thoughtful questions, such as "How does this current event compare to a historical event?" or "Why should we study algebra?" or "Why does man create?" demonstrate an awareness that goes beyond answering multiple-choice questions on a state test.

HOW SHOULD WE ASSESS LEARNING LOGS AND JOURNALS?

Learning logs and journals are usually considered formative methods of assessment that can be assigned numerical or letter grades or point values to provide a grade or effective feedback on how well students are meeting goals. The following methods of assessment may be helpful:

1. Jeroski, Brownlie, and Kaser (1990b) developed indicators to describe the depth and personalization of students' responses to readings. They scored sixth graders' responses to a poem using the following criteria: powerful, competent, partial, and undeveloped (see Figure 6.4).

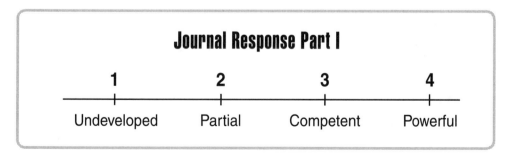

Figure 6.4

2. Another way to assess journal responses is by the level of thoughtfulness: no evidence, little evidence, some evidence, and strong evidence (see Figure 6.5).

Journal Response Part II

No Evidence of Thoughtfulness 1	Little Evidence of Thoughtfulness 2	Some Evidence of Thoughtfulness 3	Strong Evidence of Thoughtfulness 4
• No response	• Response only • Not supported by specific examples	• Response • Supported by specific examples	• Response • Supported by specific examples • Supported by personal reflections

Figure 6.5

3. Teachers can assign point values for logs or journals:

    20 points for completing all logs or journals

    10 points for completing all logs or journals within the time allotment

    15 points for originality of ideas

    15 points for evidence of higher-order thinking

    15 points for making connections to other subject areas

    10 points for personal examples

    15 points for personal reflections or insights

    _____

    100 total points for log and journal assignments

4. Sample criteria and indicators used to assess logs and journals on a checklist or rubric include the following:
    • descriptive words
    • use of specific examples
    • length of response
    • use of similes or metaphors
    • appropriate dialogue
    • connections to other subjects
    • thoughtfulness
    • originality
    • creativity
    • ability to answer essential questions posed in the lesson
    • insight toward grasping the big idea of the lesson

5. Students turn in journals on a periodic basis for feedback and/or a grade. The grade could be based on the number of entries, the quality of entries (based on predetermined criteria), or a combination of quantity and quality.

6. Students share journal entries with a buddy or a cooperative group. Peers provide both oral and written feedback based on predetermined criteria.

7. Students complete a self-assessment of their journal entries based on predetermined criteria provided in a checklist or a rubric, such as the one shown in Figure 6.6.

8. Students and teachers select a few of the journal entries to be rewritten and turned in for a grade or be placed in the final portfolio.

9. Students and teachers create a visual rubric that correlates to standards and benchmarks and can be used for self-assessment.

Brain research suggests that all teachers—not just English teachers—need to provide more opportunities for students to process what they have learned and to reflect on how that learning affects their lives. Keeping logs and journals reinforces reflective teaching and learning by helping students construct knowledge for themselves. Figure 6.6 is an example of a journal checklist used by science teachers in a unit about rocks and minerals. Notice how the journal checklist includes specific terms included in the third-grade science standard.

Self-Assessment Questions

Bellanca and Fogarty (2003) suggest a series of questions called "Mrs. Potter's Questions" to help individuals and groups process and reflect on their individual work or their group work (see Figure 6.7 on page 121).

Stiggins (2002) believes that teachers need to engage students in regular self-assessment with the standards held constant so that "students can watch themselves grow over time and thus feel in charge of their own success" (p. 762). By dating log and journal entries and reviewing them over time, students trace their growth and reflect on how their ideas have changed. They also recognize how they are improving and set new goals for meeting and exceeding the standards.

T-Chart for the Reflective Classroom

Bellanca and Fogarty (2003) believe that teachers should prepare students for reflection and foster the collaborative culture in the classroom by establishing behavior norms encouraging all students to think independently and interdependently. The T-chart graphic organizer helps students know what the reflective classroom looks like and sounds like. By making the characteristics more concrete, students are better able to understand the meaning of reflection. The example in Figure 6.8 on page 123 shows their T-chart for the reflective classroom. If it is posted in the room, teachers can refer to it in order to reinforce reflective behaviors.

Checklist for Science Journal

Science Standard (Grade 3): Student will investigate the physical attributes of rocks and minerals.

Assignment: Write a journal entry to document your findings from your investigations, graphic organizers, vocabulary study, and notes.	**Not Yet** 0	**Some Evidence** 1
Explain the difference between a rock and a mineral.		
• Did you include the definition of a rock?		
• Did you include the definition of a mineral?		
• Did you complete the Venn diagram to compare and contrast rocks and minerals?		
Recognize physical attributes of rocks and minerals.		
• Did you record your observations of shape, color, and texture?		
• Did you record the weights of each rock and mineral?		
• Did you record the results of the hardness tests?		
Compare similarities and differences in topsoils.		
• Did you record the similarities and differences of clay, including texture, particle size, and color?		
• Did you record the similarities and differences of loam, including texture, particle size, and color?		
• Did you record the similarities and differences of sand, including texture, particle size, and color?		
• Did you record the similarities and differences of potting soil, including texture, particle size, and color?		
Research and observe changes in rocks and minerals caused by water and wind over time.		
• Did you record your research results and observations of erosion by water?		
• Did you record your research results and observations of erosion by wind?		

Figure 6.6

Source: © Created in 2008 workshops sponsored by Dr. Mark Tavernier, Director of Curriculum, and the Clarke County Curriculum Department and facilitated by Kay Burke. Used with the permission of Patty Birchenall, Susan Bolen, Mia Jordan, Pamela Stevens, Claudia Taxell, Donna Ware, and the Clarke County School District, Athens, GA.

Mrs. Potter's Questions

1. What were you expected to do?

2. In this assignment, what did you do well?

3. If you had to do this task over, what would you do differently?

4. What help do you need from me?

Figure 6.7

Wait Time

Wait time is the period of silence after the teacher poses a question before he or she calls on the first student for a response. When Rowe (1974) first conducted research on wait time, she found that high school teachers had an average wait time of just over one second, whereas elementary teachers waited an average of three seconds. In these time frames, slower retrievers, many of whom may know the correct answer, do not have enough time to locate the answer in long-term memory storage and retrieve it into working memory. Rowe found that if teachers extended the wait time to at least five seconds or more, the length and quality of student responses increased, there was greater participation by slower learners, students used more evidence to support inferences, and there were more higher-order thinking responses.

Rowe (1974) also found that allowing additional wait time *after* a student responds to a question provides the student more time to amend or extend his answer. In addition, the other students have the opportunity to provide more information or ask follow-up questions. It takes time to think and the more time devoted to building in wait time, the more time for thoughtfulness.

Another strategy teachers can use is to instruct students not to raise their hands to volunteer to answer the questions. If teachers call on students by using a seating chart or by randomly selecting cards with names on them, more students will pay attention and be prepared to answer the question.

Group Processing

Students also need to reflect on their participation in group work and continually ask themselves and their fellow group members what they can do to improve their social skills. An example of a group processing strategy using a car-race metaphor can be found on Figure 6.10 (page 125). Too often, teachers put too much emphasis on the group project or performance and neglect one of the most important reasons for assigning group work—cooperation. The group may produce a "killer" project but almost "kill" each other in the process. By assessing participation, collaboration, and social skills, teachers show students that those traits are valued. It has been said that "we assess what we value" and if teachers only give feedback or grades on content, they signal the students that working together in teams, listening, cooperating, sharing, and coming to consensus is not valued.

FINAL THOUGHTS

Teachers in the twenty-first century graduate from college with a content-knowledge base they hope to share with their students. But, just knowing the content is not enough. Of course, students need a body of factual knowledge upon which to base their thinking, but merely covering the material and asking students to memorize information is not sufficient. Brady (2008) discusses how some teachers believe that their job is to provide the raw factual materials because many students are incapable of getting beyond the basics. He believes, however, that most kids are already using higher-order thought processes when they enter kindergarten. "They don't need to be taught to think; they need to learn how to examine, elaborate, and refine their ways of thinking and put this thinking to deliberate use converting information into knowledge and knowledge into wisdom" (p. 67). To add to this, Epstein (2008) believes, "To help children to become creative thinkers and problem solvers, teachers must exercise critical thinking themselves. The mechanism is the same regardless of age. Critical thinkers plan and reflect" (p. 42). Teachers in today's standards-based classroom not only prepare students to pass high-stakes tests but also prepare them to develop a full range of thinking skills that are applicable to the classroom and the wider world.

EXAMPLES
The Reflective Classroom

PRIMARY

THE REFLECTIVE CLASSROOM

Looks Like	Sounds Like
Waiting for the talker to finish	"That's a good idea."
Nodding agreement	"I'd like to clarify"
Taking notes on peer's ideas	"Let's see if I understand_____."
Heads together	"Good thinking...."
Making journal entries	"I agree..."
Taking turns	"Way to go_____."
Low voice	"Here's another idea...."
High fives	"You can do it."
Thumbs up	"Thanks for sharing."

MIDDLE SCHOOL

DOUBLE-ENTRY JOURNAL

Name: Juan   **Date:** September 3

Grade: 7

Topic: Life Skills (looking)

Initial Observation (Sept. 3)	Upon Reflection (Sept. 15)
I think it's really stupid that boys have to take a "Family Living" course. Why should I have to learn to sew and cook? I don't plan on ever doing it. I'd rather take a computer or another physical education course. There's only five guys in this class. I'm going to go to my counselor during homeroom tomorrow and try to get out of here!	Well, the counselor said all the sections of the computer were full, so I'm stuck in here for the quarter. I still don't believe it but my Apple Brown Betty was pretty good! I guess it wouldn't hurt to learn a few cooking tricks. Maybe this won't be so bad. Besides, I've met a lot of cool girls!

HIGH SCHOOL

REFLECTION

Name: Josh   **Date:** October 6
Course: Science – 9th grade   **Topic:** AIDS

Circle One: (Lecture) Discussion Video Written material

1. Key Ideas:
   - It's spreading fast.
   - No cure
   - Kids can get it from transfusions.
2. Questions I have:
   - Can you get it by kissing?
   - Is the blood supply safe?
3. Connections I can make with other subjects: social studies
   - AIDS reminds me of the Black Death during the Middle Ages.
4. How I can apply these ideas to my own life:
   - I better find out if you can get it by kissing—I need to learn more.
5. My insights or reflections from these ideas:
   - I really don't know that much about AIDS. We'll see the video tomorrow. Maybe I'll learn more.

COLLEGE

SELF-ASSESSMENT

Name: Cedric   **Date:** Jan. 7
Assignment: Speech 101

1. What were you supposed to do?
   Give a speech on my favorite hobby.
2. What was your favorite part?
   Bringing my baseball card collection to college—no one in my class has ever seen it before.
3. What was your least favorite part? Why?
   Having to write an outline—my mind doesn't think in roman numerals.
4. If you did this task over, what would you do differently? Why?
   Get a better ending—I just stopped! I should have thrown a baseball or something dramatic.
5. What grade do you think you deserve and why?
   B—People remember the last thing you say, and my last thing wasn't too memorable.
6. What new goal can you set for yourself?
   Practice a better ending—some of the other speeches had quotes or jokes—mine had a fact—Blah!

Figure 6.8

Source: "Looks Like/Sounds Like" reflective T-chart taken from Bellanca, J., & Fogarty, R. (2003). *Blueprints for achievement in the cooperative classroom,* 3rd ed. Thousand Oaks, CA: Corwin. Used with permission.

EXAMPLES

Transfer Journal

Name: _____   **Class/Course:** _____   **Date:** _____

Idea	Interpretation	Application
What's the Big Idea? (Copy phrase or sentence exactly)	**What does it mean?** (Write in your own words)	**How can you apply or transfer the idea to another subject or your life?**
Example: Vietnam became President Lyndon Johnson's *Achilles' heel.*	Soft spot, weakness—In mythology Achilles was dipped in the River Styx to make him invincible. His mother held him by the heel, which wasn't protected. He was later killed when someone shot him in the heel.	I can say that when I diet, chocolate is my *Achilles' heel*—my weak spot—my downfall. In the book *A Separate Peace,* Gene's *Achilles' heel* (downfall) was jealousy. He envied Finny, and his envy caused Finny's death.

Signed: _____   **Date:** _____

Figure 6.9

ON YOUR OWN

Group Processing: How Did We Do?

1. How did we stay on task?

2. How did we listen to each other?

3. How did we encourage each other?

4. What do we need to work on next time?

5. How do we want to celebrate our successes?

Figure 6.10

ON YOUR OWN

Wraparound

The wraparound is an effective reflective strategy that teachers can use in the middle or at the end of a lesson to find out how students feel and what they remember about a lesson. Write a few stem statements on the board and divide the room so that students know what stem question they will answer. Give enough wait time to allow everyone time to reflect. Go around the room and call on each student to complete the stem statement assigned, or let the students select any one to complete.

Sample Wraparound Stems

One idea I learned today is . . .

The fact that really surprised me is . . .

One thing I'll remember 25 years from now is . . .

One idea I would like to learn more about is . . .

Create your own wraparound stems to use with your class.

Wraparound Stems

Stem: _____

Stem: _____

Stem: _____

Stem: _____

Ask your students to help create their own stems.

Figure 6.11

O N   Y O U R   O W N

JOURNAL STEMS

1. Create some original stem statements that would motivate your students to write in their logs or journals.

Example: My worst nightmare is . . .   My friends would never believe that . . .

Journal Stem Statements

- _____   - _____

- _____   - _____

- _____   - _____

2. Response journals require students to respond to a particular stimulus such as a field trip, an assembly speaker, or a newspaper article. List some activities that your students could respond to in a journal.

Response Journal Topics

_____   _____

_____   _____

_____   _____

_____   _____

_____   _____

Figure 6.12

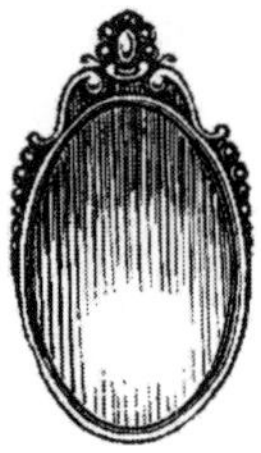

REFLECTION

THINKING AT RIGHT ANGLES

Directions: In section A, list all the facts you know about metacognition. In section B, list your feelings and associations. In section C, write a summary statement about metacognition.

TOPIC: *Metacognition*

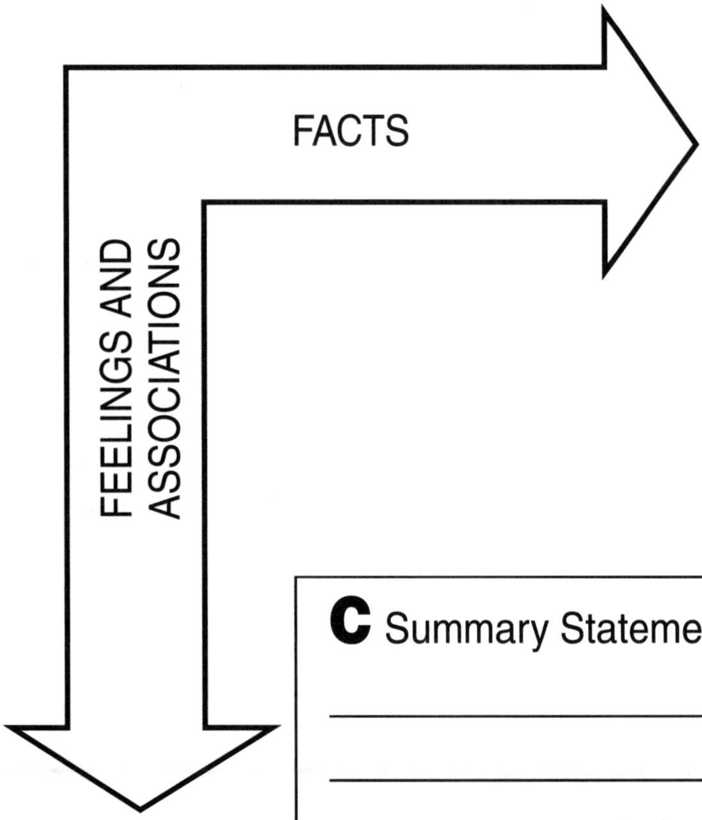

FACTS

A _____

FEELINGS AND ASSOCIATIONS

B

C Summary Statement

_____

Figure 6.13

Source: Adapted From Bellanca, J., & Fogarty, R. © 2003. (pg. 147) *Blueprints for Achievement in the Cooperative Classroom, 3rd edition.* Thousand Oaks, CA: Corwin.

Graphic Organizers 7

WHAT ARE GRAPHIC ORGANIZERS?

Graphic organizers are mental maps that involve students in active thinking through representation of key skills such as sequencing, comparing and contrasting, and classifying. These mental maps depict complex relationships and promote clearer understanding of content lessons. They also "provide tools to help students organize and find patterns among the overwhelming amount of information available today, as well as to make sense out of it and evaluate it" (Costa, as cited in Hyerle, 1996, p. x). Since so many students are visual learners, it makes sense to provide more graphics that will help them understand complex ideas and remember them longer.

As Hyerle (1996) says, "Visual tools are for constructing representations of knowledge. In educational terms, visual tools are for constructing and remembering, communicating, and negotiating meanings, and assessing and reforming the shifting terrain of interrelated knowledge" (p. 11). One of the most important learning experiences involves students making connections so they can see patterns. Using a Venn diagram to compare and contrast World War I and World War II helps students see the similarities of causes leading up to both wars, the leaders during each time period, and the effects of the war on the people and the countries. Students may be able to make some generalizations about what wars throughout time have in common as well as pinpoint major differences.

Graphic organizers serve as effective tools for helping both teachers and students graphically display their thinking processes. They also help represent abstract information in more concrete forms so students can better grasp the meaning of the concepts. They help students organize information, relate it to prior knowledge, and then connect it with new information. Since graphic organizers are so visual, many students say they can remember the information better than they could if it was just in a written format. Graphic organizers are often used as instructional tools to teach new information to students, but they also serve as unique assessment tools because they target the visual learners and allow them to demonstrate their understanding in a format different than multiple-choice test items.

129

Graphic organizers such as the web, Venn diagram, concept map, and many others help students make their thinking visible. They also "become a metacognitive tool to transfer the thinking processes to other lessons which feature the same relationships" (Black & Black, 1990, p. 2). The brain seeks patterns, and students who recognize the pattern when it is used with one content area can transfer the pattern to another content area to see similar relationships.

In the book *What Works in Schools: Translating Research into Action,* Marzano (2003) examined the research on categories of instructional strategies that have the greatest effect on student achievement. His metanalysis of the research showed that nonlinguistic representations that ask students to make mental images, pictures, and graphic organizers help students recall what they already know about the content and help them organize or think about the content by synthesizing new information. Shores and Chester (2009) believe graphic organizers are effective differentiation strategies that affect student achievement in the classroom by allowing the "big picture" view of concepts by helping students organize the relationship between concepts. They recommend that teachers use familiar graphic organizers such as webs or concept maps, sequence chains, flowcharts, and Venn diagrams as follows: "*Before* instruction to activate prior knowledge and provide a conceptual framework for new information. *During* instruction, students use graphic organizers to process the information. *After* instruction, organizers are used for summarizing, elaborating, organizing, structuring, and assessing learning" (p. 71). Within this framework, different thinking skills can be activated at different times throughout the lesson.

Introducing Graphic Organizers

Teachers can do the following when introducing new graphic organizers:

1. Show and explain the new organizer, then model how to use it with the whole class by selecting a topic that is easily understood by all of the students (e.g., web of attributes of school lunches).

2. Allow students to practice using the graphic organizer in small groups. Let them select a topic of their choice.

3. Ask individual students to complete a graphic organizer on their own in class or for homework.

4. Encourage students or groups to create an original organizer to share subject content with the class.

Once students become comfortable using a variety of graphic organizers, they will begin to incorporate them in their note taking, projects, and performances.

WHY SHOULD WE USE GRAPHIC ORGANIZERS?

Many students experience difficulty connecting or relating new information to prior knowledge because they have trouble remembering things. Graphic organizers help because they function as blueprints or maps that make abstract ideas more visible and concrete. Students also need to make connections between prior knowledge, what they are doing today, and what they can apply or transfer to other things tomorrow. Graphic organizers help bridge those connections and make them stronger. Students who are visual learners need graphic organizers to help them organize information and remember key concepts.

Sprenger (1999) says that when semantic memory is not processed in several ways, the brain has a hard time making neural connections. Semantic memory operates word by word and it uses working memory. Each learning experience should be organized to present a short chunk of information. She discusses devices such as peer teaching, questioning strategies, summarizing, role playing, debates, outlining, timelines, paraphrasing, mnemonic devices, and graphic organizers that can be used to help students build semantic memories. She says, "The brain must process the information in some way after the presentation of each short chunk. This processing may take many forms [. . .] Graphic organizers can help students retain semantic information" (p. 65). While teachers may not be able to use a graphic organizer for every learning experience, teachers who maintain a repertoire of the devices mentioned above can make their teaching more motivating by addressing the different learning styles of their students.

Graphic organizers also help students make sense of expository texts. The organizers reflect overarching text patterns such as problem-solution, comparison-contrast, cause-effect description, and sequence. Vacca (2002) explains, "Graphic organizers enable students to identify what ideas in an expository text are important, how these ideas are related, and where to find specific information about these ideas in the text" (p. 10). They help students make sense of what they are reading and lead to better reading comprehension.

Visual tools such as graphic organizers are becoming key teaching, learning, and assessing tools because students are faced with an overwhelming and ever-changing quantity of data they are attempting to synthesize into a quality representation. They are also trying to construct knowledge for themselves and engage in simulation and interactive learning experiences (Hyerle, 1996). One size does not fit all and one of the basic principles of differentiated learning is to allow students to learn in different ways, find their own voice, express themselves creatively, and demonstrate what they have learned in various ways. Graphic organizers provide these additional options for teachers and students.

HOW SHOULD GRAPHIC ORGANIZERS BE USED FOR ASSESSMENT?

Graphic organizers have frequently been used in the learning process, but they should also be used more often as assessment tools. If students learn differently, they should also be assessed differently. Graphic organizers work as constructed response questions because students do not have to worry about fitting the answer into a structured multiple-choice format like they do on restricted-response questions. Many state-mandated tests include questions using graphic organizers, and it is important to practice this type of test items in the classroom.

Lang, Stanley, and Moore (2008, pp. 56–57) show how a two-part constructed mathematics response question could be posed:

- *Part A:* How would you compare the relative size of common U.S. customary units such as foot, yard, inch, mile to its metric unit counterpoints; e.g., mile and kilometer, gallon and liter, pound and kilogram?
- *Part B:* Place the units of measure, U.S. and metric, in their proper order from largest to smallest.

This question lends itself very well to a couple of graphic organizers. Part A could require the students to fill in a compare-and-contrast chart such as a Venn diagram. Part B could ask the students to complete a largest-to-smallest chart. Notice how this question changes when using graphic organizers.

- *Part A:* Complete the Venn diagram below (Figure 7.1) comparing the relative size of a common U.S. customary unit to its metric unit counterpart.

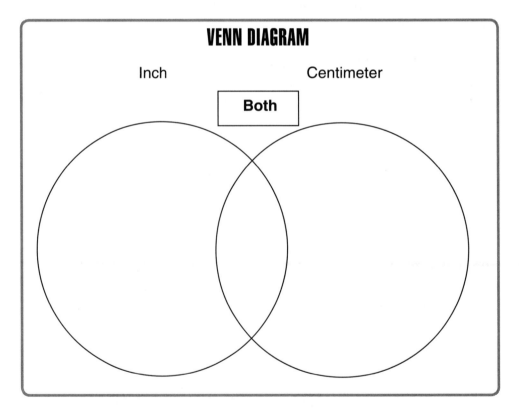

Figure 7.1

Source: Lang, S., Stanley, T., & Moore, B. (2008). *Short cycle assessment: Improving student achievement through formative assessment.* Larchmont, NY: Eye On Education.

- *Part B:* Place the following units of measure (inch, kilometer, yard, millimeter), U.S. and metric, in their proper order from largest to smallest by filling out the chart in Figure 7.2.

UNITS OF MEASUREMENT

Part B. Place the following units of measure, U.S. and metric, in their proper order from largest to smallest by filling out the chart below. Units: inch, kilometer, yard, millimeter.

Largest   Smallest

_____   _____   _____   _____

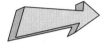

Figure 7.2

Source: Lang, S., Stanley, T., & Moore, B. (2008). *Short cycle assessment: Improving student achievement through formative assessment.* Larchmont, NY: Eye On Education.

A constructed response question using a graphic organizer targets higher-order thinking skills more so than multiple-choice questions. "An advantage of using graphic organizers whenever you can is that the students will get used to seeing a question in different forms. It lets students know constructed response questions do not have to be presented only in words" (Lang, Stanley, & Moore, 2008, p. 57). Using these types of questions on teacher-made tests will help students demonstrate thinking skills and will prepare them to answer the same type of questions on high-stakes tests such as end-of-course tests, state-mandated tests, or college entrance tests.

Why not ask students to complete a graphic organizer to take the place of an essay? Why couldn't students complete a right-angle thinking model listing the facts on the right and their feelings or associations about the topic on the bottom? Why couldn't an English teacher ask students to fill in a Venn diagram comparing the works of Hemingway and Faulkner? (See Figure 7.3.) Students could get points for every correct characteristic they feel the authors have in common (middle area) and points for each of the characteristics they feel are different (outside circles). Including graphic organizers on tests would be more creative, challenging, and fun than traditional objective-style items. Teachers could also require students to write a paragraph or make an oral presentation discussing the different elements of the graphic organizer as part of a test.

Graphic organizers can be used as assessment tools in the following ways:

1. Include graphic organizers on quizzes and tests.

2. Require groups to complete an assigned graphic organizer on a topic on chart paper. Give a group grade for the final graphic organizer and oral presentation.

3. Assign students to select one graphic organizer to use to analyze a lecture, video, book, a piece of nonfiction, speech, news story, or textbook reading. Grade the assignment on accuracy, originality, and creativity.

4. Allow the students to select one or two graphic-organizer assignments from their work to include in their portfolios.

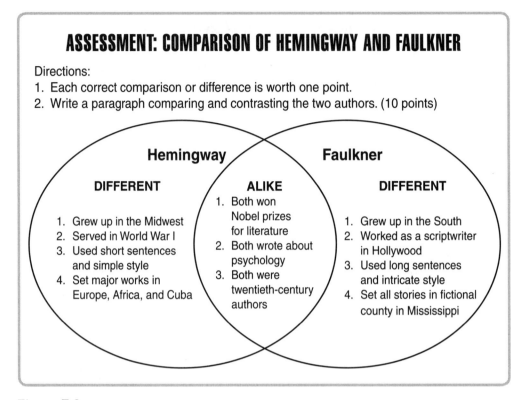

Figure 7.3

5. Ask the students or the cooperative group to invent an original graphic organizer. Grade the assignment on the basis of originality, creativity, usefulness, and logic.

6. Require students to utilize a graphic organizer in a project or oral presentation. Grade on the quality and effectiveness of the graphic organizer in enhancing the presentation.

7. Create a picture graphic organizer (such as the modified Venn diagram shown in Figure 7.4) that includes outlines of objects rather than circles or lines.

Hoerr (2008) asserts, "Let's give our assessments the kind of creativity that we want to see in our students and allow students to show what they know by constructing flow charts or diagrams, or by creating dioramas, drawings, or paintings" (p. 94). Hoerr believes that while students need to be able to perform well on paper-and-pencil tests, teachers who rely too heavily on these assessments are overlooking learning differences. Differentiated learning helps meet the diverse needs of learners, and differentiated assessments—such as graphic organizers—assess students' growth and development using different modalities.

FINAL THOUGHTS

In today's world of iPods, YouTube, iPhones, MySpace, and rapid-fire television montages, it is no wonder so many students learn best when their visual/spatial

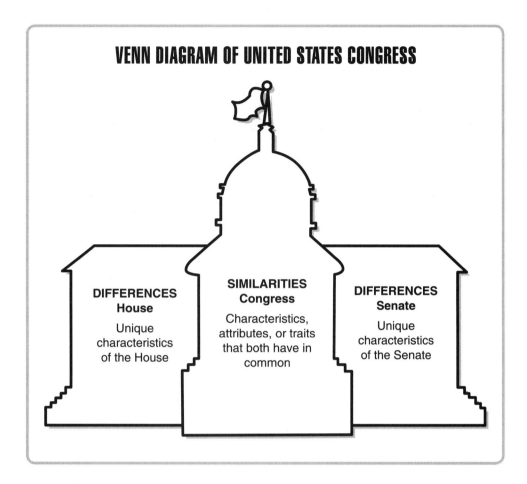

VENN DIAGRAM OF UNITED STATES CONGRESS

**DIFFERENCES
House**

Unique
characteristics
of the House

**SIMILARITIES
Congress**

Characteristics,
attributes, or traits
that both have in
common

**DIFFERENCES
Senate**

Unique
characteristics
of the Senate

Figure 7.4

intelligence is activated. The creativity of today's technology surpasses the routine textbook learning that so many students endure in schools. It is no wonder that students have a difficult time seeing the relevance of school as it relates to the real world. Moreover, students with reading problems or language barriers have difficulty with tests that require only verbal/linguistic and logical/mathematical skills. If today's students are going to construct knowledge for themselves, they will need what Hyerle (1996) describes as dynamic, new mental tools to "help them unlearn and relearn what we have taught them so that they may build new theories of knowledge and also have the experience and capacity to create new tools for making sense of their world" (p. 127). Today's world is difficult enough to make sense of using only reading and writing tools. Graphic organizers provide other ways to showcase student learning.

EXAMPLES
GRAPHIC ORGANIZERS

PRIMARY
VENN DIAGRAM

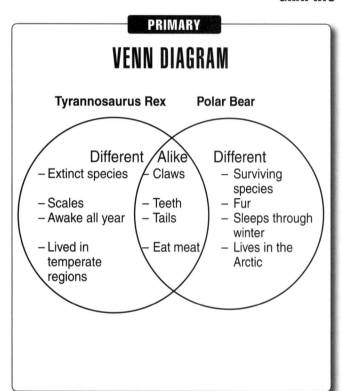

Tyrannosaurus Rex   **Polar Bear**

Different
– Extinct species
– Scales
– Awake all year
– Lived in temperate regions

Alike
– Claws
– Teeth
– Tails
– Eat meat

Different
– Surviving species
– Fur
– Sleeps through winter
– Lives in the Arctic

MIDDLE SCHOOL
MIND MAP

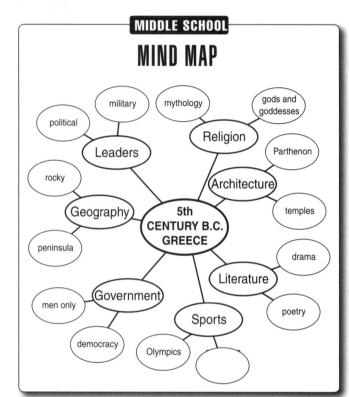

military · mythology · gods and goddesses
political · Religion · Parthenon
Leaders · Architecture
rocky · temples
Geography · **5th CENTURY B.C. GREECE**
peninsula · drama
Literature
men only · Government · poetry
Sports
democracy · Olympics

HIGH SCHOOL
AGREE/DISAGREE CHART

SUBJECT: Health/Physical Education
TOPIC: Alcohol/Drug Unit

STATEMENT	BEFORE		AFTER	
	Agree	Disagree	Agree	Disagree
1. Marijuana is a safe drug.	KB	BR MC		KR BR MC
2. Alcoholism is a disease.	MC	BR KB	MC	BR KB
3. Steroids are legal.	KB BR MC			KB BR MC
4. Crack is not as lethal as cocaine.	KB	BR MC		KB BR MC
5. Alcoholism runs in families.		KB BR MC	KB BR MC	
6. Men can drink more than women.	KB MC	BR	KB BR MC	

COLLEGE
THINKING AT RIGHT ANGLES

SUBJECT: United States History
DIRECTIONS: Complete the thinking at right angles graphic organizer by listing the facts about the topic in section A and your feelings or associations about the topic in section B.

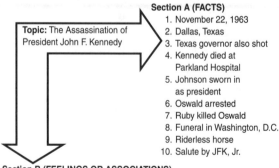

Topic: The Assassination of President John F. Kennedy

Section A (FACTS)
1. November 22, 1963
2. Dallas, Texas
3. Texas governor also shot
4. Kennedy died at Parkland Hospital
5. Johnson sworn in as president
6. Oswald arrested
7. Ruby killed Oswald
8. Funeral in Washington, D.C.
9. Riderless horse
10. Salute by JFK, Jr.

Section B (FEELINGS OR ASSOCIATIONS)
1. Betrayal: Who can we trust?
2. Loss of innocence: Nation experienced tragedy
3. Glued to TV for days: Nation was paralyzed
4. End of Camelot: Death of King Arthur
5. Sadness: Fear of a conspiracy
6. Just the beginning in a series of national tragedies

Figure 7.5

ON YOUR OWN

AGREE/DISAGREE STATEMENTS

Directions: Write statements about a unit your students will study. Give this list to groups of students *before* and then again *after* the unit and ask them to write their initials in the Agree or Disagree columns. Discuss why they changed their opinions.

Topic: _____

STATEMENTS	BEFORE		AFTER	
	Agree	Disagree	Agree	Disagree
1.				
2.				
3.				
4.				
5.				
6.				
7.				
8.				
9.				
10.				

Figure 7.6

Source: Adapted from Bellanca, J. (1990). *The Cooperative Think Tank: Graphic Organizers to Teach Thinking in the Cooperative Classroom.* Arlington Heights, IL: SkyLight.

ON YOUR OWN

THINKING AT RIGHT ANGLES

Directions: Select a topic and ask students to list the facts about it in column A and their feelings and associations in column B.

Topic: _____

FACTS

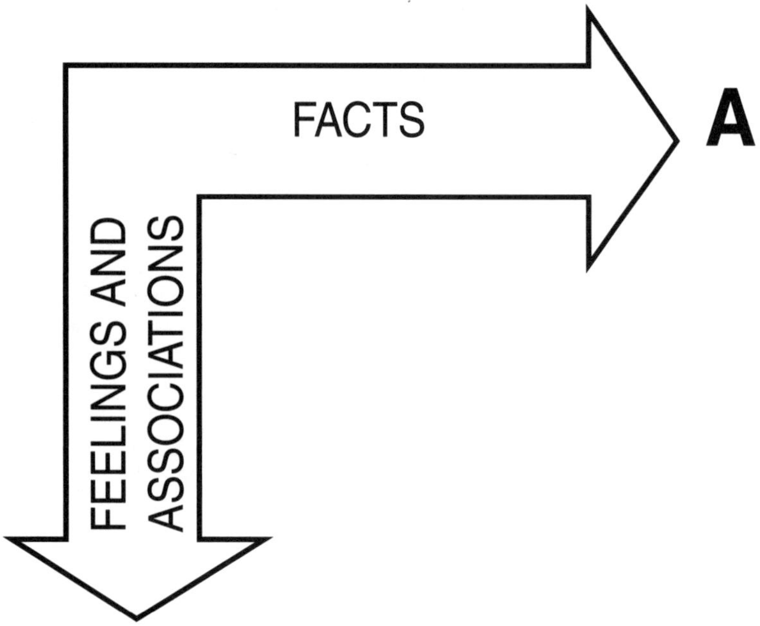

FACTS → **A**
_____
_____
_____
_____
_____
_____
_____
_____
_____

FEELINGS AND ASSOCIATIONS

B

FEELINGS AND ASSOCIATIONS

_____

_____

_____

_____

_____

Figure 7.7

Source: Adapted From Bellanca, J., & Fogarty, R. © 2003. *From Blueprints to Achievement in the Cooperative Classroom, 3rd edition.* Thousand Oaks, CA: Corwin.

REFLECTION

GRAPHIC ORGANIZERS

1. Take this survey and in the *Before* column check off what you believed about authentic assessment *before* you started to read this book. In the *After* column, check off your answer *after* reading this book.

Agree/Disagree Chart on Authentic Assessment

STATEMENT	BEFORE		AFTER	
	Agree	Disagree	Agree	Disagree
1. Formative assessments are ongoing.				
2. Portfolios always contain final products.				
3. Metacognition is illegal in 23 states.				
4. Letter writing is more authentic than grammar exercises.				
5. Rubrics are puzzle cubes.				

2. Review any statement where you changed your opinion and reflect on what you have learned that caused you to change your opinion.

Figure 7.8

Source: Adapted from Bellanca, J. (1990). *The Cooperative Think Tank: Graphic Organizers to Teach Thinking in the Cooperative Classroom.* Arlington Heights, IL: SkyLight.

8 Teacher-Made Tests

WHAT ARE TEACHER-MADE TESTS?

A test is the process of evaluating students' knowledge or skills by performance on a particular instrument or task that is presented in a controlled manner. A test is intended to serve as an objective measure of learning. The types of questions used vary widely in their format (e.g., true-false, essay, multiple-choice) and the environment can also vary (paper-and-pencil, oral interview, computer, time or untimed, open note, open book, take home; (Musial, Neminen, Thomas, & Burke, 2009). Even though tests have existed since schooling began, creating effective tests designed to measure what they are supposed to measure (validity) and measuring what they are supposed to measure consistently (reliability) is still a challenge.

Teacher-made tests are written or oral assessments that are not commercially produced or standardized—in other words, they are tests teachers design specifically for their students. *Testing* refers to any kind of school activity that results in a mark or comment being entered in a checklist, grade book, or anecdotal record. The term *test*, however, refers to a more structured oral or written evaluation of student achievement. Teacher-made tests consist of a variety of formats, including matching, fill-in-the-blank, short answer, true-false questions, or essays.

Tests can be important parts of the teaching and learning process if they are integrated into daily classroom teaching and are constructed to be part of the learning process—not just the culminating event. Tests allow students to see their own progress and allow teachers to make adjustments to their instruction on a daily basis. However, the tests themselves are often inadequate or used incorrectly (Hills, 1991). Many teachers feel they were not adequately prepared in undergraduate or graduate courses to construct quality teacher-made tests. As a result, teachers often use textbook or workbook tests provided by publishers because they are convenient. Many of those tests, however, may measure the objectives and content of the textbooks, but they do not necessarily measure the state standards that will be used to determine whether or not a student passes the end-of-year courses or the state standardized tests. The data that determine whether students meet adequate yearly practice (AYP) as part of the

NCLB legislation are derived from the standards-based assessments administered by the department of education in each state.

Constructing effective teacher-made tests is time consuming and difficult. Nevertheless, it is important for classroom teachers to consider technical issues in order to have confidence in results of the assessments. The term *validity* is frequently used when discussing tests because it asks the question, "Does the assessment measure what it is supposed to measure?" The term *content validity* refers to matching instructional objectives or standards to the assessment. While validity is concerned with the accuracy of an assessment, *reliability* focuses on the consistency of the scores. Terms such as "test-retest reliability," "alternate-forms reliability," and "interrater reliability" are used by standardized test experts, but rarely heard among teachers (Ataya, 2007). Despite the tremendous impact of testing in today's schools, the lack of training provided for teachers calls into question the validity and reliability of teacher-made tests. Teachers at the same school teaching the same courses, targeting the same standards could create tests of differing quality that produce dramatically different results. Unfortunately, these teacher-generated tests, regardless of their validity and reliability, affect the final grades and the lives of their students as well as the lives of their families.

Because of these concerns, teacher-made tests do not carry the same importance as standardized tests in the eyes of most district and state officials, and the public in general. Even though many teacher-made tests may have the same objective-style format that allows for easy comparisons, they are not seen as reliable and valid because the world looks to standardized tests as the yardstick by which academic achievement is measured.

Stiggins (1994) notes that although standardized, large-scale assessments command all the media attention, day-to-day classroom assessments have the greatest impact on student learning. Stiggins asserts that classroom assessments are "most influential in terms of their contribution to student, teacher, and parent decision making" (p. 438). The balanced assessment model in the Introduction shows how teacher-made and standardized tests fall under traditional types of assessment. Since developing quality teacher-made tests plays a major role in the overall assessment cycle, it needs to be addressed more in preservice education courses as well as ongoing professional development workshops.

WHY DO WE NEED TEACHER-MADE TESTS?

Even though district and state officials, parents, and the media seem to value standardized-test scores, most teachers do not rely solely on standardized tests to tell them what their students know and don't know. Standardized tests occur so infrequently, and often at the end of the year; therefore, one aggregate score posted in May is not very helpful in determining future instructional goals. Teacher-made tests, however, allow teachers to make decisions that keep instruction moving and provide feedback to guide the teaching and learning process. Teachers are able to make changes immediately to meet the needs of their students rather than waiting until the end of an assessment cycle to try to figure out, "What went wrong?"

The key to teacher-made tests is to make them a part of assessment—not separate from it. Tests should be instructional and ongoing. Rather than being "after-the-fact" to find out what students did not learn, they should be more "before-the-fact" to target essential learnings and standards. Popham (1999) explains, "Assessment instruments prepared prior to instruction operationalize a teacher's instructional intentions . . . The better you understand where you're going, the more efficiently you can get there" (p. 12). The expression "begin with the end in mind" indicates how all assessments should be developed. It is difficult for teachers and students to aim for the target if the target is not created until the night before the test!

Teachers also need to make adjustments in their tests for the various learning styles, multiple intelligences, and learning problems of the diverse students in their classes. It would be impossible to address every student's needs on every test, but efforts should be made to construct tests that target learning goals and make allowances for individual differences.

HOW CAN WE DESIGN BETTER TEACHER-MADE TESTS?

Most educational experts recommend that teachers create their tests *before* they begin to teach the material. That task is a challenge for beginning teachers because they don't have any of last year's tests to use or revise. Teachers in middle school and high school are often teaching five different classes, preparing the lessons and also preparing five different tests at the same time. The best of intentions may not always be realistic. According to Gareis and Grant (2008):

> Designing a good test is like building a house. You have to begin with the end in mind. You have to think about how it will look holistically and then think about how each part will look and how each part will function. To first build the house, you have to know what you want from the house. The same is true with a test. How should the test function? What information will be gleaned from the test? As with a house, creating a test involves first planning for the test itself. (p. 55)

Because of all the time and effort involved in developing effective teacher-made tests, teams of teachers sometimes work together to share the work by contributing test items all the teachers can use. Teachers select the items they feel will meet their goals and, of course, mix them up on the test to help prevent students in the same class from "borrowing" answers from their neighbors or writing down answers to give to friends in the next period or another teacher's class.

Students should be brought into the test-making process. They can help construct meaningful tests based on essential learnings. Brown (1989) maintains that nothing helps a person master a subject better than having to ask and debate fundamental questions about what is most important about that subject—and how someone could tell if he or she has mastered it. Students focus on "what's on the test"; therefore, quality tests improve learning. One of the most critical guidelines for creating valid and reliable teacher-made tests is to include vocabulary words, people, and concepts from the state standards and benchmarks. Even textbook tests and the practice-test booklets that accompany textbooks do not always use the specific terminology from each state's standards. Even though textbook companies claim they are "aligned" to each state's standards, they may be aligned to the abstract standard of "Students will write a narrative essay." But, they may not be aligned to all the elements, indicators, or criteria in the benchmarks. If the benchmarks include terms such as thesis statement, controlling ideas, plot, setting, tone, dialogue, figurative language, sensory details, and organizational structures, then those terms should be used to construct the teacher-made tests, as well as every other type of performance assessment. *Begin with the end in mind* by creating the test before teaching the material and include the vocabulary, concepts, big ideas, people, and processes of the standards.

Guidelines for Constructing Teacher-Made Tests

The following guidelines may help teachers construct better teacher-made tests:

1. Create the test before beginning the unit.

2. Incorporate the vocabulary and concepts of the state standards into the test questions.

3. Give clear directions for each section of the test.

4. Arrange the questions from simple to complex (concrete to abstract).

5. Give point values for each section (e.g., true-false [2 points each]).

6. Vary the question types (true-false, fill-in-the-blank, multiple-choice, essay, matching). Limit the number of questions to five to ten per type.

7. Group question types together so students can follow each set of directions.

8. Type or print clearly. (Leave space between questions to facilitate easy reading and writing.)

9. Make sure the appropriate reading level is used.

10. Include a variety of graphic organizers used as assessment tools.

11. Make allowances for students with special needs (see next section on modifications for students with special needs).

12. Give students some choice in the questions they select (e.g., a choice of graphic organizers or essay questions).

13. Vary levels of questions by using the three-story intellect verbs to cover gathering, processing, and application questions (see Figure 8.3 on page 151).

14. Provide a grading scale so students know what score constitutes a certain grade (e.g., 93–100 = A; 85–92 = B; 75–84 = C; 70–74 = D; below 70 = not yet!)

15. Give sufficient time for all students to finish. (The teacher should be able to work through the test in one-third to one-half the time given students.)

Modifications for Students With Special Needs

In the inclusive classroom, teachers are expected to meet the needs of students with learning disabilities, behavior exceptionalities, physical exceptionalities, and intellectual exceptionalities. In addition, as today's society is a "salad bowl" of many ethnic groups, teacher-made tests must allow opportunities for students whose first language is not English. Authentic tests can celebrate diversity by allowing students a wide variety of ways to demonstrate what they know and what they can do. To help ensure success on tests for all students, the Board of Education for the City of Etobicoke (1987) introduced strategies for teachers to use in test design. Some of those initial ideas are included in this adapted list of modifications teachers can make on tests for all students, but especially those who are at most risk of failing:

1. Read instructions orally.

2. Rephrase oral instructions if needed.

3. Ask students to repeat directions to make sure they understand.

4. Monitor carefully to make sure all students understand directions for the test.

5. Provide alternative methods of evaluations (e.g., oral testing, use of tapes, test given in another room, dictation).

6. Provide a clock so students can monitor themselves and learn to manage their time.

7. Use both oral and written tests.

8. Leave enough space for answers because some students write large.

9. Use visual demonstrations for some test items.

10. Use white paper because colored paper is sometimes distracting for students with disabilities.

11. Do not crowd or clutter the test so that it is difficult to read or follow directions.

12. Give choices so students can demonstrate what they know in different formats.

13. Go from concrete to abstract in each section of questions so students build their confidence.

14. Don't deduct for spelling or grammar on tests unless that is the objective of the test. Students need to focus on the content being tested and not be distracted by focusing on using only words they can spell. Validity calls for measuring the objectives of the test.

15. Use some take-home tests so students have more time and a more relaxed atmosphere.

16. Provide manipulative experiences whenever possible for the tactile learners.

17. Allow students to use notes and textbooks (open-book tests) during some tests to assess students' abilities to organize in advance, access

information, and demonstrate understanding of text features such as headers, graphs, and charts included in many state research standards.

18. Allow students to write down key math or science formulas, literary terms, or social-studies people, places, and dates on a note card so that students are not always penalized for poor memory or spelling.

19. Include visuals such as graphic organizers, charts, graphs, or pictures.

20. Give specific point values for each group of questions so students allocate their time appropriately based upon the weight of the questions or section (e.g., 20 points for essay question shows students the importance of the item).

21. List criteria for all essay questions (length, key points, logic, coherence, originality, specific examples, interpretation, analysis, evaluation, sentence structure, spelling, grammar) so students know how they will be assessed prior to writing the essay.

22. Provide immediate feedback on all tests so students know what they got wrong and why they got it wrong.

23. Allow students to correct mistakes and/or to retake tests to improve scores and understand what they didn't understand on the first test.

24. Consider allowing all students to drop one or two tests scores, especially those early in the marking period, and emphasize tests scores at the end of the period more to value progress and final results more than initial attempts.

25. Ask students to submit sample questions for each teacher-made test along with the answers. Select student-made questions to include in the test.

Source: Adapted from the Board of Education for the City of Etobicoke, 1987, pp. 208–211.

These strategies will work with all students because many regular education students experience anxiety and frustration while they are taking tests. Some students need much more time; others become fixated on one question and lose sight of the time requirements; some spend too much time trying to understand what the question is asking because of reading problems. If teachers are asked to differentiate their teaching, it seems realistic to have them differentiate their testing to meet the diverse needs of their learners.

Constructing Effective Selected-Response Test Questions

It is important for teachers to consider the types of questions that should be included on a test. Teachers should create test items that measure whether students have achieved the targeted learning objectives, benchmarks, or standards. *Selected-(or select-)response items* are items that have predetermined responses from which students may choose. Types of selected-response items include true-false, matching, and multiple-choice. Effective selected-response tests provide formative feedback about particular strengths or areas that need improvement. They provide diagnostic information, allow for comparisons among students or classes, are relatively easy to grade, and prepare students to take the same type of format as standardized tests. The biggest criticism of selected-response tests items is the possibility of students guessing the right answer and the teachers' lack of insight into a student's reasoning as to why he or she selected the answer (Musial, Nieminen, Thomas, & Burke, 2009). Figure 8.1 provides some guidelines for writing selected-response test questions.

Writing Selected-Response Test Questions

True-False Items

The true-false format requires students to classify a statement into one of two categories: true or false, yes or no, correct or incorrect, fact or opinion. They are used primarily to assess factual knowledge, but their main limitation is their susceptibility to guessing (Airasian, 2000).

- Place only one idea in the true-false statement.
- Avoid absolute words such as *all, never,* and *always.*
- Make sure items are clearly true or false and not ambiguous.
- Avoid opinion statements.
- Avoid negatives in the statement.
- Consider asking students to make false questions true to encourage critical thinking.

Matching Items

Matching items consist of a column of premises, a column of responses, and directions for matching the two. "The matching exercise is similar to a set of multiple-choice items, except that in a matching question, the same set of options or responses is used for all the premises. Its main disadvantage is that it is limited to assessing mainly lower-level behaviors" (Airasian, 2000, p. 110).

- Limit the list to between five and ten items.
- Use homogeneous lists. (Don't mix names with dates.)
- Give clear instructions. (Write the letter, number, etc.)
- Give more choices than there are questions.
- Keep the matching set short.
- Order items in a logical manner.

Multiple-Choice Items

Multiple-choice items are relatively easy to construct and very easy to score. They represent the most common type of questions on state standardized tests and national tests such as the SAT and ACT. They also can assess a variety of learning outcomes and levels of understanding. Multiple-choice questions can be constructed to assess a range of learning from recall of information to an understanding of basic processes and principles (Musial, Nieminen, Thomas, & Burke, 2009).

- State the main idea in the core or stem of the question and keep the wording as short and clear as possible. (Don't use vague stems.)
- Ask a question in the stem for which there is either one correct or best answer.
- Use plausible distracters. (Don't use ridiculous incorrect answers.)
- Make options the same length. (Don't use anything very long or very short.)
- Make sure the choices are grammatically parallel.

Avoid multiple correct answers (a and b, all of the above, none of the above) because they have several drawbacks such as "all of the above" answers must all be entirely correct.

Figure 8.1

Higher Cognitive Level Multiple-Choice Items

Many educators feel that multiple-choice tests narrow the curriculum, focus too much on recall of factual information, and do not challenge students to think and solve problems. Teachers also sometimes feel pressured to use multiple-choice test questions on their own tests because they simulate the types of questions included on most standardized tests. Schools and districts all over the country are asking teams of teachers to spend summers writing sample "benchmark" test questions based on their state standards. Districts place the questions in an electronic data bank so all teachers access them to provide practice tests for the students. These periodic, checkpoint tests are administered at least once a quarter, but more often if students are at risk of failing the tests. The results are used to modify instruction and help teachers refocus on the specific skills each student needs. A controversy exists about whether or not these benchmark assessments are formative assessments that guide instruction or mini-summative assessments designed to prepare students for the final standardized tests. Regardless of the label, multiple-choice tests provide feedback and are an integral part of both classroom and standardized testing.

Gardner (as cited in Scherer, 1999), states, "I am not a fan of short-answer tests because they can't really assess understanding. The world does not come with four choices, the last one being 'none of the above'" (p. 13). He also says that the more time we spend trying to isolate bits of information that lend themselves to assessment in a short-answer instrument, "the less time that we have to present materials that are rich in content and that can engender understanding" (p. 13). The key is to create and use multiple-choice tests, but strive to create better questions that lead to higher cognitive levels.

According to Gareis and Grant (2008), many people have the misconception that multiple-choice items only assess lower cognitive levels. Even though it is very difficult for multiple-choice items to assess the high levels of synthesis, evaluation, and creativity, they can tap cognitive levels of comprehension, application, and analysis. Gareis and Grant describe five principles for writing higher cognitive level multiple-choice items in Figure 8.2.

Five Principles for Writing Higher Cognitive Level Multiple-Choice Items

Principle #1: Refine your understanding of *content* and *cognitive levels*.

Target the content from the standard (statistics) and the cognitive levels from the verbs (analyze, interpret).

Principle #2: Introduce novelty.

Ask students to interpret what a symbol means in a story that was *not* discussed in class to see if they have learned the process of recognizing and interpreting a literacy device rather than asking a multiple-choice question about a symbol that was discussed in class. See if the students can transfer understanding to another situation rather than just memorize the answer they were told.

(Continued)

(Continued)

Principle #3: Focus on complex content.

Rather than asking students in science a question like, "When water evaporates it turns into A: liquid; B: solid; C: gas; D: solution," ask a question that requires students to know the process of the water cycle and engage with this content at a higher level. "On a very hot day, there is a brief rain shower, followed by the return of the sun. The small puddles of water on the streets will *most likely* turn into A: gases; B: liquids; C: solids; D: solutions."

Principle #4: Use an extended prompt.

Provide students with an extended prompt that includes more background information and gives contextual information needed to answer the questions.

Principle #5: Provide stimulus material.

Have students use the information provided to them to answer the question (similar to extended prompt). It includes diagrams, charts, maps, pictures, excerpts from documents, and short passages that require students to interpret the information or data. Several test questions can be based upon the stimulus material.

Figure 8.2

Source: Adapted from Gareis, C. R., & Grant, L. W. (2008). *Teacher-made assessments: How to connect curriculum, instruction, and student learning.*Larchmont, NY: Eye On Education.

Writing Effective Constructed-Response Test Questions

Constructed-response assessments require students to generate and supply a response by filling in the blank with a single word or a short phrase, label a diagram or a map, show their work solving a problem, or write the steps they went through to arrive at an answer or solution to a problem. These are short-answer items that assess primarily factual recall-names, dates, places, or specific persons. The students must create their own answer since the response is not provided for them as it is with selected-response assessments (Carr, 2007). The advantages of using fill-in-the-blank or short-answer test items is that students are less likely to guess because correct responses cannot be identified by simple recognition as they can for multiple-choice questions. The disadvantage is that short-answer items focus only on recall of information and not on higher-level thinking. "They require careful attention to clarity in the stem to avoid ambiguity. The scoring also may be more subjective than with other simple types of assessment items, and for this reason would be more time-consuming" (Musial, Nieminen, Thomas, & Burke, 2009, p. 139.). Since students may use a variety of different answers, teachers have to spend more time considering each answer separately.

Completion Items or Fill-in-the-Blank Items

Completion items or fill-in-the-blank items are constructed of a sentence from which one or more words are missing and the student is to write in the missing words. They are useful for assessing lower cognitive levels such as knowledge and comprehension. These types of items can help eliminate guessing because a student must know the correct answer and cannot choose from a supplied list of possible responses. They are fairly easy to grade and allow for an efficient use of test time (Gareis & Grant, 2008). Another format option is the question where the teacher asks a direct question such as, "Name the literary term that describes the high point of a story. The student would write in "climax" for the answer. The following guidelines can help teachers construct more effective completion and fill-in-the-blank tests:

- Structure clearly in order to get a brief and specific answer for each item.
- Avoid ambiguous stems, such as "Abraham Lincoln was born in _____." The student could write "1809" or "a log cabin" or "Kentucky" and all answers would be correct. Be specific, such as "Abraham Lincoln was born in the *state* of _____," in order to get the intended answer (Musial, Nieminen, Thomas, & Burke, 2009).
- Position the blank at the end of the stem statement.
- Avoid multiple blanks that sometimes make a sentence too confusing.
- Use blanks of equal length so as not to give students a clue.
- Avoid passages lifted directly from text (emphasis on memorization).

Essay Items

Essay items provide teachers with opportunities to assess higher-level cognitive skills. Essays may require students to analyze, synthesize, evaluate, or compare and contrast in order to show their levels of understanding and a greater depth of content. It is important that the essay questions are not too broad and are developmentally appropriate so that students have enough time to respond to the essay prompt. Essay items are used extensively in state assessments, particularly when evaluating writing ability, so students need in-class practice on writing essays within a specific time frame (Gareis & Grant, 2008).

Essay items allow students more choice in constructing their answers and consequently permit greater individuality, creativity, and personalization. On the other hand, students tend to "write around" the answer if they do not know it. In addition, scoring essays is time consuming and can be subjective because teachers could be biased about their perception of the quality of work a student usually does. They can also get distracted by sloppy handwriting, lack of subject-verb agreement, or misspellings, and then lose sight of the intended outcome of an essay that, for example, focused on "understanding of nuclear waste problems." The following guidelines can help teachers construct more effective essay tests:

- Avoid general questions. ("Discuss" is ambiguous because it could mean "Tell all you know about a subject.")
- Make the length of the response clear to the student (one paragraph, a five-paragraph essay, one page).

- Define criteria for evaluation by using point values or a rubric so students know the expectations.
- Give specific point values for all questions so students know how much time and effort to spend on them.
- Use higher-order thinking verbs such as *predict* or *compare and contrast* rather than all recall verbs such as *list* and *name* that could be tested with short-answer questions.
- Avoid options within the question because they assess different content and it is difficult for teachers to draw inferences about student learning.

Even though objective-style questions play a role in the assessment process, they must be incorporated appropriately into the balanced assessment philosophy. Too much of any one type of test question will not work. Students who do not do well on one type of question should not be penalized by having to answer all the same type of questions. Students who have poor writing skills will not do well if their teachers use only essay questions on all of their tests. The key word again is "repertoire." Vary the types of tests and the types of test items to meet the needs of all students—especially the poor test takers.

Questioning Techniques and Three-Story Intellect Verbs

Marzano, Pickering, and Pollock (2005) identified nine families of strategies that significantly increase student achievement. The first family deals with finding similarities and differences, specifically comparing and contrasting, classifying, metaphors, and analogies. Teachers can include questions on tests that require students to compare and contrast, an analysis skill of finding similarities and differences. Students are asked to compare the attributes that are alike, but contrast the ones that are different. Classifying is another important skill. Classifying organizes by sorting according to similarities. Things that have similar attributes are separated from those that don't share these similarities. Pete and Fogarty (2003) state that "classification is like an egg carton: both have compartments that separate and divide, providing a specified place for each thing and a unifying element that brings the individual items into a connected whole" (p. 5). Asking effective questions on tests challenges students to go beyond memorization and requires them to think for themselves.

Bellanca and Fogarty (2003) have created a graphic based on Bloom's Taxonomy called the three-story intellect to show what verbs teachers can use when they ask questions. First-story verbs such as *count, describe,* and *match* ask students to *gather* or *recall* information. Second-story verbs such as *reason, compare,* and *analyze* ask students to *process* information. Third-story verbs such as *evaluate, imagine,* and *speculate* require students to *apply* information. An effective teacher-made test includes verbs from all three stories of the intellect. Many teachers use this graphic organizer in Figure 8.3 to guide them when asking questions in class as well as creating teacher-made tests that require students to use higher-order thinking skills.

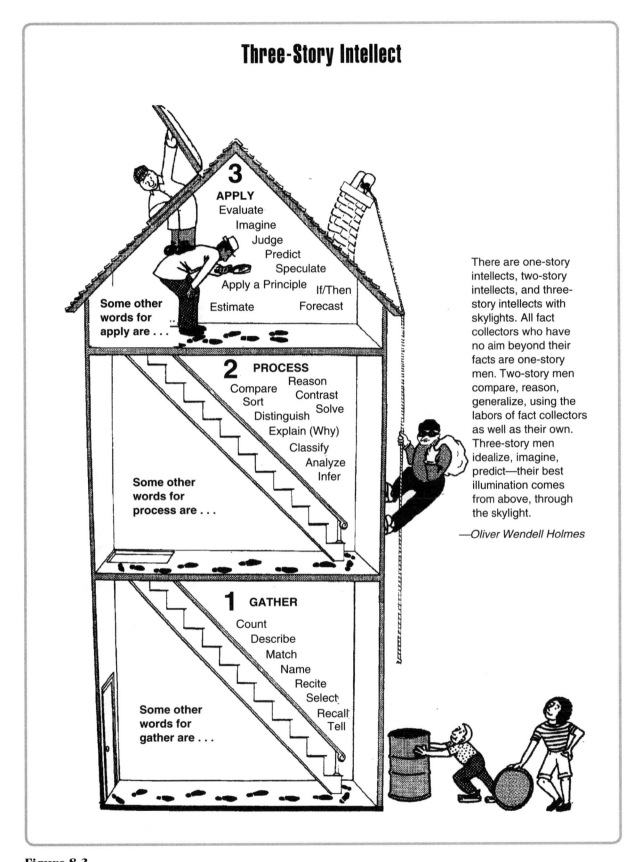

Figure 8.3

Source: From Bellanca and Fogarty (2003), *Blueprints for achievement in the cooperative classroom, 3rd edition.* Thousand Oaks: Corwin.

One self-check teachers use to evaluate the effectiveness of teacher-made tests and commercially made tests is included in Figure 8.6. "The Three-Story Intellect Verbs Review" provides one method to analyze tests and determine how many questions address each of the three levels of learning—gathering, processing, and applying. A well-balanced test should include questions from all levels to assess students' recall of factual information, their ability to process that information, and, most importantly, their ability to apply that information by doing something with it.

FINAL THOUGHTS

The balanced assessment model in the Introduction (Figure 0.3) of the book shows how assessment is divided among traditional tools such as teacher-made and standardized tests; portfolios that show process, product, and growth and provide reflection and insight; and performance that requires application of knowledge in skills. These are just three categories discussed in this book, but there are multiple dimensions of classroom assessment. According to Ataya (2007), assessments can be classified by their method of development (teacher-made versus standardized), the nature of the task (traditional versus alternative), the instructional purpose (formative versus summative), the grading standard (criterion reference versus norm reference), the type of item format (selected versus constructed response), and the type of scoring procedure (objective versus subjective). It is no wonder that assessment is such an essential yet complicated component of education today.

Colleges of education need to focus on preparing preservice and graduate teachers to navigate the multiple dimensions of assessment challenges. Professional development programs in school districts should introduce courses or workshops to help teachers become more proficient in designing and interpreting quality teacher-made tests while at the same time preparing students for the high-stakes tests. Taking one college course in educational measurement that focuses on how to compute the "mean," the "medium," and the "mode" for student grades is no longer sufficient for educators enrolled in preservice or graduate programs. Assessment drives instruction in the twenty-first century, and educators today need to become "assessment literate" in all areas if they want to improve student achievement.

E X A M P L E S

MATCHING QUESTIONS

Language Arts Test on Authors

Directions: On the line to the left of each book in Column A, write the letter of the person in Column B who wrote the book. Each name in Column B may be used only once or not at all.

Column A

____ 1) *Huckleberry Finn*

____ 2) *The Call of the Wild*

____ 3) *The Pearl*

____ 4) *The Red Badge of Courage*

A. Stephen Crane

B. John Steinbeck

C. Mark Twain

D. Jack London

E. Ernest Hemingway

GRAPHIC ORGANIZER

History

Directions: Complete the mind map on the Middle Ages by filling in the main components in the big circles and the subpoints in the smaller circles (1 point per circle).

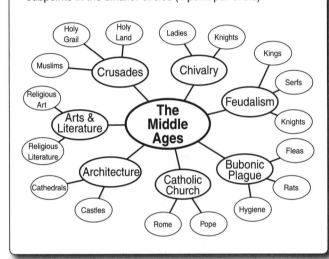

TRUE-FALSE QUESTIONS

English

Directions: Please circle *true* next to the number if the statement is true; circle *false* if the statement is in any way false (2 points each). You will receive an additional 2 points if you rewrite the *false* statements to make them true.

T or F 1. Mark Twain wrote *Huckleberry Finn*.
Rewrite: _____

T or **F** 2. Tom Sawyer is the protagonist in *Huckleberry Finn*.
Rewrite: Tom Sawyer appears in *Huckleberry Finn*, but Huck Finn is the protagonist.

T or F 3. Mark Twain's real name is Samuel Clemens.
Rewrite: _____

T or **F** 4. The runaway slave, Jim, hid on Hanibal Island after he left Aunt Polly.
Rewrite: He hid on Jackson Island.

T or **F** 5. Mark Twain was a wealthy man all of his life.
Rewrite: Twain made a lot of money, but he went bankrupt by investing in bad businesses.

ESSAY QUESTIONS

Science

Point Value: 20

Directions: Select *one* of the following topics for your essay question. Your essay will be evaluated on the following criteria:

- accuracy of information
- organization of information
- use of support statements
- clarity and effectiveness

Select *one* topic.

1. Predict what will happen if the ozone layer continues to deplete at its current rate.
2. Evaluate the effectiveness of our government's research and regulations regarding acid rain.
3. Speculate what will happen if a cure for AIDS is not found within five years.
4. Compare and contrast the bubonic plague to AIDS. You may draw a Venn diagram to help you organize your thoughts before you write.

Figure 8.4

ON YOUR OWN

The Big Ten Checklist for Teacher-Made Tests

Test: _____   Date: _____

Grade Level/Class: _____

1. ____ I wrote my test *before* I taught the subject matter.

2. ____ I have listed my standards and benchmarks on the test.

3. ____ I have listed my grading scale on the test.

4. ____ I have varied the question types to include _____ types.

5. ____ I have provided point values for each section.

6. ____ I have included tasks to address the multiple intelligences and learning modalities of my students.

7. ____ I have given students some choice of questions.

8. ____ I have used all three levels of the Three-Story Intellect verbs in my questions.

9. ____ I have made allowances for students with special needs.

10. ____ I have made sure that all students have time to finish the test.

Teacher's Signature: _____   Date: _____

Figure 8.5

ON YOUR OWN

Three-Story Intellect Verbs Review

1. Analyze one of your own teacher-made tests. Classify the questions by marking them first, second, or third level according to the Three-Story Intellect (see page 151). Tally the results.

   a. Number of first-story gathering questions. _____

   b. Number of second-story processing questions. _____

   c. Number of third-story applying questions. _____

2. Analyze a chapter test from a textbook or any commercially prepared-content test in terms of the guidelines used above. Tally the results.

   a. Number of first-story gathering questions. _____

   b. Number of second-story processing questions. _____

   c. Number of third-story applying questions. _____

3. Compare and contrast the analysis of your original teacher-made test to your analysis of the commercially prepared test. Comment on your findings.

4. Construct an original teacher-made test to use with your students. Follow the guidelines discussed in this chapter and use The Big Ten Checklist for Teacher-Made Tests on page 154 to self-assess your test.

Figure 8.6

REFLECTION

Teacher-Made Tests 3–2–1

List *three* things you have learned about teacher-made tests.

3
1. _____

2. _____

3. _____

List *two* things you would like to try on your next teacher-made test.

2
1. _____

2. _____

List *one* insight you have about teacher-made tests.

1
_____

_____

_____

Figure 8.7

Source: Adapted From Lipton, L., & Wellman, B. © 1999 From *Pathways to Understanding: Patterns and Practices in the Learning Focused Classroom.* Gilford, VT: Pathways Publishing.

Interviews and Conferences 9

WHAT ARE INTERVIEWS AND CONFERENCES?

Interviewing is an interaction in which the teacher presents a student with a planned series of questions, listens to the responses, asks follow-up questions, and then records the data (Musial, Nieminen, Thomas, & Burke, 2009). The interview is a viable assessment tool to ascertain students' understanding of key concepts and determine indicators about each student's level of achievement. During the teaching and learning process, teachers can gather a great deal of information about student achievement by asking questions, listening to answers, conducting conferences and interviews, evaluating student reasoning, conducting oral examinations, and engaging in conversations with students (Stiggins, 1994). Additionally, teachers can gather information about how to modify or differentiate their curriculum, instruction, and assessment, using it as another tool to gather information about students who do not do well on paper-and-pencil assessments or who are not comfortable asking or answering questions in front of other students. Some teachers, however, are reluctant to utilize direct personal communication such as interviews or conferences with students as legitimate assessment because they feel it is too subjective. Imagine how a teacher would feel telling a parent, "I have an intuition or gut feeling that Bradley doesn't cooperate effectively." Without documentation or concrete evidence, it is difficult to pass judgment or assign grades based upon an impression or opinion, regardless of its accuracy. Yet, conferences and interviews structured effectively and documented appropriately yield legitimate assessment data.

Musial, Nieminen, Thomas, & Burke (2009) believe:

> Interviews provide opportunities to develop rapport with your students as you probe their thinking. As you question a student about how or why she came to a certain conclusion, you learn more about how she thinks, and you can ask follow-up questions to probe more deeply. Besides listening to a student's responses, you have the opportunity to observe him

closely. Are there long pauses as he gathers his thoughts? Is he fidgeting in his seat or with a pencil? Does he make eye contact with you? These reactions may give you further insight into a student's abilities and provide you with data that you could not get in other ways. (p. 192)

Oral communication is a critical component of the assessment process. Often teachers find out more about what students know in a two-minute conversation than from their answers on a forty-question objective test. Unfortunately, many educators don't feel comfortable using the information they gather from interviews and conferences because it is "informal" and subjective compared to the results of the more formal objective tests scored by a Scantron machine.

Types of Interviews and Conferences

Interviews can be unstructured or structured. In an *unstructured* interview, teachers ask a series of developmentally appropriate questions that occur naturally in the conversation. It is similar to a news conference where the interviewee makes a short statement and the reporters ask a series of follow-up questions based upon what he said. They may have come to the press conference with predetermined questions, but the questions evolve depending on the person's response to questions. In a *structured* interview, the teacher has prepared the questions in advance. That way all interviews have the same purpose, the same directions, the same materials, and the same questions. In other words, the interview is more standardized to validate the data gathered. The guidelines in Figure 9.1 will help teachers prepare structured interview questions.

Tips for Preparing Structured Interview Questions

1. Word the questions carefully so students understand what they are being asked.

2. Use the language of the standards (LOTS) to reinforce key vocabulary that will be used on state standardized tests.

3. Determine time allotments for each question.

4. Prepare an instrument to record data.

Figure 9.1

Teachers utilize a wide variety of both formal and informal interviews and conferences, such as the following:

1. Book interview with one student or group of students

2. Discussion about a group or an individual project

3. Interview about a research paper or project

4. Reactions to a film or video

5. Feedback on a field trip

6. Reactions to assemblies or guest speakers

7. Discussion of a piece of writing

8. Interview in a foreign language class to check for fluency and grammar in that language

9. Feelings about works of art or music composition

10. Discussion about problem solving

11. Interview about a scientific experiment

12. Discussion surrounding attitudes about a course or school

13. Conference about a portfolio

14. Discussion about dynamics of cooperative groups

15. Discussion of students' grades and future goals

16. Discussion about sportsmanship and ethics

17. Interview about procedures

18. Questions about the process in a paper or project

19. Conversations about meeting standards

20. Discussion of grades

Student interviews and conferences reinforce communication. Students should be encouraged to engage in oral interactions on a daily basis, and these authentic assessments provide the opportunity to assess their knowledge, insights, and feelings as qualitative data.

Another type of conference that is used effectively to provide feedback to students is the three-minute conference. Chappuis, Stiggins, Arter, and Chappuis (2005) recommend teachers confer with students as a way to offer feedback on their work by asking them to do some thinking prior to the meeting. Teachers should also identify a focus for the feedback by narrowing the aspects of quality to just a few rather than trying to discuss an entire paper or project. They also recommend providing the students with a scoring guide in advance so they can identify what aspects of quality are present in a particular piece. If the feedback from the teacher matches the feedback of the student, the teacher can point out a strength that may have been overlooked. The goals should be mutually set based upon the input from the teacher and the students. Chappuis, Stiggins, Arter, and Chappuis (2005) say, "At first, students may set large, unmanageable, or nonspecific goals. Help them, if needed, focus their plan on what is doable in the short term" (p. 146). Multiple three-minute conferences that focus on specific goals that can be met quickly are probably more valuable than several thirty-minute conferences that focus on too many aspects and too many goals for students to absorb in one sitting. The "less is more" philosophy applies to teacher-student conferences, especially if there are thirty-five students in the class.

WHY SHOULD WE USE INTERVIEWS AND CONFERENCES?

Interviews and conferences provide opportunities for teachers to not only develop a friendly rapport with their students but also to probe for deeper understanding or areas of misunderstanding. Many students are not able to express complex ideas through their writing because of language barriers or poor writing skills. Primary teachers base more assessments on direct personal communication with the student than teachers in the middle school or high school, since often talking to younger students is the most effective way to assess what they know and feel.

If teachers talk with and listen to students, they are able to gather information that sometimes cannot be gathered any other way, no matter what the ages of the learners. When talking with and listening to students, teachers use the experience to

- help clarify the students' thinking
- help students use metacognitive strategies to reflect on their own learning
- facilitate students' abilities to self-assess their own thinking
- help children set future goals
- build better teacher-student relationships
- help students monitor their own progress and growth toward personal goals

In interviews, conferences, and conversations, students have the opportunity to refine and clarify their thinking and respond to others. Additionally, talking about what they have done and what they plan to do is essential if students are going to learn how to evaluate themselves. The interactions that take place in a learner-focused classroom enhance the communication skills of the students and provide valuable assessment tools for the teacher.

HOW SHOULD WE ASSESS INTERVIEWS AND CONFERENCES?

It is important to develop a recording tool to capture the information provided by the students in interviews and conferences. Anecdotal records, checklists, rating scales, and rubrics can all be used. Teachers usually take brief notes during the interactions but should avoid distracting the students and interrupting their flow of thoughts. Some teachers audiotape or videotape the interviews to allow more time to transcribe the results or to share the information with parents or administrators as needed. While teachers know the value of one-on-one conferences with students, many worry about classroom management and time management issues, especially if they have large classes. What are the other students supposed to be doing when the teacher is conferencing with a student? Many teachers are experimenting with allowing the rest of the class members to do group work or independent work while they are conversing with one student. Some teachers conduct group conferences or allow students to conduct peer conferences using guiding questions to help the students focus on key points. Since some students may feel intimidated when teachers question them directly, pairing students to conduct peer interviews provides a more comfortable climate for interaction.

Most teachers would prefer to conduct longer and more in-depth interviews with students to really discover what they know and what they don't know, but they are limited in their time. Since they may only have a few minutes to assess each student, teachers should concentrate on thoughtful questions that will illicit whether or not students understand the big idea. For example, if a teacher had a chance to interview author Ernest Hemingway, she should avoid asking questions such as "Where were you born?" or "How many books have you written?" that an encyclopedia could provide. Instead, the teacher would ask more provocative questions that only the author himself could answer. Questions like "Did you really have a death wish?" or "Which of your characters most represents you?" or "How did your early jobs in journalism influence your writing style?" will elicit much more interesting answers. "Less is more" is what Hemingway supposedly learned from writer Gertrude Stein. The lesson can be applied to questioning techniques as well as writing style. Higher-order questions that assess the student's thoughts or feelings in a few minutes are more valuable than short-answer recall questions that could be answered on an objective test.

Sample Questions for Student Interview

- How did you feel about our unit on poetry?
- How do you feel about your writing?
- How would you describe your mathematical abilities to a famous mathematician?
- In your opinion, why is it important to keep a portfolio?
- Do you think you are meeting the standards? Why or why not?
- What are you learning? How can you use your new learning?

Personal communication is one of the oldest forms of assessment and teachers should utilize this valuable tool more frequently and more effectively. Establishing data collection tools will make the students' thoughts, questions, and answers a valued component of assessment and evaluation.

FINAL THOUGHTS

Interviews and conferences should play a more important role in the assessment process in all classrooms—from prekindergarten to graduate school. After all, communication skills dominate most state standards, and speaking and listening skills are equally as important as reading and writing skills— not only in school but throughout life. Even parent teacher conferences are changing by including the students and allowing them to talk about what they have learned instead of the teachers showing grades to parents while the students sit at home. Richard Sagor (2008) describes the time he attended his daughter's first open house in preschool. He was expecting the teacher to give a presentation, share handouts, and talk with each parent. Instead, his daughter used a 3 × 5 index card that listed all her lessons to show her parents what she could do. "For the next 40 minutes, Ellisa led us around the room and treated us to demonstrations of things she had learned. Her pride in her accomplishments was palpable, and as I looked around, I saw the same scene repeated child after child" (p. 29). Sagor's first experience with student-led parent conferences illustrates how even a four-year-old can show more about student accomplishment and classroom activities than what is typically shared in a more traditional conference. Just because oral communication is not often tested on high-stakes state tests does not mean it is not a vital instructional and assessment tool. More importantly, it is a critical life skill that all students need to practice and master in order to be successful in school and in life.

EXAMPLES

PRIMARY

TEACHER-STUDENT CONFERENCE

Student: _Bruce_   **Date:** _March 15_

Purpose of Conference:
To discuss Bruce's work with his group

What items were discussed?
1. _frequent absences_
2. _personality conflict with David_
3. _refusal to accept role assignments_

Student's Reaction to Conference: (Complete and return within 2 days)
I stay home from school because I hate my group.
David always makes fun of me when I'm the recorder
because I can't write well.

Teacher's Reaction to Conference:
I will work with your group on the social skill of helping one
another and encouragement. I will also monitor your group
more often.

Date and Time to Follow-up Conference: _March 25, 3:30_

MIDDLE SCHOOL

BOOK REVIEW CONFERENCE

Title of book: _To Kill a Mockingbird_

Date: _March 15_   **Grade:** _9_

Ratings:
2 = Strong Evidence
1 = Some Evidence
0 = Not Yet

Scale:
9–10 = A
7–8 = B
5–6 = C
3–4 = Not Yet

The student demonstrates understanding of:	Plot	Setting	Characters	Theme	Symbols	Total Points	Final Grade
1. Ricardo	2	2	2	1	2	9	A
2. Sherry	1	2	1	0	0	4	Not yet
3. Joann	2	2	2	2	2	10	A
4. Rick	1	2	1	1	2	7	B
5. John	2	2	2	1	2	9	A
6. Bruce	1	1	1	0	1	4	Not yet
7. Jose	2	2	2	1	1	8	B
8. Anna	1	1	2	1	2	7	B
9. Vladic	2	2	2	2	2	10	A
10. Frank	2	2	2	1	2	9	A

HIGH SCHOOL

PEER CONFERENCE ON WRITTEN WORK

☑ First Reading   ☐ Second Reading   ☐ Third Reading
Please read or listen to my written work and help me by answering the following questions:

Title of Piece: _"My Pet Peeves"_

The part I like best is _examples_ because...
you give specifics like gum chewing— people saying "you know"

The part I am not really clear about is _why_ because...
you don't say why you have the pet peeves

Please tell me more about...
when you first realized you had these pet peeves

You might want to try...
including fewer pet peeves but describing them in more detail

Written by: _Pablo_   **Read by:** _Jim_

COLLEGE

PROBLEM-SOLVING INTERVIEW

Student: _Lynn_   **Date:** _January 5_

Type of Problem: _We want everyone on the team to compete but we also want to win the debate._

■ Self-Assessment   ☑ Peer Assessment   ☐ Teacher Assessment

	Yes	Not Yet	Questions
1.	☑		Can you explain the problem?
2.	☑		Can you brainstorm possible solutions?
3.		☑	Can you list steps to solve the problem?
4.	☑		Can you relate this problem to others like it?
5.		☑	Can you give alternative solutions?

Problem: _We have 8 people on the debate team, but only 4 people can compete._

Best Solution: _Rotate 4-person teams._

First Step: _Establish schedule._

Figure 9.2

O N   Y O U R   O W N

Plan a Portfolio Conference

Directions: Have students create a list of questions they would want their teacher or their parents to ask them during a portfolio conference. Encourage the students to write thoughtful questions that elicit reflective responses.

Questions for My Portfolio Conference

1. _____
   _____
   _____

2. _____
   _____
   _____

3. _____
   _____
   _____

4. _____
   _____
   _____

5. _____
   _____
   _____

6. _____
   _____
   _____

Figure 9.3

ON YOUR OWN

Problem-Solving Interview

Student: _____ **Date:** _____

Problem: _____

_____

■ Self-Assessment   ☐ Peer Assessment   ☐ Teacher Assessment

	Yes 0	Not Yet 1	Questions
1.			Can you explain the problem?
2.			Can you speculate what you think the real problem is?
3.			Can you brainstorm two possible solutions?
4.			Can you evaluate your solutions and select the best one?
5.			Can you describe two steps you will take to solve the problem?

Two Possible Solutions

1.
2.

Best Solution

Two Steps to Solve Problem

1.
2.

Figure 9.4

O N   Y O U R   O W N

Peer Conference on Written Work

Directions: Have students exchange their written work with a partner and critique the work by using the following form.

☑ First Reading   ☐ Second Reading   ☐ Third Reading

Please read or listen to my written work and help me by answering the following questions:

Title of Piece: _____

The part I like best is

_____

because…

The part I am not really clear about is

_____

because…

Please tell me more about…

You might want to try…

Written by: _____   **Read by:** _____

Date: _____   **Date:** _____

Figure 9.5

ON YOUR OWN

Interview on Student Projects

Student: _____ **Date:** _____

Subject Area: _____

1. Describe your project.

    _____
    _____
    _____

2. Why did you select this project?

    _____
    _____
    _____

3. What do you like best about your project?

    _____
    _____
    _____

4. If you could do anything differently, what would it be?

    _____
    _____
    _____

5. What skills or knowledge from other subject areas did you use to complete this project?

    _____
    _____
    _____

6. What have you learned about yourself by completing this project?

    _____
    _____
    _____

7. What skills, concepts, or insights have you learned from completing this project?

    _____
    _____
    _____

Teacher's Signature: _____

Figure 9.6

REFLECTION

Interviews and Conferences

1. Reflect on the value of utilizing personal communication to find out what students know and how they feel. Do you agree or disagree that "personal communication" is an important form of classroom assessment?

_____

_____

_____

_____

_____

_____

_____

2. Brainstorm four ways you can use personal communication more effectively as a valuable assessment tool.

- _____

_____

- _____

_____

- _____

_____

- _____

_____

Figure 9.7

Conclusion

Understanding [. . .] involves sophisticated insights and abilities, reflected in varied performances and contexts [. . .] We also suggest that different kinds of understandings exist, that knowledge and skill do not automatically lead to understanding, that misunderstanding is a bigger problem than we realize, and that assessment of understanding therefore requires evidence that cannot be gained from traditional testing alone. (Wiggins & McTighe, 1998, p. 5)

This quotation points out a very important problem in education. Despite all the emphasis on state standards, standardized tests, formative and summative assessments, differentiated learning, and response to intervention, how do educators really know if students *understand* the essential concepts? How do educators recognize and assess the depth of that understanding? And, most importantly, how can educators clear up misunderstandings?

Students memorize facts and demonstrate skills, but do they really understand why they are doing what they do? Do they know their learning goals? Do they have any idea about how they will apply these skills throughout their lives?

How can the overall assessment system support effective teaching and learning outcomes and enhance student understanding? Darling-Hammond et al. (2008) discuss the need to create performance assessments that encourage the kinds of higher-order thinking and performance skills students will need to use in the outside world. If teachers focus on balancing their assessments, they can meet the needs of all their students. As Burke (2006) states, "Assessment, like diets and budgets, needs to be balanced. The balanced assessment model that integrates traditional teaching and testing, portfolio or work samples, and performance tasks and projects meets the needs of the national mandates, state accountability, and the students" (p. 152). Teachers need to create formative assessments that improve their own teaching and their students' learning.

The whole purpose of the standards movement is to improve education for all students. And, the improvement that is needed includes much more than just raising test scores. The standards movement should also improve students' abilities to think critically and creatively, make informed decisions based on data and logic, access and analyze information, solve problems, communicate effectively, collaborate with others, contribute to society and the world, self-assess and reflect on one's actions, and strive to improve personally and academically.

The assessment ideas in this book represent the tip of the iceberg. If the schools of the twenty-first century plan to succeed in meeting the needs of their students, they must go beyond standardized testing; go beyond worksheets and chapter tests; and go beyond meeting the standards. Teachers must teach more than content; they must teach students how to use effective cognitive structures. As Garner (2008) says:

> With immense pressure to raise test scores, it often seems more efficient to simply cover the material as best we can and hope it sticks. It is truly more efficient, however, to equip students for ongoing learning by using the everyday curriculum to fortify cognitive structures. Investing teaching energy in cognitive structures helps students learn how to learn. (p. 38)

The educated students of tomorrow must be able to "learn how to learn" by explaining, interpreting, applying, synthesizing, evaluating, and creating. They must also be able to develop their own perspective of the world, empathize with others, develop a sense of self-knowledge about their strengths and weaknesses, and recognize their prejudices that could impede their understanding.

It is self-awareness that helps students become *independent learners.* Independent learners do not need a teacher with a red pen following them through life correcting their mistakes. They rank at the highest level of understanding— the ability to self-evaluate. The ultimate goal of education is for students to be able to analyze their own actions: What did I do well? If I did this task over, what would I do differently? Do I need help? Where do I go if I don't know what to do? The ancient Greek playwright Sophocles used a powerful theme of "know thyself" in his dramas. Intelligent behavior is "knowing what to do when you don't know what to do." Sophocles' theme of "know thyself" from the fifth century B.C. continues to be a powerful theme for education in the new millennium.

Resource A

*Investigating Rocks, Minerals, and
Soils in Third-Grade Science*

Dr. Geologist Needs Us!

Resource A includes excerpts from a science performance-task unit created by members of the mathematics/science team in Clarke County School District in Athens, Georgia, in the fall of 2008. The workshops were facilitated by Mark Tavernier, Director of Teaching and Learning; Kay Burke, educational consultant; and content specialists Kate Arnold, Glenda Huff, Claude Gonzalez, Barbara Michalove, and Julie Bower. The unit was created by the following:

Patty Birchenall

Susan Bolens

Mia Jordan

Pam Stevens

Claudia Taxel

Donna Ware

Source: Clarke County School District, Athens, GA. Used with permission.

Resource A.1

Dr. Geologist Needs Us!

Key Standard: Students will investigate the physical attributes of rocks and soils.

Problem Scenario: Help! Dr. Geologist needs help researching rocks and minerals for his latest book. He has called upon our class to form geological teams to collect, create, and present information. Each of the teams will be responsible for the following: Team 1: Create a bank of illustrated riddles showing the physical attributes of rocks and minerals; Team 2: Create a picture dictionary of science words; Group 3: Create a photo-story presentation of your investigations of soil; and Group 4: Create a sample book page using photos and other sources to explain erosion of rocks and minerals by wind and water. Be prepared to share your work with Dr. Geologist next week when he visits our school. Come on everybody. *Let's get rockin'!*

Whole-Class Instruction: List the content or skills that will be introduced by the teacher to prepare students for the group and individual work.
- Conduct investigations on rocks and soils from our science text.
- Take a field trip to Sandy Creek to investigate rocks and soils there.
- Take notes and make observations while viewing a Bill Nye video.
- Read books, magazines, and explore the Internet to gain information about rocks and soils.
- Explore *Magic School Bus* books to make sure we know our science.

Group Work: Students may select their group topic or presentation method.

Group 1: We noticed that Dr. Geologist uses riddles in his books, so we are going to create a bank of illustrated riddles, using PowerPoint, about the physical attributes of rocks and minerals.

Group 2: Dr. Geologist uses lots of interesting words in his books, so we will create a picture dictionary of the science words that we used in our work together (e.g. *field trip, video, investigations*).

Group 3: In his new book, Dr. Geologist wants to include photographs along with his illustrations, so we will create a photo-story presentation of our investigations of soil to share with him.

Group 4: Because we are using real pictures, Dr. Geologist would like us to create a sample book page. We will use our photos and other sources, including the Internet, to explain erosion of rocks and minerals by wind and water.

Individual Work: Each student will complete the following:
- Document findings in science journals (i.e., write-ups of investigations, graphic organizers, vocabulary, notes . . .).

Methods of Assessment: List all the methods of assessment used in this unit.
- Teacher observation
- Checklists and rubrics
- Benchmark tests and chapter and unit tests
- Journals and portfolios

Source: © Created in 2008 workshops sponsored by Mark Tavernier, Director of Curriculum, and the Clarke County Curriculum Department and facilitated by Kay Burke. Used with the permission of Patty Birchenall, Susan Bolen, Mia Jordan, Pamela Stevens, Claudia Taxell, Donna Ware, and the Clarke County School District, Athens, GA.

Resource A.2

Dirty Investigations: Group 3 Checklist

Group 3: Dirty Investigations: Photo Story on Soil	Not Yet 0	Some Evidence 1
Content:		
• Does your photo story have a title?		
• Did you include captions for each photo?		
• Did you include a photo for each type of soil and each investigation?		
• Did you include appropriate vocabulary words?		
• Did you include an introduction and conclusion for each investigation and the photo story?		
Mechanics:		
• Did you use common rules of spelling?		
• Did you use common rules of capitalization and punctuation?		
Appearance:		
• Did you include each group member's name?		
• Is it neatly organized?		
• Is your work detailed?		
Social Skills:		
• Did you respect the opinions of others?		
• Did you stay on task?		
• Did you contribute to the group?		
• Did you help others?		
• Did you listen to others?		
• Did you offer encouragement?		

Total Points: _____
(16)

Student Reflection:

How did you contribute to the group?

What did you learn about the soil?

Teacher Feedback:

Scale:
15–16 = Great Job
13–14 = On Track
0–12 = Not Yet

Source: © Created in 2008 workshops sponsored by Mark Tavernier, Director of Curriculum, and the Clarke County Curriculum Department and facilitated by Kay Burke. Used with the permission of Patty Birchenall, Susan Bolen, Mia Jordan, Pamela Stevens, Claudia Taxell, Donna Ware, and the Clarke County School District, Athens, GA.

Resource A.3

Rockin' Rubric

Standard: Students will investigate the physical attributes of rocks and soils.

Elements:	1 **Missed the Bus** (below the standard)	2 **Keep Exploring** (approaching the standard)	3 **You Rock!** (meets the standard)	4 **Move Over, Dr. Geologist!** (exceeds the standard)	**Score**
Shape of Venn Diagram • Has two large circles • Overlaps • Room to write 5 lines in each circle	I included **1** element.	I included **2** elements.	I included **3** elements.	I included visual details.	/4
Physical Attributes • Shape • Color • Texture • Hardness • Weight	I included **1–2** attributes.	I included **3–4** attributes.	I included **5** attributes.	I included **5** attributes and added one more.	/4
Comparisons • Shape • Color • Texture • Hardness • Weight	I included **1–2** attributes.	I included **3–4** attributes.	I included **5** attributes.	I included **5** attributes and then some more.	/4
Organization & Mechanics • Title for all sections • Words are spelled correctly • My work is easy to read and understand	I included **1** element.	I included **2** elements.	I included **3** elements.	My diagram was edited by a peer.	/4

Grade Equivalents: Exceeds Expectations = 14–16 pts. **Total Points:____/16**
Meets Expectations = 10–13 pts.
Approaching the Standard = 6–9 pts.
Below the Standard = 5 pts. or fewer

Source: © Created in 2008 workshops sponsored by Mark Tavernier, Director of Curriculum, and the Clarke County Curriculum Department and facilitated by Kay Burke. Used with the permission of Patty Birchenall, Susan Bolen, Mia Jordan, Pamela Stevens, Claudia Taxell, Donna Ware, and the Clarke County School District, Athens, GA.

Resource B

A Middle School
Economics Performance Task

Money Doesn't Grow on Trees!

Resource B includes excerpts from a middle school social studies performance-task unit on economics created by Cobb County Area Lead Teachers in the fall of 2007. The workshop was facilitated by Nancy Larimer, Professional Learning Supervisor, and Kay Burke, educational consultant, and created by the following:

Nathifa Carmichael

Tracy Gutierrez

Jennifer Hogan

Mary Jo Martucci

Marcia McComas

Brandi Miller

Denise Reynolds

Tameka Walker

Source: Cobb County School District in Georgia. Used with permission.

RESOURCE B.1

MONEY DOESN'T GROW ON TREES!

Key Standard: The student will explain choices in term of income, spending, credit, savings, and investing.

Problem Scenario:

In America, millions of people file bankruptcy and our state has one of the highest number of foreclosures in the nation. Due to the huge number of people who struggle managing their finances, Governor Perdue and the Consumer Credit Counseling Services (CCCS) has initiated a program to address the needs of our state's citizens of all ages including teens, single adults, couples, and families. Our class has been selected to create a proactive plan for middle school students to teach them how to make wise money-management choices. Let's get started. *Money doesn't grow on trees!*

Whole-Class Instruction: List the content or skills that will be introduced by the teacher to prepare students for the group and individual work.

- Invite a guest speaker to discuss investments to help students understand different types of investments: real estate, 401K and 403B, and stock market.

- Read expository articles regarding financial concepts that also include the key vocabulary terms.

- Watch a video that addresses the key concepts and terms.

- Groups complete a Frayer model on the key terms from the standard: *income, spending, credit, savings & investments.* (Each group member is responsible for a different section of the Frayer.)

- Whole class will complete a word sort on other key vocabulary terms to demonstrate understanding.

- Visual Aids:
   Savings - Account ledger
   Investments - Documents from guest speaker
   Debt free - Sample financial plan
   Income - Sample pay stub
   Spending - Sample budget
   Credit - Credit cards, loans, etc.

Group Work: Students will create a financial plan for the following individuals that would allow them to become debt free and develop a consistent savings and investment plan. Each group has four members responsible for a different section of the financial plan (spending, credit, savings, and investments).*

Group 1	Group 2	Group 3	Group 4
Teen employed part-time	Single woman employed full-time	Couple both employed full-time	Family of four one spouse employed full-time & one spouse employed part-time

* Scenarios would include income and debt information for each.

Individual Work: Each student will complete the following:
- Create a financial-planning guide (handout) for targeted middle school students to help them avoid financial mismanagement.

Methods of Assessment: List all the methods of assessment used in this unit:
- Test on terminology from the standards
- Test on budget form (information is located in each section)
- Financial-planning checklist for group
- Reflection/learning logs
- Note sheet during guest speaker
- Scavenger hunt during video
- Checklist and rubric for individual tasks

Source: © Created in a 2007 workshop for Area Lead Teachers facilitated by Nancy Larimer, Professional Learning Supervisor, and Kay Burke. Used with the permission of Nathifa Carmichael, Tracy Gutierrez, Mary Jo Martucci, Denise Reynolds, Tameka Walker, Brandi Miller, Marcia McComas, and Jennnifer Hogan and the Cobb County School District in Georgia.

RESOURCE B.2

GROUP 1: TEENAGER SCENARIO

Income: You are a fourteen-year-old working part-time, making $50.00 per week. You have a mandatory expense of $20.00 per month that you need to pay for your cell phone bill.

Spending: You like to spend money on other items such as going to the movies, clothing, shoes, other social activities, sports events, going out to eat, and school supplies. You will need to think about how much money you need for your discretionary spending.

Credit: You have established credit with your parents on a personal loan because you borrowed money from them to purchase an iPod and your monthly installment payment is $10.00.

Savings: You are planning a trip for spring break so it is necessary for you to save enough money to use as spending money. You will need to think about how much spending money you will need because your parents are paying for all other expenses of your trip.

Investment: You and two of your friends are planning a lawn care business. You have to purchase a lawn mower and gas supplies for this business. You will need to think of equipment and supplies, advertising expenses, and the fees you will charge for your lawn-care services.

Task: You will create a budget to meet your financial needs based upon your income, spending, monthly expenses, and savings. As you make decisions in completing your budget, you need to answer the following questions:

1. Based on your earnings, how much do you make per month? _____

2. How much are your monthly expenses? (Include your loan payments and other mandatory expenses.) _____

3. How much will you save for your spending expenses on spring break? _____

4. How much will you invest in your business venture? _____

5. How much money will you have for discretionary spending during the month? _____

Complete the financial ledger to determine if your income is enough to meet all of your monthly expenses.

Source: © Created in a 2007 workshop for Area Lead Teachers facilitated by Nancy Larimer, Professional Learning Supervisor, and Kay Burke. Used with the permission of Nathifa Carmichael, Tracy Gutierrez, Mary Jo Martucci, Denise Reynolds, Tameka Walker, Brandi Miller, Marcia McComas, and Jennnifer Hogan and the Cobb County School District in Georgia.

RESOURCE B.3

BALANCED BUDGET

Beginning Monthly Net Income: _____

Spending

Item	M = Mandatory O = Optional	Dollar Amount	Balance

Credit

Item	Dollar Amount	Balance

Savings

Item	Dollar Amount	Balance

Investments

Item	Dollar Amount	Balance

Summary

Please justify your budget.

> **Guiding Questions:**
>
> - Did you explain how you spent your net income? (mandatory vs. optional spending)
> - Did you explain your decision about how much to send your creditor(s)?
> - Did you explain your savings decisions?
> - Did you explain your investment decisions?

_____

_____

_____

_____

Source: © Created in a 2007 workshop for Area Lead Teachers facilitated by Nancy Larimer, Professional Learning Supervisor, and Kay Burke. Used with the permission of Nathifa Carmichael, Tracy Gutierrez, Mary Jo Martucci, Denise Reynolds, Tameka Walker, Brandi Miller, Marcia McComas, and Jennnifer Hogan and the Cobb County School District in Georgia.

RESOURCE B.4

CHECKLIST FOR BUDGET FOR A TEENAGER

Assignment: Prepare a budget for a teenager. Use this checklist to self-assess your budget.	Not Yet 0	Some Evidence 1
Spending		
• Did you pay all your required expenses?		
• Did you select at least two optional spending items? If so, which ones? _____ _____		
• Did you include an amount for each spending item?		
Credit		
• Did you pay all your creditors?		

• How much did you pay?
  ○ minimum _____
  ○ additional amount _____		

Savings		
• Did you decide how much to save? If so, how much? _____		
• Did you determine when you would be able to make the purchase? If so, when? _____		
• Did you decide which investments to make? If so, which ones? _____ _____		
• Did you make a decision on how much to invest? If so, how much? _____		
Summary/Explanation		
• Did you explain how you spent your net income? (mandatory vs. optional spending)		
• Did you explain your decision about how much to send your creditor(s)?		
• Did you explain your savings decisions?		
• Did you explain your investment decisions?		
Cooperative Learning		
• Did you work well with your team? If not, why? _____		
• Did you contribute?		

Assignment: Prepare a budget for a teenager.	Not Yet 0	Some Evidence 1
Cooperative Learning		
• Did you listen?		
• Did you participate?		
• Did you help others?		

Student Comment:

Scale:

A = 17–18
B = 15–16
C = 13–14
12 or under—redo!

Teacher Comment:

Student Signature: _____ Date: _____

Teacher Signature: _____ Date: _____

Source: © Created in a 2007 workshop for Area Lead Teachers facilitated by Nancy Larimer, Professional Learning Supervisor, and Kay Burke. Used with the permission of Nathifa Carmichael, Tracy Gutierrez, Mary Jo Martucci, Denise Reynolds, Tameka Walker, Brandi Miller, Marcia McComas, and Jennnifer Hogan and the Cobb County School District in Georgia.

RESOURCE B.5

CHECKLIST FOR MONEY-MANAGEMENT BROCHURE

Assignment: Prepare a money-management brochure to share with your peers.	Not Yet 0	Some Evidence 1
Cover		
• Did you include your name?		
• Did you include the name of your school and school system?		
• Did you include a creative title for your brochure?		
• Did you include a subtitle that states the purpose?		
• Did you include a corresponding graphic? What is it? _____		
Money Statistics		
• Did you include at least three money management statistics? If so, which did you use? 1. _____ 2. _____ 3. _____		
• Did you use reliable sites on the Internet to find the statistics?		
• Did you include a graphic that enhances the meaning of the text?		
• Did you include at least three key terms? If so, which terms? 1. _____ 2. _____ 3. _____		
Recommended Budget Guidelines		
• Did you designate percentages of income for each area of the budget?		
• Did you include at least three key terms? If so, which terms? 1. _____ 2. _____ 3. _____		
• Did you include rationales for each guideline?		
• Did you include a graphic that enhances the meaning of the text?		

Prepare a money-management brochure to share with your peers.	Not Yet 0	Some Evidence 1
Methods of Growing Your Money		
• Did you include at least one pro and one con for each option? If so, what are they? _____ _____		
Shoe • Pro #1 _____ • Con#1 _____ Savings • Pro#1 _____ • Con#2 _____ CD • Pro #1 _____ • Con#2 _____ Stock Market • Con#1 _____ • Con#2 _____		
• Did you include at least three key terms? If so, which terms? 1. _____ 2. _____ 3. _____		
• Did you include a graphic that enhances the text?		
• Are the pros and cons easily distinguished?		
Glossary of Terms		
• Did you define the ten words used in the pamphlet (including terms used in the pamphlet)?		
• Did you create kid-friendly definitions?		
• Did you include a graphic that enhances the text?		
• Are your definitions accurate?		
Visual Appeal		
• Does the pamphlet use a clearly organized structure?		
• Did you use vivid colors and bold print for section headings?		
• Is your material presented in a neat manner?		
• Did you include borders around each section of text?		

Student Reflection:

New Student Goal:

Source: © Created in a 2007 workshop for Area Lead Teachers facilitated by Nancy Larimer, Professional Learning Supervisor, and Kay Burke. Used with the permission of Nathifa Carmichael, Tracy Gutierrez, Mary Jo Martucci, Denise Reynolds, Tameka Walker, Brandi Miller, Marcia McComas, and Jennnifer Hogan and the Cobb County School District in Georgia.

RESOURCE B.6

BROCHURE TEMPLATE

Money Statistics

Recommended Budget Guidelines

F. Y. I.

Methods of Growing Your Money

Shoebox under bed:
Pro   Con

Savings Account:
Pro   Con

Certificate of Deposit (CD):
Pro   Con

Stock Market:
Pro   Con

Source: © Created in a 2007 workshop for Area Lead Teachers facilitated by Nancy Larimer, Professional Learning Supervisor, and Kay Burke. Used with the permission of Nathifa Carmichael, Tracy Gutierrez, Mary Jo Martucci, Denise Reynolds, Tameka Walker, Brandi Miller, Marcia McComas, and Jennnifer Hogan and the Cobb County School District in Georgia.

Resource C

Using Algebra to Plan a Garden Party

Extreme Makeover!

Resource C includes excerpts from a high school algebra performance-task unit on quadratic equations and factoring created by Cobb County Area Lead Teachers in the fall of 2007. The workshop was facilitated by Nancy Larimer, Professional Learning Supervisor, and Kay Burke, educational consultant, and created by the following:

April Gwyn

Marianne Mitchell

Source: Cobb County School District, Cobb County, GA. Used with permission.

RESOURCE C.1

EXTREME MAKEOVER

Key Standards, Math I—Algebra in Context: The student explores the concepts of quadratic equations and factoring. Math: Sets up equations, uses appropriate methods to solve equations, and compares solutions to the graphs of the equations using a variety of means.

Problem Scenario:

Attention math gurus! The courtyard behind the cafeteria has been abandoned. Established as a gift from the senior class of 1992, the fence is now falling apart, the trees and shrubs in the courtyard are dead, and no one uses the courtyard anymore. The principal has decided that the courtyard is an eyesore and needs a makeover. The rectangular courtyard takes up 300 square feet of space. Going back to the original invoice of the fence, 80 feet of fencing were ordered to surround the courtyard. Unfortunately, the area has been deemed unsafe as it stands, so students are not allowed to take measurements of the space at the site. The principal knows that you are an ideal candidate to work on this job, so your challenge is to determine the dimensions of the courtyard and use this information for the makeover. The principal has agreed to provide $2,000 to work on this project. The project includes four tasks: (1) Write an action plan to provide to the principal that includes reasons for the makeover; (2) Create a scaled blueprint showing the plans for the new courtyard; (3) Create a Web Site that displays different items that could be used to makeover the courtyard; and (4) Develop a PowerPoint presentation to present to the faculty that explains the specifications for the project. Let's get busy! The faculty needs our recommendations for their next meeting on Friday.

Whole-Class Instruction: The whole class will be involved in the following learning experiences:

- Use lecture and textbook to explain how to solve quadratic equations.
- Review methods for graphing.
- Discuss interpretations of solutions.
- Review other math content such as area, perimeter, ratios, and systems of equations.
- Train on graphing utilities.
- Review appropriate research techniques.
- Review letter writing.

Group Work: Students may select their group topic or presentation method.

Group 1: Write an *action plan* to provide to the principal that includes reasons for the makeover; who will benefit from its use; and a written budget explaining materials used and the cost using the dimensions you found, and reasons for going under, over, or meeting budget.

Group 2: Create a *scaled blueprint* showing the plans for the new courtyard that includes the dimensions of the courtyard, as well as a landscape plan for plants, benches, tables, or any other items that will be displayed in the courtyard.

Group 3: Create a *Web site* that displays different items that could be used for the makeover, including a comparison of prices of other big name home-improvement and landscaping stores. It should also give a history and current status of the courtyard and have visual representations of the courtyard that include the dimensions and varying costs based on materials used.

Group 4: Develop a *PowerPoint presentation* to present to the faculty that explains the specifications for the project, shows a timeline for the makeover, the plans to stay within budget, as well as services that you may ask the faculty and community to donate to the project.

Individual Work: Each student will complete the following:

- Write a letter to the principal explaining why each of the four components plays an important role in the extreme makeover. You must also include your mathematical methods and computations for finding the dimensions of the courtyard as well as why you chose to perform your particular component.

Methods of Assessment: List all the methods of assessment used in this unit.

- Checklists for group work
- Checklist and rubric for letter to the principal
- Teacher-made test on solving quadratic equations

Source: © Created in a 2007 workshop for Area Lead Teachers facilitated by Nancy Larimer, Professional Learning Supervisor, and Kay Burke. Used with the permission of Marianne Mitchell, April Gwyn, and the Cobb County School District in Georgia.

RESOURCE C.2

CHECKLIST FOR GROUP 1: ACTION PLAN FOR PRINCIPAL

Performance: Write an action plan to provide to the principal that includes reasons for the makeover; who will benefit from its use; and a written budget explaining materials used and the cost, and reasons for going under or over or meeting budget.

Scale: **Action Plan for Principal** **Criteria:**	**1** Novice	**2** Apprentice Builder	**3** Builder	**4** Master Builder
Content • Are the math problems listed and solved correctly?				
• Did you give three reasons for the makeover? (1) _____ (2) _____ (3) _____				
• Did you give three benefits of the makeover? (1) _____ (2) _____ (3) _____				
• Did you provide a budget for the makeover?				
Organization • Does the plan consider your audience?				
• Has the plan been edited by a peer?				
• Does the budget have all necessary explanations?				

Social Skills				
• Has everyone respected the rights of his or her group members?				
• Has everyone contributed to the group project?				
• Did everyone encourage each other?				

Student Reflection:

Student Goal:

Teacher Comment:

Student Signature: _____   Date: _____

Source: © Created in a 2007 workshop for Area Lead Teachers facilitated by Nancy Larimer, Professional Learning Supervisor, and Kay Burke. Used with the permission of Marianne Mitchell, April Gwyn, and the Cobb County School District in Georgia.

RESOURCE C.3

INDIVIDUAL CHECKLIST FOR LETTER TO THE PRINCIPAL

Assignment: Write a letter to the principal explaining why each of the four components plays an important role in the extreme makeover, your mathematical methods and computations for finding the dimensions of the courtyard, and why you chose to perform your particular component.

Scale: Letter to the Principal Criteria:	1 Blog Writer	2 High School Paper Writer	3 Atlanta Journal Writer	4 New York Times Writer
Accuracy of Computations				
• Did you draw and label the courtyard with the appropriate expressions? Show.				
• Did you set up appropriate equations? What are they?				
• Did you find the accurate solutions? What are they? Do all of them work?				
Letter Content				
• Did you include all mathematical computations in your letter?				
• Does your letter show a strong understanding of solving quadratic equations?				
• Does your letter provide the principal with a clear understanding of the four components and their importance?				
• Does it give a clear understanding of why you chose your component?				

Letter Content				
• Date				
• Inside Address				
• Salutation				
• Body				
• Closing				
• Signature				
Mechanics				
• Capitalization				
• Punctuation				
• Spelling				
Usage				
• Grammar				
• Sentence Structure				
• Transitions				

Student Comment:

Peer Comment:

Teacher Comment:

Source: © Created in a 2007 workshop for Area Lead Teachers facilitated by Nancy Larimer, Professional Learning Supervisor, and Kay Burke. Used with the permission of Marianne Mitchell, April Gwyn, and the Cobb County School District in Georgia.

RESOURCE C.4

INDIVIDUAL RUBRIC FOR ACTION PLAN FOR PRINCIPAL

Key Standards, Math I—Algebra in Context: The student explores the concepts of quadratic equations and factoring. Math: Sets up equations, uses appropriate methods to solve equations and compares solutions to the graphs of the equations using a variety of means.

Action Plan for Principal (Group 1)	1 Below the Standard	2 Approaching the Standard	3 Meets the Standard	4 Exceeds the Standard	Score
Math Problems	Set up incorrectly, and does not have solutions	Set up correctly, with two or more mathematical errors	Set up and solved correctly	Set up and solved correctly and incorporated correctly throughout the project	
Reasons and Benefits for Makeover	Fewer than three reasons listed and not described	Fewer than three reasons listed and described	Three reasons listed and described clearly or accurately	Three reasons listed, described, and incorporated the throughout project	
Budget • Expenses • Funds • Balanced	Lists expenses	Expenses and funds are listed, but may not balance	Balanced without any additional reference made to it	Balanced and has been referenced throughout the project	
Organization • Consider audiences • Peer Edit • Exploration	Meets one component	Meets two components	Meets three components	Meets all three components accurately and coherently	
Social • Respect • Contribution • Encouragement	Demonstrated one social skill	Demonstrated two social skills	Demonstrated three social skills	Demonstrated additional leadership skills	

Total Points:

Resource D

Foreign Language Performance Task for Middle and High School

Are We a Match?

Resource D includes excerpts from a middle school or high school foreign language performance task created by Cobb County Area Lead Teachers in the fall of 2007. The workshop was facilitated by Nancy Larimer, Professional Learning Supervisor, and Kay Burke, educational consultant, and created by the following:

Sheree Altmann

Amy Lacher

Deborah Marker

Suzanne Schott

RESOURCE D.1

Are We a Match?

Key Standard, Modern Languages Presentational Mode of Communication: The student presents information orally and in writing that contains a variety of vocabulary, phrases, and patterns.

Problem Scenario: The International Student Exchange Program has received your application to host a foreign exchange student in your home for the next school year. Before officials can select your family to be a part of this program, the director of the exchange program will need to come to your home and interview you and your family to determine if you would be a suitable host family. The director will want to match your family with a student who will be comfortable with your family routines and activities. Be prepared because you and your family are about to find out, *"Are we a match?"*

Whole-Class Instruction: List the content or skills that will be introduced by the teacher to prepare students for the group and individual work.
- Grammar, verbs, and vocabulary necessary to discuss family, school routines, and activities
- Verbs and structures necessary to express likes and dislikes

Group Work: Students may select their group topic or presentation method.

Group 1: Through the use of dramatization, show and tell us about your family routines and chores. Who does what? At what time? Where?

Group 2: Interview two or three family members. Find out about their likes, dislikes, activities, ages, and pets.

Group 3: Create and explain a family calendar that shows family and school activities.

Individual Work: Each student will complete the following:
- Write a letter to the director describing yourself, your family, school routines, chores, activities, likes and dislikes. Be sure to include the names and ages of your family members. Include your pets!

Methods of Assessment: List all the methods of assessment used in this unit.
- Oral presentations for group work
  - Written letter for individual work
  - Daily participation (Q & A, conversations)
  - Quizzes and tests including sections to assess listening, reading, and writing skills

Source: © Created in a 2007 workshop for Area Lead Teachers facilitated by Nancy Larimer, Professional Learning Supervisor, and Kay Burke. Used with the permission of Sheree Altmann, Suzanne Schott, Deborah Marker, Amy Lacher, and the Cobb County School District in Georgia.

RESOURCE D.2

Individual Checklist for "Letter to the Director"

Assignment: Write a letter to the director describing yourself, your family, school routines, chores, activities, likes and dislikes. Be sure to include the names and ages of your family members. Include your pets!

Letter to the Director:	Scale:	0	1
Did you complete the task?			
• Are your ideas developed and organized?			
• Did you include information about your family?			
• Did you include information about your school routines?			
• Did you include information about your chores?			
• Did you include information about your activities?			
• Did you include information about your likes and dislikes?			
• Did you mention your pets?			
How accurate is your grammar?			
• Did you check your subject/verb agreement?			
• Did you check your adjective agreement?			
Did you check your conventions?			
• Did you check your spelling?			
• Did you check punctuation?			
Can your letter be understood by others?			
• Is your letter logical?			
• Can the reader easily understand your letter?			
• Did you organize your ideas?			

Source: © Created in a 2007 workshop for Area Lead Teachers facilitated by Nancy Larimer, Professional Learning Supervisor, and Kay Burke. Used with the permission of Sheree Altmann, Suzanne Schott, Deborah Marker, Amy Lacher, and the Cobb County School District in Georgia.

RESOURCE D.3

Individual Rubric for "Letter to the Director"

Key Standard, Modern Languages Presentational Mode of Communication: The student presents information that contains a variety of vocabulary, phrases, and patterns.

"Letter to the Director"	1 Below the Standard	2 Approaching the Standard	3 Meets the Standard	4 Exceeds the Standard	Score
Task Completion	Minimal completion of task and/or content frequently inappropriate	• Partial completion of task • Content mostly appropriate • Ideas are underdeveloped	• Completion of the task • Appropriate content • Ideas are adequately developed	• "Above and beyond" completion of task • Content appropriate • Ideas well developed well organized	
Grammar Accuracy	Five or more grammar errors	Three-four grammar errors	No more than two grammar errors	No grammar errors—"Grammar Guru"	
Conventions	Four or more spelling/ punctuation errors	Three spelling/ punctuation errors	No more than two spelling/ punctuation errors	No spelling/ punctuation errors	
Comprehensibility	Information is not logical and cannot be understood	Some content is logical but difficult to understand	Most content is logical and can be early understood	All content is logical and clearly understood	

Total Points: _____

Student Reflection:

Teacher Comment:

Scale:

15–16 = A
13–14 = B
11–12 = C
Not Yet

Source: © Created in a 2007 workshop for Area Lead Teachers facilitated by Nancy Larimer, Professional Learning Supervisor, and Kay Burke. Used with the permission of Sheree Altmann, Suzanne Schott, Deborah Marker, Amy Lacher, and the Cobb County School District in Georgia.

Resource E

Thinking About Themes Through Texts and Tasks in Literature, Grades 9–12

Resource E includes excerpts from a high school language arts performance-task unit on reading and writing created by Cobb County Area Lead Teachers in the fall of 2007. The workshop was facilitated by Nancy Larimer, Professional Learning Supervisor, and Kay Burke, educational consultant, and created by the following:

Kristen Carwile

Elizabeth Cobia

Sylvia M. Spruill

Source: Cobb County School District, Cobb County, GA. Used with permission.

Resource E.1

Thinking About Themes Through Texts and Tasks

Key Standards: 1. The student identifies, analyzes, and applies knowledge of theme in literary works from various genres and provides evidence from the works to support understanding. 2. The student produces writing that establishes an appropriate organizational structure, sets a context and engages the reader, maintains a coherent focus throughout, and signals closure. 3. The student participates in student-to-teacher, student-to-student, and group verbal interactions.

Problem Scenario: We have an opportunity to visit the fifth-grade classes at Clay Elementary School. The fifth-grade teachers there are having difficulty selecting texts to teach the concept of theme in literary works. They want to select texts that engage their audience, contain age-appropriate themes, and represent the various cultures in their classrooms. They have asked us to make a presentation recommending five texts to teach theme. The texts must address the criteria specified by the fifth-grade teachers. The class will make the presentation to the teachers at the end of the month (date/time). We will need groups to complete all of the following for each one of the texts our class selects:

1. Write a rationale for how the text meets the criteria.
2. Create a movie poster to promote the text.
3. Perform a two-minute skit summarizing the text.
4. Write and deliver an "elevator speech" (no more than one minute) about the text.

Whole-Class Instruction: List the content or skills that will be introduced by the teacher to prepare students for the group and individual work.

- Identify theme in various genres/texts.
- Compare and contrast themes in various genres/texts (Venn diagram).
- Explain the elements of style related to theme.
- Practice interviewing skills.
- Identify audience, tone, and purpose in a variety of genres/texts.

Group Work: Students may select their texts based on the fifth-grade teachers' criteria. Students will be grouped to incorporate a variety of multiple intelligences in each group.

Individual Work: Each student will complete the following:

- Write a critical review of a grade-level (their grade-level 9–12) appropriate text focusing on theme.

Methods of Assessment: List all the methods of assessment used in this unit.

- Observation
- Question/answer
- Student checklist
- Rubric

Source: © Created in a 2007 workshop for Area Lead Teachers facilitated by Nancy Larimer, Professional Learning Supervisor, and Kay Burke. Used with the permission of Sylvia M. Spruill, Elizabeth Cobia, Kristen Carwile, and the Cobb County School District in Georgia.

Resource E.2

Checklist for Written Rationale

Standards: 1. The student identifies, analyzes, and applies knowledge of theme in literary works from various genres and provides evidence from the works to support understanding. 2. The student produces writing that establishes an appropriate organizational structure, sets a context and engages the reader, maintains a coherent focus throughout, and signals closure.

Assignment: Explain how the selected text meets the fifth-grade teachers' criteria. Before "checking" the item, write in the answer if there is a question.	**Not Yet** **0**	**Some** **Evidence** **1**
Content		
• Does your rationale directly address the theme? State the theme: _____		
• Does your rationale include evidence from the text (quotations) that supports the theme? Give one example: _____		
• Does your rationale have a hook to engage your audience? What is it? _____		
• Do you explain how the theme is age appropriate?		
• Do you explain how the text represents the various cultures in the classroom?		
Organizational Structure		

• Are the ideas in your paragraphs grouped in a logical order?
  State which way (chronological, cause and effect, similarities and difference, posing and answering a question):
  _____		

Grammar/Mechanics/Style		
• Is your writing free of grammatical errors?		
• Is your writing free of spelling errors?		
• Is your writing free of capitalization errors?		
• Is your writing punctuated correctly?		
• Do you use a variety of sentence structures (simple, compound, complex, compound-complex)?		
• Do you use words (diction) that are descriptive and appropriate for your audience and purpose?		
Length		
• Is your rationale no longer than two typed pages using MLA formatting? (12 point Times New Roman, 1-inch margins, double-spaced)		

Source: © Created in a 2007 workshop for Area Lead Teachers facilitated by Nancy Larimer, Professional Learning Supervisor, and Kay Burke. Used with the permission of Sylvia M. Spruill, Elizabeth Cobia, Kristen Carwile, and the Cobb County School District in Georgia.

Resource E.3

Checklist for Movie Poster

Assignment: Create a movie poster to promote the selected text. Before "checking" the item, write in the answer if it is a question.	**Not Yet** **0**	**Some** **Evidence** **1**
Content		
• Does your poster include the title of the text? What is it? _____		
• Does your poster include the author of the text on your poster? Who is it? _____		
• Does your poster include a visual representation/symbol of the text? Describe it: _____		
• Does your poster include a tagline that engages the viewer? What is it? _____		
• Do you represent the theme of the text? How? (check one or both) _____ with pictures _____ with words		
• Does your movie poster include the names of the main characters in the text? List them _____		
Mechanics		
• Is your poster free of spelling errors?		
• Is your poster free of capitalization errors?		
• Is your poster free of punctuation errors?		
• Do you use correct sentence structure in your tag line?		
Appearance		
• Is your poster on poster board?		
• Do you use at least five colors on your poster?		
• Is your poster neat? (No obvious error corrections and no smudges)		
• Does the visual appearance (font, pictures, art) support the theme?		

Source: © Created in a 2007 workshop for Area Lead Teachers facilitated by Nancy Larimer, Professional Learning Supervisor, and Kay Burke. Used with the permission of Sylvia M. Spruill, Elizabeth Cobia, Kristen Carwile, and the Cobb County School District in Georgia.

Resource E.4

Checklist for Skit

Standard: 1. Student delivers narrative, expository, or persuasive presentations that incorporate the same elements found in that mode or genre of writing.

Assignment: Create and present a skit summarizing the text. Before "checking" the item, write in the answer if it is a question.	**Not Yet** **0**	**Some Evidence** **1**
Content		
• Does your skit directly address the theme? What is the theme? _____		
• Does your skit represent a summary of the complete story?		
• Does your skit interject plot tension, suspense, and closure where appropriate?		
Presentation		
• Is your skit two minutes long? How many minutes? _____		
• Does each person in your group have at least one speaking line?		
• Is your enunciation and pacing in your skit appropriate for conveying the text?		
• Can every line be heard?		
• Are you using appropriate props and/or costumes?		
• Are your lines memorized?		

Student Reflection:

Teacher Feedback:

Source: © Created in a 2007 workshop for Area Lead Teachers facilitated by Nancy Larimer, Professional Learning Supervisor, and Kay Burke. Used with the permission of Sylvia M. Spruill, Elizabeth Cobia, Kristen Carwile, and the Cobb County School District in Georgia.

Resource E.5

Checklist for Elevator Speech

Standard: 1. Student delivers narrative, expository, or persuasive presentations that incorporate the same elements found in that mode or genre of writing.

An elevator speech should be as long as it takes an elevator to go up and down (short and sweet). **Assignment:** In one minute, present your text to your audience.	**Not Yet** **0**	**Some** **Evidence** **1**
Content		
• Do you use a hook to engage your audience? What is it? _____		
• Do you state the title of the text? What is it? _____		
• Do you explain how the text is age appropriate?		
• Do you explain how the text represents the various cultures in the classroom? Give one example: _____		
• Does your speech directly address the theme of the text? What is the theme? _____		
• Do you include at least one specific example from the text to support the theme? What is it? _____		
• Do you end your speech with an effective closing statement? What is it? _____		
Presentation		
• Is your speech memorized?		
• Are you speaking loud enough?		
• Are you maintaining consistent eye contact while delivering your speech?		
• Are you using appropriate gestures?		
• Are you emphasizing key points?		

Student Self-Assessment:

Source: © Created in a 2007 workshop for Area Lead Teachers facilitated by Nancy Larimer, Professional Learning Supervisor, and Kay Burke. Used with the permission of Sylvia M. Spruill, Elizabeth Cobia, Kristen Carwile, and the Cobb County School District in Georgia.

Resource E.6

Checklist for Critical Review of Grade-Level Appropriate Text

Assignment: Write a critical review of a grade-level appropriate text focusing on theme.	**Not Yet** 0	**Some Evidence** 1
Content		
• Did you explain how the theme represents a universal view or comments on life or society?		
• Did you include textual evidence to support your explanation?		
• Did you explain how the author's choice of words (diction) advances the theme?		
• Did you evaluate the author's choice of words (diction)?		
• If your text contains more than one theme, did you address the second theme? State: _____		
• Did you compare the theme of your text with the theme of another text you have read? Identify the text to which you compared it: _____		
Organizational Structure		
• Do you have an introduction with a hook to grab your reader's attention?		
• Do you have a focus/thesis statement? State: _____		
• Do you have at least four paragraphs? How many? _____		
• Are your explanations and evidence organized into paragraphs?		
• Do your paragraphs contain topic sentences? Write two: 1) _____ 2) _____		
• Do you provide supporting sentences for your topic sentences?		
• Do you have transitions between your ideas and paragraphs?		

(Continued)

(Continued)

• Did you select an organizing structure? (Check which one) ___ Chronological ___ Cause and effect ___ Similarities and differences ___ Posing and answering a question		
• Do you have a satisfying closure/conclusion that leaves your reader with a better understanding of the text?		
• Did you write in third person?		
• Do you use precise language, action verbs, and sensory details to engage the reader?		
• Did you explain how the theme is age-appropriate for your audience?		
Format		
• Is your rationale typed in 12 pt. Times New Roman font?		
• Do you have the correct MLA heading? (Name, teacher, class, date on the left)		
• Is your rationale double-spaced?		
• Do you have 1-inch margins?		
• Do you have a header and page number on every page?		
Conventions		
• Did you check for spelling and mechanical errors?		
• Did you check for usage errors?		
• Did you check for comma splices, run-on, and fragments?		

Student Self-Assessment: Total Points _____

                                                           (out of 26)

Scale
23–26 = A (90%) 21–22 = B (80%) 18–20 = C (70%) Not Yet

Peer Assessment:

Source: © Created in a 2007 workshop for Area Lead Teachers facilitated by Nancy Larimer, Professional Learning Supervisor, and Kay Burke. Used with the permission of Sylvia M. Spruill, Elizabeth Cobia, Kristen Carwile, and the Cobb County School District in Georgia.

Resource E.7

Individual Rubric for Thinking About Themes Through Texts and Tasks

Key Standards: 1. The student demonstrates comprehension by identifying evidence and main ideas in a variety of texts representative of different genres and uses this evidence as a basis for interpretation. 2. The student identifies, analyzes and applies knowledge of theme in literary works and provides evidence from the works to support understanding. 3. The student demonstrates competence (in writing) in a variety of genres.

Criteria/Scoring	**1** **Below the** **Standard**	**2** **Approaching** **the Standard**	**3** **Meets the** **Standard**	**4** **Exceeds the** **Standard**	**Score**
Content					
Explanation of theme to a universal view	Little explanation	Explanation is confusing	Explanation is coherent	Explanation is mature and insightful	___x 3___ (12)
Use of textual evidence to support explanation	No textual evidence	Includes one–two references to text	Includes three–four references to text with limited analysis	Includes four or more references to text with mature analysis	___x 3___ (12)
Evaluation of author's diction	No mention of author's diction	Author's diction mentioned as an afterthought	Evaluation of diction coherent	Evaluation of diction mature and insightful	___x 3 ___ (12)
Comparison of theme to another text	Lacks specific comparison	Comparison vague	Comparison developed and coherent	Comparison developed and thought provoking	___ x 3 ___ (12)
			Total Score for **Content** Section= ____/48		
Organizational Structure					
Introduction	Weak	Attempts to engage reader	Captures the reader's attention	Grabs reader's attention	___x 1 ___ (4)
Topic sentences	None	Main idea wrong or invalid	Main idea correct and stated coherently	Main idea clear and controlling	___x 1 ___ (4)

(Continued)

(Continued)

Criteria/Scoring	1 **Below the Standard**	2 **Approaching the Standard**	3 **Meets the Standard**	4 **Exceeds the Standard**	**Score**
Supporting sentences	Show marginal relationship to topic sentence	One supporting sentence related to topic sentence	Two supporting sentences related to topic sentence	Three or more well-written sentences related to topic sentence	___ x 1 ___ (4)
Organizing structure	Does not fully align with topic	Adequately aligns with topic	Complements topic	Complements topic and advances the theme	___ x 1 ___ (4)
Conclusion	Weak	Attempts to pull things together	Helps create cohesion for paper	Helps create cohesion and leaves the reader with a thought-provoking statement	___ x 1 ___ (4)
Explanation of age-appropriateness	Weak	Attempts to show why theme is appropriate	Developed and is sound	Developed and is mature and insightful	___ x 1 ___ (4)
Total Score for **Organizational Structure** Section=____/24					
Format					
Format from individual checklist is followed	Only one element followed	Two elements followed	Three–four elements followed	All five elements followed	___ x 2 ___ (8)
Total Score for **Format** Section=____/8					
Conventions					
Spelling and mechanical errors	Four or more errors; begins to affect the meaning of the work	Two–three errors	One error	No errors	___ x 1 ___ (4)
Usage	Four or more errors; begins to affect the meaning of the work	Two–three errors	One error	No errors	___ x 1 ___ (4)

Criteria/Scoring	1 **Below the Standard**	2 **Approaching the Standard**	3 **Meets the Standard**	4 **Exceeds the Standard**	Score
Comma splices, run-on sentences, and fragments	Four or more errors; begins to affect the meaning of the work	Two–three errors	One error	No errors	___ x 1 ___ (4)
			Total Score for **Conventions** Section= ____/12		

Student Comments: (Worth 8 points):

Final Score: _____

(92)

+   Comments: _____

Final Grade: _____

Peer Comments:

Teacher Comments:

Student's Signature: _____   Date: _____

Peer's Signature: _____   Date: _____

Teacher's Signature: _____   Date: _____

Source: © Created in a 2007 workshop for Area Lead Teachers facilitated by Nancy Larimer, Professional Learning Supervisor, and Kay Burke. Used with the permission of Sylvia M. Spruill, Elizabeth Cobia, Kristen Carwile, and the Cobb County School District in Georgia.

References

Airasian, P. W. (1994). *Classroom assessment* (2nd ed.). New York: McGraw-Hill.

Airasian, P. W. (2000). *Assessment in the classroom: A concise approach* (2nd ed.). Boston, MA: McGraw-Hill Higher Education.

Archbald, D. A., & Newmann, F. M. (1988). *Beyond standardized testing: Assessing authentic academic achievement in the secondary school.* Madison: University of Wisconsin, National Association of Secondary Principals.

Ardovino, J., Hollingsworth, J., & Ybarra, S. (2000). *Multiple measures: Accurate ways to assess student achievement.* Thousand Oaks, CA: Corwin.

Ataya, R. L. (2007). Policy and technical considerations for classroom assessment. In P. Jones, J. F. Carr, & R. L. Ataya (Eds.), *A pig don't get fatter the more you weigh it: Classroom assessments that work* (pp. 71–86). New York: Teachers College Press.

Belgrad, S., Burke, K., & Fogarty, R. (2008). *The portfolio connection: Student work linked to standards* (3rd ed.). Thousand Oaks, CA: Corwin.

Black, H., & Black, S. (1990). *Organizing thinking: Graphic organizers, Book II.* Pacific Grove, CA: Midwest Publications Critical Thinking Press and Software.

Black, P., & Wiliam, D. (1998). Assessment and classroom learning. *Assessment in Education, 5* (1), 7–75.

Blythe, T., Allen, D., & Powell, B. S. (2008). *Looking together at student work* (2nd ed.). New York: Teachers College Press.

Board of Education for the City of Etobicoke. (1987). *Making the grade: Evaluating student progress.* Scarborough, Ontario, Canada: Prentice-Hall Canada.

Brady, M. (2008). Cover the material—or teach students to think? *Educational Leadership, 65* (5), 64–67.

Brown, R. (1989). Testing and thoughtfulness. *Educational Leadership, 467* (7), 31–33.

Brownlie, F., Close, S., & Wingren, L. (1988). *Reaching for higher thought: Reading, writing, thinking strategies.* Edmonton, Alberta, Canada: Arnold.

Brownlie, F., Close, S., & Wingren, L. (1990). *Tomorrow's classroom today.* Portsmouth, NH: Heinemann.

Burke, K. (2006). *From standards to rubrics in six steps: Tools for assessing student learning, K–8.* Thousand Oaks, CA: Corwin.

Burke, K. (2008). *What to do with the kid who . . . Developing cooperation, self-discipline, and responsibility in the classroom* (3rd ed.). Thousand Oaks, CA: Corwin.

Butler, S. M., & McMunn, N. D. (2006). *A teacher's guide to classroom assessment: Understanding and using assessment to improve student learning grades K–12.* San Francisco: Jossey-Bass.

Carr, J. F. (2007). Classroom assessments that work. In P. Jones, J. F. Carr, & R. L. Ataya (Eds.), *A pig don't get fatter the more you weigh it: Classroom assessments that work.* (pp. 1–10). New York: Teachers College Press.

Chappuis, S., & Chappuis, J. (2007/2008). The best value in formative assessment. *Educational Leadership, 65* (4), 14–18.

Chappuis, S., Stiggins, R. J., Arter, J., & Chappuis, J. (2005). *Assessment for learning: A action guide for school leaders: Vision + Competence + Action=Student success.* Portland, OR: Educational Testing Service.

Chen, J., & McNamee, G. D. (2007). *Bridging: Assessment for teaching and learning in early childhood classrooms, PreK–3.* Thousand Oaks, CA: Corwin.

Costa, A. L. (2008). The thought filled curriculum. *Educational Leadership, 65* (5), 20–24.

Costa, A. L. (2008). *The school as a home for the mind: Creating mindful curriculum, instruction, and dialogue.* Thousand Oaks, CA: Corwin.

Cranton, P. (1996). *Professional development as transformative learning: New perspectives for teachers of adults.* San Francisco: Jossey-Bass.

Crow, T. (2008). An interview with Richard F. Elmore "Practicing Professionals." *Journal of Staff Development, 29* (2), 42–47.

Darling-Hammond, L. (1997). *The right to learn: A blueprint for creating schools that work.* San Francisco: Jossey-Bass.

Darling-Hammond, L., Barron, B., Pearson, P. D., Schoenfeld, A. H., Stage, E. K., Zimmerman, T. D., Cervetti, G. N., & Tilson, J. L. (2008). *Powerful learning: What we know about teaching for understanding.* San Francisco: Jossey-Bass.

Elmore, R. F. (2008). *Bridging the gap between standards and achievement: The imperative for professional development in education.* Washington, DC: Author (ERIC Document Reproduction Service No. ED475871).

Epstein, A. S. (2008). An early start on thinking. *Educational Leadership, 65* (5), 38–42.

Flynn, L., & Flynn, E. M. (2004). *Teaching writing with rubrics: Practical strategies and lesson plans for grades 2–8.* Thousand Oaks, CA: Corwin.

Fogarty, R. (2001). *Differentiated learning: Different strokes for different folks.* Chicago: Fogarty & Associates.

Fogarty, R., & Stoehr, J. (2008). *Integrating curricula with multiple intelligences: Teams, themes, & threads* (2nd ed.) Thousand Oaks, CA: Corwin.

Foriska, T. J. (1998). *Restructuring around standards: A practitioner's guide to design and implementation.* Thousand Oaks, CA: Corwin.

Gardner, H. (1983). *Frames of mind: The theory of multiple intelligences.* New York: Basic Books.

Gareis, C. R., & Grant, L.W. (2008). *Teacher-made assessments: How to connect curriculum, instruction, and student learning.* Larchmont, NY: Eye on Education.

Garner, B. K. (2007). *Getting to got it! Helping struggling students learn how to learn.* Alexandria, VA: Association for Supervision and Curriculum Development.

Garner, B. K. (2008). When students seem stalled. *Educational Leadership, 65* (6), 32–38.

Gottlieb, M. (2006). *Assessing English language learners: Bridges from language proficiency to academic achievement.* Thousand Oaks, CA: Corwin.

Graham, P., & Ferriter, B. (2008). One step at a time. *The Journal of Staff Development, 29* (3), 38–42.

Gregory, G. H., & Chapman, C. (2002). *Differentiated instructional strategies: One size doesn't fit all.* Thousand Oaks, CA: Corwin.

Groeber, J. F. (2007). *Designing and using rubrics for reading and language arts, K–6.* Thousand Oaks, CA: Corwin.

Gronlund, N. E. (1998). *Assessment of student achievement* (6th ed.). Boston: Allyn & Bacon.

Guskey, T. R. (2007). Using assessments to improve teaching and learning. In D. Reeves (Ed.), *Ahead of the curve: The power of assessment to transform teaching and learning.* Bloomington, IN: Solution Tree.

Guskey, T. R., & Bailey, J. M. (2001). Developing grading and reporting systems for student learning. In T. R. Guskey & R. J. Marzano (Eds.), *Experts in assessment*. Thousand Oaks, CA: Corwin.

Hansen, J. (1992). Literacy portfolios: Helping students know themselves. *Educational Leadership, 49* (8), 66–68.

Hargreaves, A., & Shirley, D. (2008). Beyond standardization: Powerful principles for improvement. *Phi Delta Kappan, 90* (2),135–143.

Herman, J. L., Aschbacher, P. R., & Winters, L. (1992). *A practical guide to alternative assessment*. Alexandria, VA: Association for Supervision and Curriculum Development.

Hills, J. R. (1991). Apathy concerning grading and testing. *Phi Delta Kappan, 72* (7), 540–545.

Hoerr, T. R. (2008). Data that count: The Principal Connection. *Educational Leadership, 66* (4), 93–94.

Hyerle, D. (1996). *Visual tools for constructing knowledge*. Alexandria, VA: Association for Supervision and Curriculum Development.

Jacobs, H. H. (1997). *Mapping the big picture: Integrating curriculum and assessment K–12*. Alexandria, VA: Association for Supervision and Curriculum Development.

Jensen, E. (1998). How Julie's brain learns. *Educational Leadership, 6* (3), 43.

Jeroski, S., Brownlie, F., & Kaser, L. (1990a). *Reading and responding: Evaluating resources for your classroom: 1–3, Grades 4–6*. Toronto, Ontario, Canada: Nelson Canada.

Jeroski, S., Brownlie, F., & Kaser, L. (1990b). *Reading and responding: Evaluation resources for your classroom: 1–2, Late primary and primary*. Toronto, Ontario, Canada: Nelson Canada.

Jonson, K. F. (2002). *Being an effective mentor: How to help beginning teachers succeed*. Thousand Oaks, CA: Corwin.

Knight, J. (2007). *Instructional coaching: A partnership approach to improving instruction*. Oxford, OH and Thousand Oaks, CA: National Staff Development Council and Corwin.

Lachat, M. A. (2004). *Standards-based instruction and assessment for English Language Learners*. Thousand Oaks, CA: Corwin.

Lang, S., Stanley, T., & Moore, B. (2008). *Start cycle assessment: Improving student achievement through formative assessment*. Larchmont, NY: Eye on Education.

Lougy, R., DeRuvo, S., & Rosenthal, D. (2007). *Teaching young children with ADHD: Successful strategies and practical interventions for PreK–3*. Thousand Oaks, CA: Corwin.

Majesky, D. (1993). Grading should go. *Educational Leadership, 50* (7), 88–90.

Mansilla, V. B., & Gardner, H. (2008). Disciplining the mind. *Educational Leadership, 65* (5), 14–19.

Martin-Kniep, G. O. (2000). *Becoming a better teacher: Eight innovations that work*. Alexandria, VA: Association for Supervision and Curriculum Development.

Marzano, R. J. (2003). *What works in schools: Translating research into action*. Alexandria, VA: Association for Supervision and Curriculum Development.

Marzano, R. J. (2006). *Classroom assessment and grading that work*. Alexandria, VA: Association for Supervision and Curriculum Development.

Marzano, R. J., & Kendall, J. S. (1996). *A comprehensive guide to designing standards-based districts, schools, and classrooms*. Alexandria, VA: Association for Supervision and Curriculum Development.

Marzano, R., Pickering, D., & Pollock, J. (2005). *Classroom instruction that works: Research-based strategies for increasing student achievement*. Boston: Allyn & Bacon.

McCombs, B. L., & Miller, L. (2007). *Learner-centered classroom practices and assessments: Maximizing student motivation, learning and achievement.* Thousand Oaks, CA: Corwin.

Moody, M. S., & Stricker, J. M. (2009). *Strategic design for student achievement.* New York: Teachers College Press.

Musial, D., Nieminem, G., Thomas, J., & Burke, K. (2009). *Foundation of meaningful educational assessment.* Boston: McGraw-Hill Higher Education.

Niguidula, D. (2005). Documenting learning with digital portfolios. *Educational Leadership, 63* (3), 44–47.

Noddings, N. (2008). All our students thinking. *Educational Leadership, 65* (5), 9–13.

O'Connor, K. (2002). *How to grade for learning: Linking grades to standards.* Thousand Oaks, CA: Corwin.

Paulson, F. L., Paulson, P. R., & Meyer, C. A. (1991). What makes a portfolio a portfolio? *Educational Leadership, 48* (5), 60–63.

Payne, R. C. (2008). Nine powerful practices. *Educational Leadership, 65* (7), 48–52.

Pete, B., & Fogarty, R. (2003). *Nine "best practices" that make a difference.* Chicago: Robin Fogarty & Associates.

Popham, W. J. (1999). *Classroom assessment: What teachers need to know* (2nd ed.). Boston: Allyn & Bacon.

Popham, W. J. (2001). Teaching to the test? *Educational Leadership, 58* (6), 16–20.

Popham, W. J. (2006). *Assessment for educational leaders.* Boston: Pearson Education.

Popham, W. J. (2008). *Transformative assessment.* Alexandria, VA: Association for Supervision and Curriculum Development.

Price, H. B. (2008). *Mobilizing the community to help students succeed.* Alexandria, VA: Association for Supervision and Curriculum Development.

Reeves, D. B. (2003). *Making standards work: How to implement standards-based assessments in the classroom, school, and district.* Englewood, CO: Advanced Learning Press.

Reflect. (1974). Webster's New World Dictionary of the American Language. (p. 1193, 2nd college ed.). Englewood Cliffs, NJ: Prentice Hall.

Rowe, M. B. (1974). Reflections on wait-time: Some methodological questions. *Journal of Research in Science Teaching, 1* (3), 263–279.

Sagor, R. (2003). *Motivating students and teachers in an era of standards.* Alexandria, VA: Association for Supervision and Curriculum Development.

Sagor, R. (2008). Cultivating optimism in the classroom. *Educational Leadership, 65* (6), 26–31.

Scherer, M. (Ed.). (1999). The understanding pathway: A conversation with Howard Gardner. *Educational Leadership, 57* (3), 12–16.

Schmöker, M. (1996). *Results: The key to continuous school improvement.* Alexandria, VA: Association for Supervision and Curriculum Development.

Shores, C., & Chester, K. (2009). *Using RTI for school improvement: Raising every students' achievement scores.* Thousand Oaks, CA: Corwin.

Shulman, L. (1988). A union of insufficiencies: Strategies for teacher assessment in a period of reform. *Educational Leadership, 46* (3), 36–41.

Solomon, P. G. (1998). *The curriculum bridge: From standards to actual classroom practice.* Thousand Oaks, CA: Corwin.

Solomon, P. G. (2002). *The assessment bridge: Positive ways to link tests to learning, standards, and curriculum improvement.* Thousand Oaks, CA: Corwin.

Sousa, D. A. (2001). *How the brain learns* (2nd ed.). Thousand Oaks, CA: Corwin.

Sprenger, M. (1999). *Learning & memory: The brain in action.* Alexandria, VA: Association for Supervision and Curriculum Development.

Sternberg, R. J. (2007/2008). Assessing what matters. *Educational Leadership, 65* (4), 20–26.

Stiggins, R. J. (1994). *Student-centered classroom assessment.* New York: MacMillan College Publishing.

Stiggins, R. J. (2002). Assessment crisis: The absence of assessment for learning. *Phi Delta Kappan, 83* (10), 758–765.

Tomlinson, C. A. (1999). *The differentiated classroom: Responding to the needs of all learners.* Alexandria, VA: Association for Supervision and Curriculum Development.

Tomlinson, C. A., & Eidson, C. C. (2003). *Differentiation in practice: A resource guide for differentiating curriculum. Grades K–5.* Alexandria, VA: Association for Supervision and Curriculum Development.

Vacca, R. T. (2002). From efficient decoders to strategic readers. *Educational Leadership, 45* (3), 52–56.

Vygotsky L. S. (1978). *Mind in society.* Cambridge, MA. Harvard University Press.

Wiggins, G., & McTighe, J. (1998). *Understanding by design.* Alexandria, VA: Association for Supervision and Curriculum Development.

Wiggins, G., & McTighe, J. (2007). *Schooling by design: Mission, action, and achievement.* Alexandria, VA: Association for Supervision and Curriculum Development.

Wiggins, G., & McTighe, J. (2008). Put understanding first. *Educational Leadership, 65* (8), 36–41.

Wiliam, D. (2007). Content then process: Teacher learner communities in the service of formative assessment. In D. Reeves (Ed.), *Ahead of the curve: The power of assessment to transform teaching and learning.* Bloomington, IN: Solution Tree.

Worthen, B. R. (1993). Critical issues that will determine the future of alternative assessment. *Phi Delta Kappan, 74* (6), 444–448, 450–454.

Index

CORWIN

A SAGE Company

The Corwin logo—a raven striding across an open book—represents the union of courage and learning. Corwin is committed to improving education for all learners by publishing books and other professional development resources for those serving the field of PreK–12 education. By providing practical, hands-on materials, Corwin continues to carry out the promise of its motto: **"Helping Educators Do Their Work Better."**